CHINA
EXPERIMENTS

CHINA
EXPERIMENTS
FROM LOCAL INNOVATIONS
TO NATIONAL REFORM

Ann Florini
Hairong Lai
Yeling Tan

BROOKINGS INSTITUTION PRESS
Washington, D.C.

Copyright © 2012
THE BROOKINGS INSTITUTION
1775 Massachusetts Avenue, N.W., Washington, DC 20036
www.brookings.edu

Library of Congress Cataloging-in-Publication data

Florini, Ann.
    China experiments : from local innovations to national reform / Ann Florini, Hairong Lai, and Yeling Tan.
        p. cm.
    Includes bibliographical references and index.
    Summary: "Using detailed and empirically grounded analysis, examines the changing relationship between the Chinese state and the society it governs, how governance choices made affect the country and the rest of the world, and how local Chinese authorities have responded to the challenges they face in coping with China's rapid transformation"—Provided by publisher.
    ISBN 978-0-8157-2200-7 (pbk. : alk. paper)
    1. Public administration—China. 2. Organizational change—China. 3. Central-local government relations—China. 4. Decentralization in government—China. 5. Local governments—China. I. Lai, Hairong. II. Tan, Yeling. III. Title.
    JQ1509.5.O73F66 2012
    352.3'670951—dc23   2011047358

9 8 7 6 5 4 3 2 1

Printed on acid-free paper

Typeset in Sabon and Optima

Composition by Cynthia Stock
Silver Spring, Maryland

Printed by R. R. Donnelley
Harrisonburg, Virginia

Contents

Foreword

Even in its first decade, the twenty-first century has provided multiple auguries that the decades ahead will be characterized by a number of transformative trends, including deepening globalization, changing demographics, shifts in economic power, and threats to the viability of our ecosphere—especially global warming. Taken together, those developments constitute a challenge to governance at the metropolitan, provincial, national, regional, and global levels.

China is at the nexus of that phenomenon, given its spectacular economic growth, its growing middle class, its robust and sometimes assertive sense of sovereignty—and, of course, its sheer size.

In this timely and trenchant book, the authors explore a very important way in which China is responding: through careful experimentation, managed with a firm hand by the central leadership. As China's leaders address the massive problems of rising inequality and social instability without jeopardizing their monopoly on power, they are carrying out—or being forced to allow—extensive experiments in political reform at localities throughout the country.

The ethos of experimentation, which has accounted for so much of China's success in recent decades, lies at the heart of this book. Local governments are taking a trial-and-error, learning-by-doing approach, from advanced metropolises like Shanghai, to impoverished townships and counties struggling to respond to rising discontent. Lessons are drawn from each initiative, with ideas spreading across different parts of China, sometimes with official encouragement from Beijing, sometimes in spite of warning signals from the central government.

The book reveals a powerful and unpredictable dynamic at work. In these pages, the conventional image of a Chinese juggernaut directed by an all-powerful party-state dissolves into a far more complex tempest of voices, interests, and powers. China's continued opening up to the rest of the world, the powerful forces of information technology, and the deepening of international production chains are all helping to fuel the government's deliberate efforts to adapt and to experiment politically.

What this means for China's future political development is an incredibly complicated question. This book explodes the common Western misperception of China as an authoritarian monolith, enabling readers to sort through China's extreme complexity and understand the significance of specific developments, including the leadership transition expected in 2012.

The authors provide useful guidelines for thinking about China's trajectory. They identify signs to watch for that would suggest the direction in which things are headed. Political experimentation could serve to entrench the current party-state by making it more efficient and less corrupt. There is a more hopeful alternative: China could serve as the basis for successful democratization as citizens develop the capacity for democratic engagement, as new conceptions of the role of the state evolve within the bureaucracy, and as appropriate institutions develop.

China's trajectory will have repercussions far beyond the country itself. It will be one of the key determinants of world order during this century. A stable, prosperous, democratic China would be a very different interlocutor for the world than a chaotic, or authoritarian, or collapsing one. Furthermore, as noted, it is not the only country that finds itself dealing with thorny challenges of governance. From political gridlock in Washington, to anti-corruption protests in New Delhi, to the problems besetting the European Union, there is plenty of evidence that large societies are hard to govern and getting harder. Some of the challenges that Chinese government officials are grappling with, such as streamlining administrative processes and managing public-private sector collaboration, will be familiar to anyone who has worked on governance reform.

This book sets a high standard and a useful model in another respect as well: the interchange of ideas and perspectives among the authors have, in their collaboration, replicated much of the dialogue that is already beginning to take place between and among China and other countries, as well as between and among key regions of China itself: Beijing, Shanghai, Hong Kong, and Guangzhou—and, crucially, between urban areas and the countryside, where some of the most promising innovations are taking place.

If the slogan "harmonious society" is to acquire concrete and beneficial meaning, it must apply to diverse communities, at both the national and the global level. It is in the fulfillment of that spirit that this book represents a major contribution that extends well beyond the subject at hand.

STROBE TALBOTT
President
Brookings Institution

Washington, D.C.
January 2012

Preface

This book is the product of an unusual collaboration across multiple countries and perspectives. It began as a conversation among the authors—one American, one Chinese, one Singaporean—over tea in Beijing, during which we discovered a mutual fascination with a profoundly important set of questions. How does a society as large, complex, and rapidly changing as China govern itself? And how will China's governance choices affect not only China itself but also the rest of the world?

To explore these vast questions, we took several approaches, bringing together work from the disciplines of political science, public policy, and international relations. First, we took advantage of the existence of a large set of case studies showing how local authorities in China have responded to the challenges they face in coping with China's rapid transformation. In 2000 the China Centre for Comparative Politics and Economics (CCCPE) at the Central Compilation and Translation Bureau, which is affiliated with the Central Committee of the Chinese Communist Party, initiated an awards program for best practice in local governance innovation, with several winners in various categories selected every two years. With the generous support of the International Development Research Centre, in 2009–10 we collaborated to translate and analyze selected case studies of the winners to date, and this book draws in part on that work. At that time Hairong Lai was deputy director of CCCPE, and Ann Florini led the Centre on Asia and Globalisation at the National University of Singapore where Yeling Tan was a research fellow. (In 2009 the China Center for Government Innovations at Peking University took charge of organizing this awards program.)

We also drew on our own ongoing field research, particularly for the discussions on electoral processes and transparency developments. We thank the Asia Foundation for its kind help in arranging meetings with government officials and academics in Hunan Province and in Beijing. We also thank the wide range of people representing China's government, academia, civil society, and the media whom we interviewed (under promises of anonymity) during the course of this research.

We are grateful to the East Asian Institute at the National University of Singapore for making its resources available to us and for facilitating important discussions by organizing a talk on the topic of this book. We also thank Yanchun Ong, Kin Ming (Osmond) Kwong, Bin Zhang, Zhengqing Xu, and Sarah Hauser for providing valuable research assistance.

The work of the community of externally based China scholars has informed our understanding of what may be unfolding in China. Many of them are cited in these pages, and we hope that the present volume contributes to the important debates they have helped to frame.

Our final thanks go to Brookings Institution Press for taking us through all the necessary stages with patience and professionalism, and to the International Development Research Centre for the support that has made this publication possible.

CHINA
EXPERIMENTS

1

China at a Crossroads

SRL Leather was upsetting its neighbors. Leather processing is not the cleanest business, and SRL Leather, like tanneries everywhere, was prone to emitting noxious odors and waste gases. The problem got so bad that exasperated residents filed multiple complaints with the local government in the early 2000s. The town's Environmental Protection Bureau responded by listing the company as a pollution standards violator from 2004 to 2009 and ordering the company to rectify the problem. SRL Leather undertook some measures to mitigate its pollution, but they were not sufficient and were not communicated to the residents—and so the complaints and unhappiness continued. In April 2009 an environmental nongovernmental organization (NGO), Friends of Nature, helped a resident to file a lawsuit demanding that the company disclose its environmental data, as required under national environmental disclosure guidelines. When SRL Leather took no action, a group of environmental NGOs called the Green Choice Alliance sent another letter again requesting that the company disclose its emissions. And when the company again failed to respond, two of the NGOs in the alliance took their complaints to the CEO of the international shoe company Timberland, one of SRL Leather's major clients.

Under this combined onslaught of citizen, government, NGO, and commercial pressure to stop its polluting activities, SRL Leather finally acted. In July 2009 the company disclosed its emissions records. Two months later, the CEO sat down with residents, representatives from Timberland, and the local media to listen to community complaints, and organized an open house for residents to visit the factory. A community representative was appointed to engage with the company regarding future environmental issues, and a direct hotline was established for pollution complaints. In addition, SRL Leather started publishing daily data on its wastewater discharge and was audited by an environmental NGO to confirm that it had indeed taken corrective actions to address its polluting practices.[1]

To North American and European readers, for whom NGOs and lawsuits are par for the course, all this sounds quite ordinary. But these events took place in Dachang, a township in the sprawling, bustling metropolis of Shanghai. China is seen by most Westerners as a very different kind of country, ruled by a Communist Party in power for more than sixty years, not a place where lawsuits and citizens groups hold sway.

Headlines about China usually tell three sorts of stories. One set focuses on China's roaring economic success over the past thirty years— and indeed, the transformation of cities such as Shanghai and Shenzhen, China's new economic clout on the world stage in forums from the International Monetary Fund (IMF) to the G-20, and the explosion of Chinese-made products in the world's marketplaces are visible for all to see. A second set of stories peers inside the country to catalog the social and environmental costs this sweeping economic transformation entails, from the tens of thousands of protests and demonstrations every year to the multiple suicides at the Foxconn iPhone factory in 2010 to the notorious pollution that had China ranked at number 121 out of 163 countries in a recent assessment of environmental performance.[2] Finally, headlines on the governance front lead abundant accounts of arbitrary arrests, censorship, and covering up of widespread official misbehavior, seeming to show a country lacking any effective political channels for feedback, participation, or dissent. Overall, the stories create the widespread impression that while the face of China has changed since Deng Xiaoping's opening up and reform policy of 1978, the political wiring within the system remains largely untouched.

Tales like that of SRL Leather, however, reveal a more deeply buried but extraordinarily important story: the rapid evolution, despite the persistence of the authoritarian one-party state, of multiple channels through which citizens can now—sometimes—express grievances and seek to solve problems. Dachang's residents started by filing complaints directly with the government, and then brought in a network of environmental NGOs. These NGOs were able to use new transparency regulations and an emerging legal system to pressure SRL Leather to improve its practices, and also leverage the international supply chain to raise the stakes on the polluting company. In the end, SRL Leather's problems were resolved not just by using formal policy rules, but through community-based discussion, and by giving citizens a stake in the management of their environment.

This story opens a window to the multitude of complex political developments that have taken place at China's subnational level, beneath the more visible transformations. The opening up and reform policy that Deng Xiaoping launched in 1978 did not simply unleash market forces on the planned economy. It also reconfigured the state's involvement in economic affairs, creating space not just for private entrepreneurship but also for subnational (or local) governments to try out different reforms.

The initial stages of reform led to what has been termed "fragmented authoritarianism"—authority divided both horizontally across different locations and vertically across different agencies and administrative levels.[3] In the ensuing years, the party-state apparatus has also gradually altered the nature of its involvement in the social sphere, allowing for more personal choices and, over time, greater scope for citizens to voice their concerns, participate in public issues, and form associations. The state structure itself has become far more decentralized, allowing for local government initiative and transforming the dynamic between central authority in Beijing and local provincial and subprovincial levels of party and government. And, crucially for a Leninist Communist system where power resides with the Communist Party far more than it does with the formal institutions of government, changes have also taken place within the party system, with the gradual emergence of some mechanisms of checks and balances, as well as restraints on the arbitrary use of power through a slowly developing system of the rule of law.

But this is not a straightforward, linear evolution toward more accountable and effective governance. The evolution of China's governing system is a story buried in layers of overlapping old and new structures, uneven implementation of intended reforms and regulations, and pushback by vested interests. On the one hand, the Chinese Communist Party (CCP) has placed increasingly strong restraints on its power in economic and social affairs and in many ways is moving incrementally toward the rule of law. On the other hand, the party's number one priority is to hold on to its monopoly of political power.

Such complexity makes it possible for observers to argue that an extraordinary range of political futures is possible for China: the triumph of authoritarian-style capitalism; the coming collapse of a nation unable to hold together in the face of rising tensions and contradictions; prolonged stagnation as a result of partial reform; or democratization as a growing middle class gains power and pushes for more rights. Where, in fact, is China heading? What kind of country is China becoming?

Through the Lens of Local Experiments

This book tries to make sense of the multitude of political changes taking place across China. In contrast to other books that focus on the party and/or elite politics,[4] our approach is to delve deeply into China's experimental approach to change at the local level—in townships, counties, and provinces. By taking this ground-level view, we aim to uncover clues about what sorts of foundations are being laid that could support future political transformations.

Local experiments are the hallmark of how China has undertaken all sorts of reforms since the end of the Mao era in the late 1970s. China's massive transformations over the past three decades are the result of multi-layered and incremental change rather than top-down shock therapy–style reform. The Chinese approach is less Big Bang and more "learning-by-doing," an incrementalist spirit often captured as "crossing the river by feeling the stones."[5] This approach is possible both because the center has actively encouraged localities to experiment with different ways of development,[6] and because of the decentralization of fiscal and administrative functions that took place in the late 1970s and early 1980s.

Decentralization brought about sweeping transfers of authority from the center to lower levels across a range of issues. Decisions over social security, health care, education, environmental protection, city planning, and so forth increasingly became the domain of local governments, by default giving local authorities a wider scope in promoting change. While overall policy objectives continued to be set by the center, localities were de facto given greater leeway to explore the specific approaches and possible instruments through which these central objectives could be met.[7]

The benefits of this experimentalist approach are clear: Given the size of the country and the relatively underdeveloped nature of its governing institutions, the repercussions of implementing a policy and getting it wrong are massive, and not easy to correct. The socioeconomic variations across the country also demand flexibility rather than a one-size-fits-all approach. The decentralized, experimentalist strategy allows the center to set an overall objective, but also allows localities to test ideas through pilot projects in different places, to gain experience from the ground up. The pilots that end up being nationalized are first endorsed by central authorities, and their adoption is then promoted through official announcements and press conferences, as well as visits and exchanges with other regions. This style of reform has been called "experimentation under hierarchy,"[8] requiring a tricky balance between control and freedom.

In practice, there is great variation in the degree to which successful experiments are the result of national orchestration, which ones end up being scaled nationally by design or simply by default, and how the national policies differ from their local models. In the early 1990s, for example, Jiangsu province started privatizing township and village enterprises (TVEs), while Shandong and Sichuan provinces experimented with the privatization of state-owned enterprises. These successful local practices were eventually endorsed by the center and spread nationwide, with tremendous impact on the trajectory of China's economic growth. However, this development was more a result of central authorities responding positively to local innovations that the former had had no role in fostering, rather than part of a larger economic design.

Continued economic growth over the past three decades has brought about increasingly complex governance challenges, from inequality and growing demands for social insurance to pollution and corruption, creating a demand for broader and stronger institutions. In response, the range of policy innovations being pioneered at local levels has expanded beyond the economic sphere, into administrative, social, and political realms. These experiments are the subject of this book. Through a series of case studies and broader analyses, we investigate how local governments across China, from provincial down to township levels, are actively experimenting with reforms to guide and adapt to, rather than resist, the broader forces of change emerging across China.

These experiments reflect a growing range of approaches to local governance that defy common assumptions about authoritarian rule. Some experiments, such as those in streamlining administrative processes, are aimed at boosting the bureaucracy's efficiency and capacity. Others, such as those dealing with social organizations and NGOs, explore ways of harnessing nonstate actors to deal with social issues and complement weaknesses in state-led approaches. Still others are trials in rewiring the innards of the party, by introducing semi-competitive elections from the township level all the way to the very top of the country's power structure. Finally, the government has experimented with using transparency as a governance tool to curb corruption and improve accountability through the proactive release of information, as well as by allowing citizens the ability to request information.

We explore the motivations for such experiments and their effects, considering how these innovations in local governance may spread, and what the implications of those experiments would be if they did spread. Thus far, the dynamic between local experimentation and central response has been different with each of type of innovation. The reform process has been spontaneous and uneven, with ideas and initiatives from provinces and cities sometimes cohering and sometimes clashing with central government interests.

The key issue we explore in this book is whether these efforts will become entrenched in the ruling regime (even while the nature of its authoritarian rule continues to evolve) or create space for significant political reform. We recognize that there is no immediate prospect for democratic rule in China, in the sense of freely contested multi-party elections backed by fully realized freedoms of press, assembly, and voice. Fundamental protection of citizen rights remains weak, and the state retains control over many aspects of society that it fears could lead to instability. These include intense media policing and control and the explicit use of force to dissipate debate or shut down dissent over a range of issues, from human rights to corruption scandals.

Nonetheless, looking beneath the surface, it is still possible to find important and interesting trends with regard to information flows, participation mechanisms, and accountability mechanisms. Those trends raise questions about what form a more democratic regime in China might take—clearly any democratic structures would necessarily grow out of China's unique historical and sociocultural context. And as the brief description of the experiments already under way makes clear, the very nature of CCP rule and the foundations of the authoritarian regime are shifting and evolving. This means that even if the CCP succeeds in entrenching its rule in the long term, it is likely to do so in ways that challenge conventional understandings of what constitutes authoritarianism. Rather than try to guess at the end state, we are more interested in whether China is developing the necessary institutions and capacity for political reform in the direction of greater voice and accountability.

The repercussions of China's gradualist approach to reform are far from straightforward. The Chinese party-state is actively attempting to address the factors that could lead to collapse, stagnation, or challenges to the party's authority, including via quite deliberate experiments in local governance innovation. We believe that it is too early to know how the extraordinary complex of factors described above may come together. Instead, what is clear is that as the party tries to walk the tightrope to reform and retain its legitimacy while maintaining its monopoly over political power, the range of actors being empowered to act and influence decisions is multiplying, and the competition between these various interests is heating up. Nothing like modern China has ever existed before. The rapidity of sustained economic growth under conditions of authoritarianism, the sheer scale of everything to do with China, and the deliberate (if not always controlled) experimentalist approach to governance all represent conditions that test the limits of social science.

The Massive Challenge of Governing China

A critical question is whether this incremental and experimental approach can sustain China in the face of the country's extraordinarily dire challenges, which would strain the capacity of the best of governments. Sustaining rapid economic development alone requires adjustments from urbanization policies to building more advanced capital markets and reforming state-owned enterprises, as well as harmonizing domestic rules with those of the global trading and financial regimes. All this must be done in the face of daunting social disruptions that the state is struggling to

Figure 1-1. *Number of Demonstrations, 1993–2008*

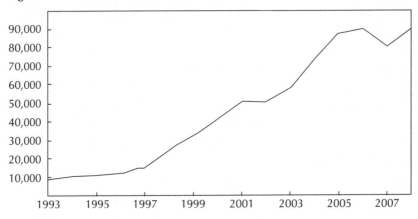

Sources: Books—*Yufang yu Chuzhi Quntixing Shijian* (Preventing and Dealing with Demonstrations) (People's Daily Press, 2009), p. 43. Chen Jinsheng, *Quntixing Shijian Yanjiu Baogao* (An Investigation on Demonstrations) (Mass Press, 2009), p. 62. Song Weiqiang, *Shehui Zhuanxingqi Zhongguo Nongmin Quntixing Shijian Yanjiu* (Peasants' Demonstration in China during Transformation) (Central China Normal University Press, 2009). Liu Zifu, *Xin Quntixing Shijian Guan* (A New Perspective on Demonstrations) (Xinhua News Agency Press, 2009), p. 1. Periodicals—Li Zhongxin, "Guanyu Shijichu Jingji Fazhan yu Shehui Wending Wenti de Taolun" (A Discussion on Economic Development and Social Stability in the Beginning of New Century), *Jiangsu Gong'an Zhuanke Xuexiao Xuebao* (Journal of Jiangsu Public Security College), no. 12 (2001), pp. 10–12. Liu Xudong, "Quntixing Shijian Shendu Pouxi (A Deep Analysis on Demonstrations)," *Dangzheng Luntan* (Forum over Party and State Issues), no. 1 (2009), pp. 44–46. In addition, data for 2000 and 2001 were based on data provided by Hu Lianhe, Hu Angang, and Wang Lei, "Yingxiang Shehui Wending de Shehui Maodun Bianhua Taishi de Shizheng Fenxi" (An Empirical Study on the Changing Trends of Social Contradictions That Affect Social Stability), *Shehui Kexue Zhanxian* (Social Science Front), no. 4 , 2006, pp. 175–85.

keep up with, from widening income disparities across and within regions, to the rapidly aging population structure, to multiplying health problems. China's economic gains have also come at the cost of catastrophic environmental degradation.[9] Pollution problems are straining not just the long-term sustainability of China's development, but also social stability, as environmental issues increasingly become a daily burden in people's lives.

As a result of all these problems, tens of thousands of (sometimes violent) protests wrack the country every year, as citizens vent their frustration over everything from labor abuses to degraded land and water to official corruption. The pace of economic growth has outstripped that of administrative (and political) adaptation. As figure 1-1 shows, the sharply rising number of demonstrations taking place across China between 1993 and 2008 reflects the growing social dislocations and strains on the existing system of governance.

For the CCP leadership, sustaining high rates of economic growth remains at the top of these competing priorities, given that economic development undergirds much of the CCP's claim to continued legitimacy. As China moves toward middle-income status, however, many questions arise as to whether the growth can be sustained, and if not, whether it will be interrupted by collapse or stagnation.[10] If such interruptions to the economy do occur, the question then is whether there are resilient institutions of social mediation that can manage the conflicts and disruptions that will hit all segments of China's state, society, and economy.

The Global Implications of Local Reform

China's future political development matters far beyond its own borders, both because of China's growing geopolitical heft, and also because of the multiplying issues on the global agenda—from nuclear nonproliferation to climate change and global economic stability—that cannot be managed without China's support and cooperation. With globalization, domestic and external challenges are becoming increasingly intertwined on multiple fronts, from resource competition and energy security, to infectious diseases and financial stability. Even as China's membership and involvement in global forums to address these issues steadily deepen, it has to deal with entrenched suspicions from the rest of the world as to its intentions, as well as domestic worries about foreign hostilities.

The question is not just whether China will choose to be a status quo power that is basically content with the rules of the existing order, or a rising hegemon out to remake the world order according to its vision and interests. The question is how the nature of the regime governing the country will shape China's global role. Would a more democratic China share values with the world's other leading powers that would make it far easier to adjust to what is seen to be an inevitable shift of power from the West to Asia? And although debates about a "democratic peace" will probably occupy scholars for decades, democracies, while not averse to waging war in general, tend not to wage war against each other, raising the crucial question of what implications the nature of China's domestic regime has for war and peace.[11]

In our view, the global implications of China's domestic political development are perhaps not so straightforward. The Chinese government's decisions about external issues will be driven in part by its willingness and ability to undertake domestic trade-offs, while its strategic calculations of external interests are in turn partially determined by domestic politics. A more democratic Chinese government may find itself with less freedom of action on the international stage if its decisions have to respond more tightly and be more accountable to domestic interest groups. A more authoritarian government could also conceivably be more supportive of the current Westphalian order if China sees sovereignty as a valuable principle to be protected and retained, so as to protect its position vis-à-vis democratic nations.

Clearly, the Chinese authorities face enormous challenges in determining how they want their relationship with society to evolve domestically, and what kind of major power they want China to be globally. These two decisions are closely interlinked, but it is not clear how much maneuvering space the party-state has to make these decisions, given the rapid changes being brought about by globalization, economic advancement, and rising social mobility within China. However, it is illuminating to examine the changes taking place within the state itself, and particularly to look beyond Beijing to the ways in which local governments are experimenting in response to multiple governance challenges. This subnational view allows for a richer set of evidence with which to consider the trajectories that the Chinese political system might take.

Understanding the implications of these experiments, however, requires some background, to which we now turn. In the rest of this chapter, we explain the context for the changes taking place within China's governance architecture and look broadly at the existing intellectual debate regarding China's political future. We then consider the various forces and experiments in new governance tools that are driving change, and explain how the subsequent chapters provide a way of understanding China's domestic changes and what factors will affect the shape of China's political future.

China's Changing Governance Architecture

China's economic rise has been accompanied by far more extensive politically relevant change than is immediately obvious. The economic structure has been utterly transformed. Citizens are now far more educated

Box 1-1. *Overview of China's Political and Administrative Structure*

Understanding the politically relevant changes in China requires a bit of background on the country's basic governance structures. China's governing system has two parallel hierarchies: a state hierarchy and a party hierarchy. These two hierarchies operate on all five administrative levels of the system: the political center (Beijing); the province; the prefecture (or municipality); the county; and the township. There are 34 provinces, autonomous regions, and special administrative regions (including Hong Kong, Macau, and Taiwan, whose distinctive political evolution is not covered in this book); 333 prefectures; 2,862 counties; and 41,636 townships.

The state hierarchy is similar to that of governments in most countries, made up of an administration, a judiciary, and a parliament (in Chinese terminology: a People's Congress is equivalent to the lower house and a People's Political Consultative Conference is equivalent to the upper house). These three different branches are in theory meant to serve as checks and balances within the state hierarchy. This parallel set of hierarchies is duplicated in each level of administration, in a fairly decentralized manner. This means that provincial and subprovincial parliaments, known as congresses, are not subordinated to the national congress but rather are parts of local states. Likewise, local judiciaries are not subordinated to the judiciary at the center but report to the local government.

This division of power and the relative autonomy of local units from the center means that local objectives often diverge from national priorities. It is the Party, which transcends all branches and levels, that brings consistency to the various levels of government. While the Party makes strategic decisions, the state implements these decisions and manages daily or routine issues. At each level of the hierarchy, a Party Committee sits parallel to the state. For example, a provincial government, a provincial judiciary, and a provincial parliament are matched by a provincial party committee. Heads of the major state organizations are usually members of the provincial party committee. The Party's main tool for managing the state organizations is its control of the leadership positions of the state through a "nomenklatura" system that reserves to the Party the right to select who is eligible for such posts. Many state officials are not Party members, but officials in decisionmaking positions (particularly at higher levels) are by and large Communist Party members.

The notion of the people's sovereignty is written into the Constitution, with the National People's Congress (NPC) as the representative body of the people. In theory, the heads of major state organizations are elected by People's Congresses at different levels. However, since only the CCP nominates candidates to these positions, and People's Congresses are largely made up of CCP members, the CCP in effect commands the appointment and dismissal of state officials. The NPC is formally China's legislative body, but the State Council, China's chief executive organ, is far more influential, with the power to submit draft

(*continued*)

Box 1-1 (*continued*)

laws to the NPC and its Standing Committee. The Legislation Law passed in 2000 restricts the power to pass laws on human rights, litigation, and taxation to the NPC, allowing the State Council, local governments, and congresses to legislate in other areas. In addition, local government legislatures are allowed to pass laws when national laws do not exist, but these must be harmonized once national legislation is established.

Aside from the Chinese Communist Party, there are eight other political parties in China, formed before the CCP took power in mainland China in 1949. Before 1949, these eight parties were aligned with the CCP in opposition to the then-ruling Kuomintang (KMT) Party. These eight parties were largely composed of and led by intellectuals and businessmen, and were fairly influential in the 1940s. Prominent figures from these eight parties took high-ranking state positions in the early 1950s, but the parties were suppressed between 1956 and 1976. The parties were restored after 1978, but their role in Chinese politics has been greatly diminished. Although the party system has been described in China as a "system of multi-party cooperation and political consultation led by the Communist Party of China," the CCP's political dominance has been essentially absolute.

and have far more scope for making choices about where to live and what to do with their lives. China has significantly (albeit somewhat haphazardly) decentralized authority over a whole host of public policy arenas, a development that brought both advantages and challenges to the task of managing a rapidly modernizing country with more than four times the U.S. population.

With a series of reforms first launched in 1978, following the upheavals of the Cultural Revolution and the death in 1976 of Mao, the CCP's role and the roles of other actors in the Chinese system began to change. Up until the end of the 1970s, the Chinese state, like its counterparts in the former Soviet Union and Eastern European countries, controlled almost every aspect of socioeconomic life. Jobs were allocated by the authorities, not chosen by individuals. Agriculture was collective, with individual farmers unable to reap individual rewards from their individual efforts. Chinese citizens had virtually no options for organizing in pursuit of their own interests. But starting in the late 1970s, China began to experiment with wide-ranging economic, social, and (to a lesser extent) political alternatives. In the past few decades, the state has greatly withdrawn its control over and intervention in economic activities, as well as greatly reined in its control over and intervention in the lives of citizens.

State Separation from the Economy

The state's changing role in economic activities includes two mutually reinforcing dimensions.[12] First came the state's retreat from central planning, starting in the 1980s with a series of steps to deregulate prices. Initially, the reforms introduced a dual-track pricing system that allowed goods produced above planned quotas to be sold at market-determined prices. Today, most prices have been deregulated, save the prices of goods and services such as oil, electricity, and railway transportation. A parallel movement away from the planned-economy model took place on the production side, with the abolition of production plans in the 1990s. Many state-owned enterprises (SOEs), which had dominated China's economy, were privatized as the government, in particular local governments, found themselves unable to continue subsidizing enterprise operations. Today there are few SOEs subordinated to local authorities. Even the large SOEs today are operating under very different conditions. While the state retains formal ownership, some are partially privatized by listings on domestic and international stock exchanges, and some of the management practices of these SOEs increasingly resemble those of large private multinational companies.[13]

The second dimension is a dramatic rebalancing of the size of the private sector relative to the state, as China's central authorities began to allow and even encourage the expansion of privately owned enterprises, foreign direct investments, and joint ventures. Figure 1-2 shows how dramatically the ownership structure of the economy changed over the three decades after the late 1970s, as the state stepped back and a private sector emerged.

Changed Citizenry

Parallel with its retreat from the planned economy, the state also rolled back its control over and intervention in the daily lives of China's citizens. The marketization of the economy meant that the state lost control over employment—people now choose their jobs and careers rather than being assigned. Mobility has greatly increased, and housing is increasingly being privatized. Well over 100 million workers have migrated from

Figure 1-2. *Changing Ownership Structure of the Economy, 1978–2006*

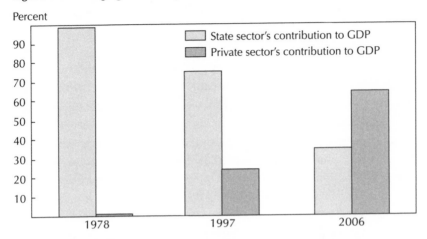

Percent

Sources: For 1978 and 1997 data, see *Jingji Ribao* (Economics Daily), November 5, 2002. For 2005 data, see Li Xinxin, "Zhongguo feigongyouzhi jingji fazhan bizhong buduan zengzhang" (The Increasing Contribution of the Non-State Sector to GDP in China), *Liaowang Xinwen Zhoukan* (Outlook News Weekly), October 1, 2007.

Note: Figure data compiled by Lai Hairong. "State sector" includes state-owned enterprises, shareholding companies where the government holds the biggest parts of the stocks, and collectively owned enterprises, which are usually run by township governments or branch administrative organizations at the upper levels. All others are included in "Private sector."

rural areas to the cities to fill jobs in China's factories. With the development of private schools and the commercialization of public schools, state control over education has decreased as well, and overseas options are rapidly expanding.

One powerful change is the degree to which China's citizens can now learn from and communicate with one another and with the outside world. The statistics are nothing short of stunning. The literacy rate rose from 66 percent in 1982 to 94 percent in 2009. The percentage of the population living in urban areas more than doubled, from 20 percent in 1981 to 44 percent in 2009. The number of Internet users rose from 2,000 in 1993 to 457 million in 2010 (see figure 1-3). A country that had one telephone line per 100 persons in 1990 had 24 lines per 100 persons in 2009, while mobile phone subscriptions per 100 persons grew from zero in 1991 to 56 in 2009.[14] With the freer flow of information and China's continuing integration into the world community, world events, new values, and mentalities are increasingly accessible and part of the

Figure 1-3. *Number of Internet Users in China, 1997–2010*

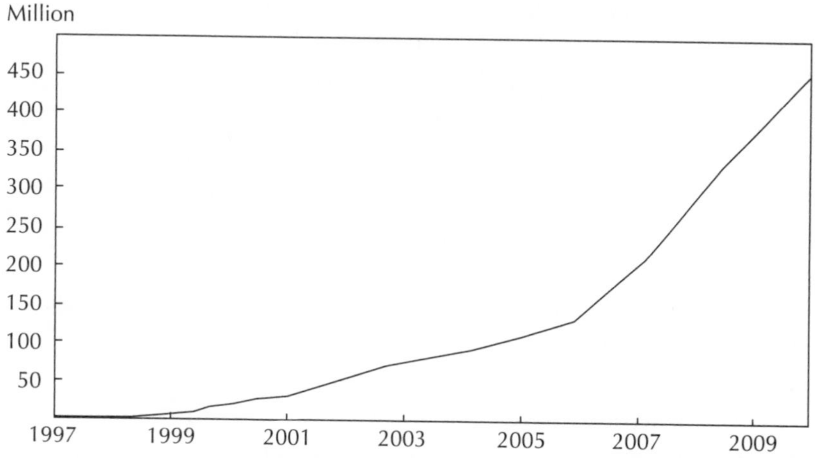

Million

Source: "Di 27 Ci Zhongguo Hulian Wangluo Fazhan Zhuangkuang Tongji Baogao" (The 27th Statistical Report on the Development of the Internet in China), issued by China Internet Network Information Center (http://research.cnnic.cn/html/1295343214d2557.html).

lives and awareness of citizens. Equally important, events and dialogue taking place in one part of China are increasingly accessible to citizens in other localities, adding up to an increasingly rich and multi-layered national consciousness.

These developments are in part reflected in rapidly changing consumer trends and lifestyles—particularly in urban areas. Fashion designer Miuccia Prada staged her spring/summer 2011 collection for the first time in Beijing in January 2011, adapting the version staged in Milan a few months earlier to the tastes of Chinese consumers.[15] New markets are also expanding. The skin care product market for Chinese men is estimated to have reached $269.6 million in 2010, outstripping the North American market of $227.4 million.[16] Pet ownership has also exploded in recent years, with 900,000 dogs officially registered in Beijing alone. This has been accompanied by the development of online dog social networks, even luxury items such as swimming pools for dogs.[17]

But China's social transformation extends far beyond flashy fashion and pampered pets. There has been a growing awareness of rights among the citizens, as witnessed by the escalating number of lawsuits against local and central government organizations. One lawyer, Hao Jinsong, has drawn public attention for his efforts to build up the rule of law in China by filing lawsuits against the authorities on small, politically non-sensitive issues. He has won a lawsuit against subway authorities, forcing them to issue (legally required) receipts for people paying six cents to use public toilets. He has also won a lawsuit against the Ministry of Railroads for its failure to issue tax receipts. His compares his brand of activism to a running track, saying "A few of the elite are leading the pack, but if ordinary people see that the track leads to jail they won't dare to get on it. My way is a way ordinary people can imitate."[18]

The expansion of the social sphere is also reflected in the rapid development of civil society and NGOs. As we explain in detail in chapter 4, NGOs were banned before the late 1970s, but the retreat and changing role of the state increased the need for organizations to step in and fill gaps in service provision and social coordination. While formal regulations exist to curtail the activities of NGOs, and the sector does not have formal autonomy, more and more NGOs have been formed to facilitate all kinds of activities: business associations, education, job finding, care of the aged, community upkeep, folk arts preservation, and trickier categories such as labor rights, environmental protection, and religious activities. According to a recent survey, the number of NGOs, including the majority that are not registered with the authorities, is about 3 million.[19]

The growth of such social organizations and evolving consumer preferences also interact with changes in social values and improvements in communications technology that have swept the country, resulting sometimes in instances of citizen activism. In April 2011, Beijing pet lover An Lidong devised a plan to disrupt the practice of eating dog meat in hotpot restaurants. He waited at a highway toll booth along a route that he knew was used by trucks transporting dogs to restaurants. Once he spotted a truck loaded with dogs, he turned on his lights, stopped the vehicle, and posted the information on his micro blog. Two hundred netizens responded and joined in his blockade, leading to a fifteen-hour standoff between the trucking company and the animal activists. Eventually, Lee Pet Vet animal hospital and an animal rights charity (Shangshan Foundation) agreed to pay 115,000 RMB to the trucking company in exchange for the dogs, and the animals were transferred to the China Small Animal Protection Association (CSAPA) shelter. Media coverage of this event sparked a nationwide debate about the long-standing practice of eating dog meat.[20]

In short, citizens are much more economically independent, mobile, and resourceful than they were in the late 1970s, with growing means to engage and even confront the state. A private sphere for citizens has gradually emerged and expanded, with the diversification of values, life-styles, and moral codes. These changes are now deeply embedded, making China a far more complex society, in which state intervention is no longer a simple or straightforward option.

Emerging Checks and Balances

Historically, the political system in China has been considered mono-lithic, marked by an absence of any checks and balances. After decades of evolution, however, some variations have emerged in balancing power and regularizing power transitions. But these political changes are more limited and gradual than the transformations in economic decentralization or in the state-society relations discussed above.

One emerging check on state power comes from the long-dormant parliamentary sphere, illustrated by an increasing number of abstentions and negative votes in the National People's Congress (NPC). Because the delegates to the NPC are selected by the party, one would expect to see no divergence between these two institutions, and indeed until recent decades the NPC was purely a rubber stamp for CCP decisions. However, starting in 1990, a small number of abstentions and negative votes began to appear in almost all the major NPC voting sessions. For example, about one-third of the NPC either abstained or voted negatively in April 1992 on the construction of the Three Gorges Dam,[21] a startling and unprecedented expression of opposition at that time. At local levels, more party-nominated candidates are being vetoed by local people's congresses.[22] Although in most cases the legislature as a whole has voted consistently with the position of the administration and the party, abstentions and negative votes now seem to have become a normal part of the legislative process.

Second, the judiciary, while still not independent, is gradually becoming more professionalized. Before the late 1980s, most judges and prosecutors were recruited from among demobilized military officers who had no formal legal education and were more inclined to make judgments on the basis of political criteria rather than legal standards, leading citizens to be highly suspicious of the judiciary. As the selection process changed

Figure 1-4. *Number of Administrative Litigation Cases Filed by Individuals against Government Organizations, 1989–2009*

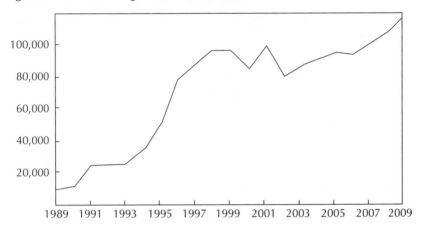

Source: Data for 1997–2009 are from *Zhongguo Tongji Nianjian* (China Statistics Yearbook), China Statistics Press; data for 1989–1996 are from *Zhongguo Falu Nianjian* (China Legal Yearbook), China Legal Yearbook Press.

in the mid-1990s, judges and prosecutors with higher education gradually replaced those former military officers. In parallel, the status of lawyers in society also shifted with the privatization of law firms from the early 1990s onward. Most lawyers now hold the status of independent professionals, and their reputations depend on their capacity to argue on behalf of their clients. Court debates have therefore become more intense and more professional. That said, these improvements remain incremental and marginal. Major problems with judicial independence persist, as local courts are still part of the local governments, with their budgets and personnel decided by those governments.

Third, citizens now have more legal rights with which to check the exercise of state power. Before the late 1980s, citizens had little legal recourse in cases of government mistreatment. In 1990, the Administrative Litigation Act came into effect, granting citizens the right to sue government organizations. About 10,000 such cases were filed nationally in initial years, and the number increased steadily to about 120,000 in 2009 (see figure 1-4). Survey data reveal that around 30 percent of these cases are won by the citizens.[23] In the mid-2000s, government organizations at the central level began for the first time to lose suits brought by individual citizens, with examples including the National Industry and Commerce Administration Agency in 2004, the Ministry of Land and Resources in 2005, and the Ministry of Finance in 2006.[24]

The 1994 State Compensation or Indemnity Law requires the state to provide either compensation or indemnity to a citizen in the event that a citizen wins a case against the government. This law places further constraints on government organizations, making them more cautious in dealing with individuals. A well-known case of state compensation occurred in Hubei province in 2005 when She Xianglin, who had been found guilty of killing his wife and sentenced to fourteen years in prison in 1995, was released after his wife reappeared. She Xianglin sued the court for the mistaken judgment, and the court ruled that the Jinshan County Government should pay him 460,000 RMB in damages.[25]

The revision of the Criminal Procedure Law in 1997 also enhanced legal rights, removing the "presumption of guilt," under which the prosecution was inclined to extort confessions by torture. However, while the 1997 revision denounced the principle of "presumption of guilt," the "presumption of innocence" was not written into the Criminal Procedure Law.

Finally, as chapter 3 explains in detail, the spread of semi-competitive elections at the village and township levels has created another layer of checks on the government. Elections in countries run by Communist Parties are usually single-candidate elections. There is no competition, and people have no choice but to accept the candidate nominated by the party. In a semi-competitive election, citizens are able to choose between multiple nominees—though from the same party, or no party at all, rather than between the ruling and opposition party. The implementation of these semi-competitive elections means that local officials have to take the needs of the residents into stronger consideration when making decisions. These bottom-up dynamics mean that local governments tend to have become more autonomous in their interactions with higher-level agencies. In addition, election campaigns can facilitate horizontal networking among the citizenry, providing another locus for social interaction and potentially strengthening deliberative processes at the local level.

Institutionalizing Transfers of Power

One merit of an electoral democracy is that mechanisms are in place to facilitate the peaceful transfer of power. However, in the former Soviet

Table 1-1. *Proportion of Peaceful Power Transfers (Generational) since 1997*

Year	Standing Committee of the Politburo (7 or 9 members)	Politburo (20–25 members)	Members of the Central Committee (190 members)	Alternate members of the Central Committee (130 members)
1997	2/7	50 percent	n.a.	n.a.
2002	6/7 (including the general secretary)	70 percent	Around 50 percent	Around 50 percent
2007	4/9	40 percent	Around 50 percent	Around 50 percent

Note: Data compiled by Lai Hairong from a database on all Party Congresses from 1921 through 2007, available on the official website of the Party at www.people.com.cn.
n.a. = Not available.

Union and most other Leninist countries, leaders held power for as long as they could. Most stayed in office until they died, or until they were demoted through cruel political struggles that often involved mass imprisonments. This was also true in China before the late 1970s.

In the early 1980s, the Chinese leadership made the crucial decision to institutionalize power holding and power transfers. Officials at all levels now have term limits: five years per term and no more than two terms. The implementation process proved to be very difficult and encountered periodic setbacks, but by the late 1990s the practice was increasingly institutionalized. The year 1997 saw a peaceful partial political succession at the very highest level in China's power pyramid, the Standing Committee of the Politburo, without any externally evident political struggle. In 2002, there was another peaceful and full transfer of power at the Standing Committee of the Politburo. In 2007, yet another peaceful and partial transfer of power at the highest level took place. Table 1-1 shows the scale of peaceful power transfers since 1997, and the ability of the party to rejuvenate its ranks with younger members through increasingly predictable and institutionalized processes.

Two factors contributed to the success of this process. One was the political will of the party elite, especially those represented by Deng Xiaoping, who had learned a lesson from the tragedy of the Cultural Revolution and the early disasters in party history. The other factor was the declining need and possibility of mobilizing the masses in power transfers, as the growing separation of politics from the economy and the separation of the state from society undermined the ability and legitimacy of would-be charismatic leaders to rule according to old-style mass mobilization. We turn now to these two trends.

Ideological Reconfiguration

Underlying the multiple shifts in the relationships between state, economy, and society is a gradual evolution in state ideology, from "Mao Zedong Thought" to "Socialism with Chinese Characteristics." This evolution has at least half a dozen dimensions.

First, the mission (and thus the legitimacy) of the Communist Party and the political system shifted from ensuring the purity of the proletarian dictatorship via class struggle to ensuring economic development and social stability. This change sparked institutional restructuring intended to facilitate individual economic initiative and to coordinate and mediate various interests to achieve social peace and "harmony."

Second, the ruling party's perception of the outside world has changed substantially. While deep suspicions remain, the outside world is increasingly viewed not solely through the lens of an enemy, but rather as consisting of potential partners from which China can benefit through peaceful and reciprocal interactions. Before the early 2000s, such mutually beneficial partnerships were struck mainly in economic affairs, but more recently, cooperation has extended to the political sphere as well. It is significant that official party messages have acknowledged this shift in perceptions, even while instances of hostility and mistrust between the Chinese government and other nations continue to take place. The political report to the 16th Party Congress in 2002 proposed the concept of "political civilization," implying an understanding of the advantages and merits of the political system in the advanced world. The party program was revised in 2002, with the important deletion of the phrase "capitalism will inevitably be replaced by socialism." The political report to the 17th Party Congress in 2007 further advocated peaceful coexistence and mutual learning between socialism and capitalism.

Third, the party-state's approach to socialism evolved in parallel with these ideological adjustments in relation to capitalism. Before the 1990s, the fundamental features of socialism were perceived to be (1) public ownership, (2) the planned economy, and (3) to each according to his work. From the early 1990s onward, the fundamental features of Socialism with Chinese Characteristics, at least, included: (1) mixed ownership (protection of private ownership was written into the 2004 constitutional revisions), (2) a market economy, and (3) mixed principles of welfare distribution, from a planned economy system of public ownership and compensation according to one's labor, to a market-based system that permits income from other sources.

Fourth, the profile of the party has changed. According to the party program before 2002, the Chinese Communist Party was the vanguard of the Chinese working class. According to the newly revised party program, the party is the vanguard of the Chinese working class, and also the vanguard of the Chinese people and the Chinese nation. In short, the CCP is moving from a class-based party to an all-encompassing party. The composition of CCP members has likewise evolved to become far more diverse, reflecting in part the growing complexity and heterogeneity of Chinese society. The first two generations of CCP members, led by Mao Zedong and Deng Xiaoping respectively, comprised mainly soldiers and peasants who were veterans of the Communist revolution. In the third and fourth generations, led by Jiang Zemin and Hu Jintao respectively, the elites who found their way to the top of the party were increasingly well educated and technocratic, schooled in engineering. The elite of the fifth generation that will replace Hu Jintao and much of the rest of the core leadership in 2012 come from even more diverse backgrounds (class, age, birthplace, and occupation—including the private sector) and are schooled in a range of disciplines including law, economics, and other social sciences.

Fifth, political values have also been changing, in part owing to decades of increasingly deeper engagement and dialogue with the international community. One notable if still evolving example is the concept of human rights, which was viewed as counterrevolutionary before the 1990s. In 1991, China issued its first White Paper on Human Rights, stating cautiously that "the evolution of the situation in regard to human rights is circumscribed by the historical, social, economic and cultural conditions of various nations, and involves a process of historical development."[26] In 2004, the protection of human rights was written into the revised constitution, with Article 33 of Chapter 2 stating that "[t]he state respects and guarantees human rights." That said, the practice of upholding human rights has lagged behind the formal changes in the constitution, and progress can seem painfully incremental and uneven. In 2009, China issued a Human Rights Action Plan for the first time, stating that "[t]he realization of human rights in the broadest sense has been a long-cherished ideal of mankind and also a long-pursued goal of the Chinese government and people," but came under criticism in 2011 for failing to meet many of the goals stated in the Action Plan.[27]

Finally, the exercise of power has also been undergoing changes. Before the 1980s, power was exercised based on revolutionary principles conducted by revolutionaries. From the 1980s onward, the ruling elite tried to replace the practice of "rule of man" with "rule of law," regarding the law as a more efficient instrument to regulate state and society. While the party-state has increasingly regularized its functions through major government reorganizations and the passage of laws and regulations, moving somewhat toward a modern bureaucratic state, such developments alone amount more to rule *by* law.[28] That is, while the exercise of power increasingly operates according to legal and regulatory guidelines, the law is used as a tool rather than a principle of governance. A "thicker," more substantive approach to governance requires that other actors, such as citizens, be able to hold the state to account and have their rights protected through the legal framework—rule of law rather than rule by law.[29] As described earlier, these changes are taking place slowly, and most observers would still characterize the situation in China as one of rule by law rather than rule of law.

Predicting China's Future

Of all the new practices, structures, laws, and values that are shaping China's political evolution, some have become firmly rooted in society, but most are still primitive, weak, and fragile. This messy transition process has led to a coexistence of the new and old, producing inconsistencies wherever one chooses to look. Norms of Confucianism sit side by side with those of socialism and capitalism. Large gaps exist between newly introduced regulations and their actual implementation in different parts of China. Income and social disparities are widening between and within regions, and even the ruling elite itself is increasingly made up of groups with different backgrounds and interests. Thus, one can find support for almost every observation and prediction about China. How can we sort through this mixture of conflicting elements to forge a relatively balanced understanding of China?

To start, it is helpful to take a look at how leading China scholars have tried to make sense of the myriad cleavages and forces of change cutting through Chinese social, economic, and political life, to forecast China's trajectory. Their thinking can be broadly grouped into four areas:[30]

(a) authoritarian resilience—the current system is adapting successfully through the creation of new institutions to manage the changes brought about by globalization and economic growth;

(b) collapse—the system cannot hold together the multiplying contradictions in society and is inherently unsustainable;

(c) democratic evolution—economic growth and the creation of market institutions will lead the way toward political reform, and eventually Chinese democracy;

(d) trapped transition—various forces have combined to impede political reform in China, leading the system to be "trapped" partway through the reform process.

Authoritarian Resilience

Andrew Nathan believes that the Chinese system is resilient (and indeed coined the phrase "authoritarian resilience"). He argues that China has successfully transitioned from a totalitarian regime to an authoritarian one, and that this authoritarian regime is becoming increasingly stable and entrenched as it institutionalizes and regularizes its processes:

—Shared norms, rather than arbitrary exercises of power, are increasingly coming to guide the process of political succession, as we describe above.

—Meritocratic criteria rather than factional identities increasingly determine the promotion of elites, a process that started with Deng's "four-way transformation" of the cadre corps, emphasizing the recruitment of candidates who were not only revolutionary, but also younger and more educated, and possessed more technical skills. This, along with the gradual fading away of personality cults or promotion based on personal loyalties, raised the use of meritocratic criteria in selecting officials at the top ranks of the party.

—Specialized functional agencies have developed over time to build up both professional expertise and technical authority and are increasingly responsible for specific tasks within the state, reflecting the increasing professionalism of the bureaucracy.[31] The roles and responsibilities of the Party center, the State Council, the National People's Congress, the military, and provincial governments have all become much more clearly delineated. As Nathan writes, "What belongs to a given agency to handle is usually handled by that agency not only without interference but with a growing sense that interference would be illegitimate."[32]

—The creation of institutions that allow for citizen participation and direct engagement with the state not only diffuses grievances that might otherwise build up, but also strengthens the legitimacy of the CCP. One example is the Administrative Litigation Act mentioned earlier, which allows citizens to sue the state.

David Shambaugh's authoritative analysis of the evolution of the CCP provides a variant of this argument. Shambaugh points to multiple successful adaptations that may portend a relatively long-term future for the party but also sees signs of party atrophy.[33] In short, in this view China is successfully adapting to changing circumstances, building an authoritarian state that is compatible both with global integration and with modernization.

Collapse

The opposing argument is that the CCP is actually massively weakened from within owing to corruption and moral decay, and has by and large lost its legitimacy in the nation. While economic growth rates have been high, the massive SOEs continue to place a strain on the economy and undermine national competitiveness. Rather than having banks serve the needs of the market, the state uses banks as a tool to push funds through the system and into the SOEs, further holding back the development of the financial sector. The growing instances of regional social protest and citizen discontent are another symptom of a system under stress. Rather than responding to citizen grievances with remedies, the state has chosen to largely respond through repression, using the heavy hand of authority to keep its power intact. And so, the argument goes, the CCP will not be able to withstand political or economic shocks, and faces collapse.[34]

Democratic Evolution

Those who believe in the inevitability of a democratic future for China argue that market reforms and the creation of market institutions in China will pave the way for political liberalization and eventual democratization, just as they did in neighboring South Korea and Taiwan.[35] The institutions required for advanced economic development, such as the rule of law, place restraints on the arbitrary exercise of power and create protection of certain rights for both the private sector and citizens. As the Chinese economy continues to integrate into global markets, this argument claims, pro-democratic values will spread. These forces will combine with a growing middle class to exert pressures on the ruling elite for reform. Some of the institutional changes explored throughout this book, such as rules for the transfer of power, semi-competitive grassroots elections, and marginal increases in legislative and judicial independence, are all seen as signs of potential political reform in the future.

Trapped Transition

The last school of thought, put forth most eloquently by Minxin Pei, argues that China's gradualist approach to reform has left its potential transition to democracy stuck at the halfway point, unable to progress to full liberalization. Real democratization will not take place for several reasons. First and foremost, the ruling elites benefit from the current authoritarian system and can now tap into the fruits of economic growth to hold back political liberalization and co-opt potential opponents. That is, economic growth reduces, rather than increases, the pressure for political change. Moreover, the incrementalist approach to reform holds back political evolution because the overriding goal of the ruling elite is to maintain its position of power, even at the cost of constraints on economic growth or efficiency losses. It is in the interests of that elite to implement only gradual, marginal reforms, protecting lucrative sectors from greater competition and maintaining their monopoly on power. At the local levels, the lack of accountability mechanisms coupled with administrative and fiscal decentralization, along with repression of civil society and the lack of legal independence for citizens groups, have opened the way for unrestrained predation by party and governmental officials. The inability of the center to monitor and control the corruption of this predatory elite throughout the system is leading to stagnation. All this leaves China in a "partial reform equilibrium," heading for neither democracy nor collapse.[36]

"Crossing the River by Feeling for the Stones"

The "trapped transition" and "collapse" schools of thought contend that China's political experiments, as detailed throughout this book, are necessarily inadequate because they cannot alter the political elite's near monopoly of power or because they represent mere tinkering around the edges that cannot meet China's enormous challenges. The "resilient authoritarianism" and "democratic evolution" schools argue that China's gradualist approach to reform is solving these problems or is evolving in directions that will lead to resolution, although they disagree on the likely end state. All these assessments respond to the understandable desire to know what to expect from this enormously important country. They represent thoughtful and informed attempts to weave a comprehensible narrative out of an extraordinary tangle of threads that will affect China's trajectory, from the rising middle class to the growing demand for services and the scale of China's domestic woes.

But in all likelihood, China's future is not predictable. So much about China is unique and unprecedented—its history, the massive scale of its perils and promise, the international environment in which its rush to modernization is occurring—that not even the deep and thoughtful reflections of the analysts cited above can be fully convincing, especially since they contradict one another so sharply. Although on paper the paths look separate and diverging (for example, between authoritarianism and democracy), in practice what is evolving on the ground is much more entangled—authoritarianism with democratic strands, and deepening contestation, along with an ever-richer debate about what kind of reform works for China. Rather than try to predict now which of the various trends shaping China's political future will win out, we look at how Chinese actors themselves are trying to shape that future.

By exploring what is happening with the many experiments China itself is undertaking, from administrative streamlining to creating semi-competitive electoral mechanisms, to engaging civil society and instituting greater transparency, we can investigate how the multifarious interests and groups are responding to the enormous social pressures building up in China. These pressures include the urgency of sustaining economic growth and reform, the need to keep up with the threats and opportunities of new information technology, and the growing demands from an increasingly vocal and empowered citizenry that is facing a diversifying set of needs. Each set of experiments in a particular type of reform is dealt with in a chapter that follows. Each innovation not only comes with its own set of success and challenges, but has also been received by central authorities with different degrees of enthusiasm.

Administrative Reforms

Chapter 2 focuses on the nitty-gritty business of government reform—efforts under way since the late 1990s to streamline bureaucratic and administrative processes and make them compatible with a modern economy and society. We present cases in which local governments have tried to build greater discipline into audit and approval procedures, as well as to transform the mind-set of officials from one of public command to one of public service. Such reforms were initiated at the local level for the practical purpose of promoting investment and economic growth, and spread to other localities owing to the race for investment among different regions. At the national level, China's accession to the World Trade Organization (WTO) provided additional impetus for the center to encourage efforts to boost the functioning of government systems. The reforms are also intended to undermine the ability of local predatory elites to extract rents—in other words, to counter the massive corruption endemic in China's governments at all levels.

Key to governance reforms everywhere are administrative processes that provide services efficiently and curb corruption. Success in both is crucial to the CCP's survival, at once deepening the party's legitimacy and changing the foundations of the CCP's rule to some degree. While falling short of democracy, the streamlining of administrative power nevertheless means a substantial step away from the totalitarianism of the pre-1980s era. Enhancing monitoring over administrative processes means the emergence of internal checks and balances within the state, which helps to improve piecemeal accountability even in the absence of broader accountability mechanisms such as free elections. These experiments have been successful to some degree, but also reveal the tremendous difficulties involved in institutionalizing restraints on the exercise of state power. Administrative powers have been substantially cut in some areas, but the dominance of the government continues to be a problem in other areas, reflecting an internal battle between reformers and those pushing to expand the power of the bureaucracy.

But even highly successful administrative reforms may not necessarily work only to support the existing political system. There may be unexpected spillovers if citizens become accustomed to demanding greater transparency and accessibility from government. To the degree that the administrative reforms also change the state-society relationship, by making people see the government as something that should serve people's needs rather than tell them what to do, these reforms could instead strengthen trends toward a more independent and demanding citizenry that feels more empowered to hold the government accountable for its performance and can overcome the capacity of local elites to be predatory.

The larger question is whether such administrative reforms are likely to go far enough to resolve the broader problems of creating a sustainable governing system for a rapidly modernizing China. To what extent can streamlining administration in itself succeed in the long run without reform in other aspects of the political system? Administrative reform has certainly been needed to support high levels of economic growth as China moves from poverty to middle-income status. But would it fall short of providing the accountability, participation, and transparency mechanisms needed to govern China's increasingly complex economy and society?

Electoral Reforms

Chapter 3 explores several innovations aimed at developing electoral capacity and mechanisms within China. China's unusual dual authority structure encompasses important roles for both party and government, such that reform within the party system has much larger ramifications for the bureaucracy compared to other countries where the civil service and political parties are separated. By focusing on the application of governance innovations, such as elections, to the party, in addition to the much better known electoral experiments at the village level, this chapter offers insights into both how China is currently governed and how those governance systems may be changing. We examine experiments in democratizing the party itself, electoral reforms within government-organized mass organizations (also known as GONGOs, or government-organized NGOs), and the relatively rare experiments with semi-competitive elections beyond the village level, into the formal administrative levels of the township and county.

Electoral competition, in however marginalized a part of the party-state, is usually thought to be the last thing that a traditional Communist regime wants to allow. However, semi-competitive elections have continued to spread to more villages, and upward to the township and county levels, although at a very slow pace.

The introduction of the semi-competitive election aims at improving the accountability of local officials to dissatisfied residents. The major reason why local party secretaries have been willing to share their power is that they have to do so in the face of limited economic resources and in order to appease increasingly independent, and in many cases discontented, local residents. But to implement competitive elections means to give up the power to appoint officials. Thus there is a constant struggle for every decisionmaker to strike a balance between keeping power over local officials and holding local officials accountable to the people. The multiple experiments with semi-competitive elections in China, and the resistance to their spread, underline this ongoing tension between the desire to hang on to a significant source of power—the power to appoint officials at the next lower level—and the need to institutionalize more meaningful forms of accountability in China's political system.

Yet confidence is clearly much greater in elections that are confined to the party itself than in those involving the general public. Intraparty democracy, as stated by the party, might not be sufficient for promoting democratization in the wider society. But it does seem likely both to transform the traditionally vertical power structure of the party to one that is more horizontal and broadly accountable and to familiarize the Party with competitive elections.

In contrast with the cautious attitude of the party-state authorities, the broader society has displayed a healthy appetite for news about competitive elections. This enthusiasm is reflected in heavy media coverage of many semi-competitive elections, particularly in new media. Stories of independent representatives striving to check the behavior of local officials, sometimes inviting retaliation by those officials, have received considerable sympathetic media coverage. The reporting and open discussion of these stories demonstrate a dynamism that has not been seen before in China, hinting at gradual changes in the political culture.

Civil Society Organizations

Chapter 4 looks at ways in which local governments are engaging with civil society groups and GONGOs (government-organized nongovernmental organizations), as well as changes within these social organizations themselves. Until recently, there was very little in the way of organized civil society in China. Social interests were gathered into government-organized associations, such as women's associations and trade unions, where the purpose was to ensure social control and meet government-directed social objectives rather than to represent the particular interests of the members. The political space that would allow nonstate groups to organize and provide a counterweight to state power was highly constrained.

However, the decentralized and fluid nature of Chinese governance, and the decline of state control in society, has created openings that citizens around the country have seized to form everything from sports clubs to religious associations and to find new openings to engage in policy processes.[37] At the same time, new pressures have emerged to provoke the realignment of the state's relations with these mass organizations. These pressures include mounting social and environmental problems that cannot be dealt with by the state alone (particularly at the local level), the rise of more independently organized civil society groups that compete to serve the interests of the associations' members, and—with the rapidly growing networks developing between Chinese state agencies, corporations, and social organizations and their international counterparts—the spread of norms related to transparency, accountability, and participation.

The chapter explores why the evolution of civil society is key to understanding the prospects for China's political development and draws on multiple cases of reform in the regulation and activities of civil society organizations. To what degree is Chinese society developing the capacity to organize and carry out collective action in search of social goals? Can social organizations and networks articulate, aggregate, and represent the multifarious interests of this increasingly complex society? As with the policy innovations examined in the other chapters, change in this area is bound up with competing interests. In the past decade, the party-state has struggled to find ways to engage the power of social organizing for what it defines as the collective good, while vigilantly opposing any organizing that could lead to threats to the party's grip on power.

The space for associations that can serve as autonomous counterweights to state authority or pose challenges to CCP monopoly via advocacy and criticism is extremely limited, although such associations do exist. Much more common are civil society organizations that provide social services, and GONGOs that are increasingly caught between their traditional role as arms of the state and the pressures they now face to serve the interests of their ostensible members. Would a more vibrant associational life bolster authoritarian resilience by having a positive effect on economic performance and social stability, or would it support political liberalization thanks to society's increased capacity to form interest-based groups able to act in defense of their interests?

Neither local nor central authorities have yet shown signs of willingness to substantially loosen controls on social organization. However, the space for negotiation and partnership with the state is far greater than formal regulations would suggest. The dynamic nature of these state-society relations makes analysis difficult, as we have to avoid the temptation to pin down what is essentially a moving target. Even what appear to be unthreatening service-provision roles carried out by GONGOs have potential political significance. Service providers often morph into advocates, as they come to see the larger systemic causes of the problems they are trying to ameliorate. And beyond this, the habits of effective collective action die hard—the skills and norms learned in a homeowners association can transfer to organizations with quite different goals.

Transparency and Scaling from Local to National

Chapter 5 considers what happens when local experiments get scaled up into national regulation, and looks at the challenge of implementation on the national level. Like all governments, Chinese authorities are grappling with the political and economic implications of the global revolution in information technology and with rapidly changing norms about who is entitled to know what. In the 1990s, numerous localities, such as the province of Guangzhou and the municipality of Shanghai, began experimenting with a variety of "right to know" rules that require government bodies to release information to citizens, both proactively and in response to citizens' requests. In addition, there have been efforts to make parliamentary processes more open and transparent. In May 2008, national regulations on "Open Government Information" (OGI) came into effect.

This chapter examines how the regulations changed in their migration from the local to the national level. Trial regulations in places such as Guangzhou and Shanghai served as sites for learning and experimentation, providing the central government with substantive evidence of the value of transparency regulations before scaling up to the national level. The national regulations, however, are circumscribed in some key ways. Unlike their local variants, the OGI regulations stop short of providing citizens with the right to know, and also lean more toward the spirit of secrecy as the norm and disclosure as the exception, rather than the other way around.

The chapter also takes a close look at how new national regulations are implemented in China's decentralized structure, highlighting examples of how effective implementation has led to important changes within the state, as well as between state and society. In a few places, there are strong signs of relatively rapid and significant implementation, buoyed by a combination of strong state leadership and active engagement by citizens and civil society. But because implementation is left up to individual localities, it is precisely where the predatory elites are most deeply ensconced that we are likely to see the least progress. This challenge will apply to all efforts to scale reforms from local to national, and will have a bearing on how all of the innovations that we look at could potentially affect the national governance architecture.

Clearly, China's transparency regulations do not necessarily operate within the same frameworks as those in democratic governance systems. The potential governance impact therefore can also play out through entirely unexpected channels as the regulations change the incentives of a wide range of actors. On one hand, if the primary effect of disclosure is to reduce corruption and promote administrative efficiency, the regulations could bolster the resilience of the one-party system, with the enhanced efficiency translating into greater legitimacy—if the party-state's conflicted relationship between openness and control doesn't cause the authorities just to shut the transparency mechanisms down. At the same time, the OGI regulations have also empowered citizens, the social elite, and civil society to advance their interests, taking advantage of the broader space provided by the disclosure regulations. As these groups continue to push for greater state accountability within the limits of the regulations, information technology and the global spread of social networking are changing the contours of citizen mobilization around the world. It is not clear whether the transparency regulations, even if comprehensively implemented, will keep up with the development of social media.

What we are left with is not a single linear path forward, but several meandering and overlapping trajectories. What is clear is that the OGI regulations, in empowering multiple interest groups, are deepening the contestation between authoritarian and democratizing forces in China.

The Unpredictable Path of China's Experiments

In the concluding chapter, we take a cross-cutting look at all of the attempts at political innovation and consider their implications for China's longer-term political trajectory. Do these reforms offer a way forward for more democratic institutions, or do they provide another way of sustaining and entrenching the rule of the CCP? The challenge of understanding China's development path is further complicated by the fact that all of these domestic events are happening in a context that extends far beyond China itself. Economic and cultural globalization is also tied in part to the development of new media and information technology, which may create new mechanisms for political organization. With globalization, points of communication are increasingly reaching behind state borders, leading to an explosion of exchanges that is affecting and changing citizen tastes, outlooks, values, norms, and expectations. The potential effects of information technology are hard to predict, given the "arms race" taking place between government controls and ongoing advances in the technology, as well as constant citizen efforts to skirt these controls.

At an even broader level, we also have to contend with the unclear and highly contested relationship between economic growth and political reform. While it could be argued that economic growth alleviates pressure for some aspects of political reform, market forces are creating pressures for change in other aspects. The question of who is reaping the rewards from growth, and how inclusive the process is, is an important one. Inequality is rising both across regions (for example, between the developed eastern cities and the more impoverished inland western provinces) and within urbanizing centers. The growing rural-urban migration, the aging population structure, and the changing burden of disease have created marginalized groups that cannot access public services and have few channels through which to voice their discontent. At the same time, sustained economic growth is creating an increasingly large and mobilized middle class, whose demands on the state are also rising.[38] If it is true, as one recent authoritative study contends, that most countries stagnate at a middle income level, unable to develop further due to lack of political reform, we must consider the possibility that China's three decade track record of explosive economic growth may falter in the near future.[39] Will China prove an exception—and if so, how? (See box 1-2 for a discussion of the Singapore model.)

Rather than predicting any single outcome, in this book we closely examine the state of intense competition pushing China in different directions, and delineate the lines of contestation. As the Chinese party-state struggles with mounting governance challenges in a rapidly transforming socioeconomic landscape, some of the most interesting battles and new ideas are taking place not in Beijing but in townships and counties. These policy experiments offer hints about the types of institutions that could evolve in the future, but China's experimentalist and ad hoc approach to reform creates dynamics that defy easy categorization. The extent to which these local experiments will have large-scale impact also depends on the response from Beijing.

The origin of each type of policy experiment, and the degree to which each innovation has been embraced by the center, is highly uneven. Trials in administrative streamlining arose spontaneously and are being strongly encouraged by central authorities, while township elections are still being watched with caution, with no final verdict on their desirability or permissibility to date. While formal regulations on civil society organizations continue to be strict, with crackdowns taking place occasionally, all manner of local, international, and government-owned NGOs are de facto operating in China and engaging with state authorities on a range of problems, revealing deep-seated contradictions within the party-state about how to act on this issue. While experiments in transparency regulations were encouraged by the center, the national policy did not go as far as local governments in places such as Guangzhou and Shanghai were willing to go, stopping short of affirming principles such as a citizen's

Box 1-2. *A Singapore Model?*

No one is more concerned with the future trajectory of China than the CCP itself. Indeed, its pragmatic and eclectic approach to reform reflects the Party's bottom line—maintaining power. Its quest for survival has meant a pragmatic willingness to examine a wide range of possible solutions to its problems, learning from foreign experiences and selectively picking and adapting these practices to try out at home. The CCP has employed analysts to study a sweeping range of political models around the world, looking not just at Communist and ex-Communist regimes, but also at democratic systems and both single- and multi-party authoritarian states.[a]

In this search, Singapore has long been of particular interest to the Party. It is often suggested that China could manage to combine a market economy with a one-party system, just as Singapore has done for the past forty-odd years. Indeed, the CCP has been sending delegations to the island nation since the 1980s, to study how the ruling People's Action Party (PAP) has retained its grip on power.[b] The lessons drawn from this detailed study are surprising. China scholar David Shambaugh quotes one article written by Chinese scholar Cai Dingjian that was published in *China Youth Daily* in 2005. In this article, Cai argues that "Singapore is basically a democratic system that practices authoritarian rule"—and that its solid hold on political power was made possible because the PAP subjected itself to general elections every five years. In his view, "[t]he danger that it may lose state power has always filled the party with a sense of crisis, always reminding it not to forget the people. This awareness is the in-built force that drives the party to truly serve the people at all times."[c]

In our view, however, there are many reasons why China's scale, and economic and population structure make such comparisons impractical. First, China's administrative structure, as previously described, is highly decentralized and fragmented. Unlike Singapore's highly integrated and compact civil service, China has to grapple with complex center-local relations, where national policy directives reach local levels through diffused channels, where monitoring and enforcement options are weak, and where local priorities can often contradict national ones.

Second, ethnic divisions in China are drawn along geographical lines that are too vast to be managed Singapore-style. In Singapore, different races live and work side by side in a fairly even mix, in part because racial quotas in public housing estates prevent any particular area from becoming dominated by one ethnicity. In China, however, ethnic identities have long been tied to regional allegiances.

Third, economic growth has spurred massive internal migration flows within China. The challenge is not just the depletion of the working-age population in rural areas, and the burgeoning work force in cities, but also dealing with large migrant populations that are marginalized and who cannot access social services. Singapore, in contrast, is small enough that internal movement of people is not a problem, and it has tightly controlled borders that allow careful management of immigration issues.

Fourth, Singapore and China have vastly different economic structures. The challenge of managing China's rural and urban economies is substantially more complex than managing Singapore's city-state economy. Singapore's Economic Development Board can make strategic bets that drive Singapore's economy and keep it competitive, while China's economy is too decentralized. China's national-level policies take place at such a large scale that they can have global repercussions. The exchange rate policy is but one example.

Finally, Singapore is governed by a highly competent and technocratic elite, which arguably is small enough such that cohesiveness can be maintained, not unlike running a very large corporation. There are 15,000 members in Singapore's ruling People's Action Party, while China's Communist Party has over 70 million members. The challenge of maintaining cohesiveness in such an immense organization is arguably unique in the world.

These differences aside, Singapore's general election in May 2011 and presidential election in August of the same year raised interesting questions about the sustainability of the PAP's approach to maintaining power. The 2011 elections also highlighted the role that formal elections play in both instilling discipline in the ruling party and providing a stable framework for political evolution. The 2011 general election was hailed as a watershed event in Singaporean politics, bringing in fresh political competition and injecting a greater sense of democracy into the system. The PAP won 60.1 percent of the vote, its worst performance since independence in 1965.[d] This translated into the highest number of opposition candidates being voted into Parliament (six, compared to four in 1991).[e] Singapore's heavyweight politician Foreign Minister George Yeo (formerly minister for trade and industry and minister for information and the arts, and a former brigadier-general in the Singapore armed forces) lost his seat when the opposition Workers Party won 54.7 percent of the vote in his constituency.

These numbers aside, the 2011 general election was seen as different for a host of reasons. First was the number and quality of candidates that joined opposition parties—people with stellar credentials from the civil service and the private and nonprofit sectors. This shift reflected a changing citizenry with shifting and far more vocal political views, challenging conventional perceptions about the political apathy of Singaporeans and revealing major cracks in the wall of fear that used to accompany anything associated with opposition politics.

It was also the first election in which political expression via new social media such as YouTube, Facebook, and blogs was freely allowed. The result was an explosion of views and commentary across these platforms, with

(continued)

Box 1-2 *(continued)*

Singaporeans creating their own videos, sharing their views, and organizing in ways not seen before. While this new dynamism was no doubt due in part to changing demographics (leading to shifting electorate characteristics), the availability of expression via new media also intersected with socioeconomic complexities and grievances that had been building for some time. Rising health care and housing prices, congestion on roads and on public transportation, high ministerial salaries, as well as swelling numbers of immigrants and foreign workers, all became sources of discontent and points of attack on the PAP—this despite the economy's having grown by an astounding 14.5 percent in 2010.[f]

The 2011 general election was also different for the level of voter anger and frustration directed at the PAP. While PAP candidates pointed to the party's track record of success and competence, voters criticized the party for its elitism and arrogance, for having lost touch with the concerns of ordinary Singaporeans, and placed it under scrutiny for high-profile mistakes over the previous five years. The discontent pointed to shifting sources of legitimacy to rule as the composition of the electorate changed over time, and as Singapore's continued development brought about new social and economic challenges.

Held just three months after the general election, the presidential election reaffirmed the major shifts in Singapore's political landscape. Despite being a largely ceremonial position with limited powers, the presidential seat was hotly contested and generated active debate that again brought the strength and legitimacy of the PAP into question. While former deputy prime minister Dr. Tony Tan, widely acknowledged as the PAP-endorsed candidate, won the vote, it was by the slimmest of margins (0.34 percent). The large number of votes garnered by the first and second runners-up only served to underscore the divergent political values across the citizenry, their dissatisfaction with the status quo, and the weakening ability of a single party to represent all interests.

It remains to be seen whether Cai's observation about the PAP is true. On one hand, the degree of political competition found in the 2011 elections may herald the steady erosion of one-party rule in Singapore. On the other hand, the PAP's slide in performance may be just the shock that the party needs to keep itself disciplined and find new ways to adapt to and evolve with changing conditions on the ground. We can be sure that analysts in the CCP will be watching future developments with great interest.

a. Shambaugh, *China's Communist Party*, p. 87.
b. Ibid., pp. 92–93.
c. Ibid., pp. 94–95.
d. The PAP won 75.3 percent of the vote in 2001 and 66.6 percent in 2006.
e. Singapore's first-past-the-postelectoral vote means that a party's representation in Parliament is not proportional to its share of electoral votes.
f. Department of Statistics, Singapore, "Time Series on GDP at 2005 Market Prices and Real Economic Growth," February 17, 2011 (www.singstat.gov.sg/stats/themes/economy/hist/gdp1.html).

right to know. The implementation process of this national regulation further sheds light on the challenges of scaling up local innovations. Change takes place unevenly, producing not one single trajectory (such as democratization or authoritarian resilience), but several overlapping and competing forces.

Therefore in the concluding chapter we draw from each realm of experimentation to identify the lines of contestation and pinpoint a set of policy areas that bear close monitoring. What we hope to provide is not a prediction about China's future, but rather a framework for thinking about the myriad ways in which local innovations could interact with broader forces of change to bring large-scale transformation to China's governance landscape.

2 | *Streamlining the State*

In 1988, nearly a decade of economic reform had not yet made doing business within China an easy task for Chinese enterprises. Fifteen months of efforts going through thirty-three administrative organizations to get 126 stamps of approval still left one state-owned enterprise at Baoshan prefecture in Shanghai municipality unable to carry out its plans for a joint venture—it needed yet more stamps of approval from yet more administrative bodies. Around the same time, an enterprise in Guizhou province spent a year going through the endless procedures for 170 stamps of approval, nowhere near enough to actually allow it to carry out a planned initiative that would shortly be outdated. The Guizhou enterprise had to pay to get another 270 required stamps in the relatively short span of only forty days, allowing it to finally legally carry out its plans.[1]

Such stories, very common and widely reported in the Chinese media in the 1980s, revealed the extraordinary level of administrative inefficiency in the early stages of China's reform process. The cumbersome red tape was not just inefficient, but also gave rise to rampant corruption, with massive bureaucracy and opaque administrative procedures facilitating rent-seeking by corrupt officials. Such inefficiency was detrimental to the party's and the government's efforts to promote economic development, which with the decline of a commitment to Communist ideology became the party's main claim to legitimate authority. Government corruption also directly eroded the legitimacy of the regime. So reforming administrative processes became a top political priority for China's leadership, crucial to its efforts to maintain the one-party system.

In this chapter we look at the ongoing attempts to fix China's administrative processes. We provide a broad picture of the reform efforts at the national level and present two detailed typical cases at the local level, followed by an assessment of the impact of the reforms.

This assessment is key to understanding whether administrative reform is likely to prove sufficient to provide China with stable and effective governance that can cope with the country's massive challenges, and to stave off pressures for broader political change. Administrative reform in China has significant political implications. Against the background of what had been a totalitarian regime until the 1980s, reducing administrative power means taking a substantial step away from totalitarianism; although it does not automatically mean the emergence of democracy. Enhancing the monitoring of administrative processes requires establishing internal checks and balance within the state apparatus, which helps to improve piecemeal accountability even in the absence of broader accountability mechanisms such as free elections (accountability and electoral processes are explored in chapter 3).

As we noted in chapter 1, one view circulating in recent years is that administrative reform, along with other procedural changes, will bolster authoritarian resilience by making the party-state more effective at meeting the needs of the people.[2] The reforms are also intended to undermine the ability of local predatory elites to extract rents. Given that corruption is one of the greatest threats to the party-state's legitimacy, successful administrative reforms that make the system less corrupt could indeed bolster the system's legitimacy.[3] Thus it is important to investigate whether administrative reforms in and of themselves could be sufficient to address the demands of an increasingly complex society.

But even highly successful administrative reforms may not necessarily work only to support the existing political system. There may be unexpected spillovers if citizens become accustomed to demanding greater transparency and accessibility to government.[4] To the degree that the administrative reforms also change the state-society relationship, by making people see the government as something that should serve people's needs rather than tell them what to do, these reforms could instead strengthen trends toward a more independent and demanding citizenry that feels more empowered to hold the government accountable for its performance and that can overcome the capacity of local elites to be predatory. Thus it is worthwhile to examine these processes in some detail.

The Administrative Reform Path

Pre-reform (that is to say, pre-1979) China was a totalitarian state dominated by a suffocating administrative apparatus that allowed no scope for initiative by its citizens. With the beginnings of economic liberalization in the late 1970s, the party-state began to allow a degree of citizen initiative. But the administrative domination continued. Any initiative to set up private enterprise activity had to be approved by an endless list of bureaucracies before the initiative could be carried out. Only after the mid-1990s did China begin to see significant reductions in the overwhelming role of the administrative apparatus.[5]

But it was not the central government that started the process of administrative streamlining. Much earlier, a process of decentralization was already under way within the government. The reforms of the 1980s brought a significant devolution of budget-making authority, substantially increasing local officials' decisionmaking power. Moreover, decisionmaking power was widely diffused among different government agencies at each level of government. Thus the Chinese administrative structure was already highly decentralized.

This high degree of decentralization led to what Kenneth Lieberthal termed "fragmented authoritarianism," with different parts of government each acting in its own self-interest, often coming into conflict with other parts of government.[6] The fragmented authoritarianism model argues that authority below the very peak of the Chinese political system is fragmented and disjointed. The fragmentation is structurally based and has been enhanced by procedural reforms. The fragmentation, moreover, grew increasingly pronounced under the reforms beginning in the late 1970s, driven by four factors.[7] First, the importance of ideology declined. Policymaking by the different parts of the government lost its ideological glue. Second, government bodies gained increasing autonomy as the decentralization of decisionmaking power accelerated. In particular, because of the existence and growth of extra-budgetary revenue, party and government organizations were inclined to make selfish decisions. Third, China's bureaucratic ranking system combined with the functional division of authority among bureaucracies to produce a situation in which it was often necessary to achieve agreement by an array of bodies, where no single body had authority over the others. Fourth, information flow within the hierarchy became increasingly fragmented. Authorities at lower levels reported to their superiors selectively. All of these factors rendered China's authoritarianism increasingly disjointed.[8]

Understanding the political impact of decentralization was a vital contribution of the literature on fragmented authoritarianism. But since this thesis, which was based on the experience of China in the 1980s, was put forth, much has changed. The country has worked to streamline its administrative processes and to change the relationship between the government and the people in new ways. The "fragmented authoritarianism" concept certainly continues to explain a great many of the politically relevant developments in China—but not all. The administrative streamlining of the past two decades improved efficiency in governance in China, which is partly embodied in the fast economic growth of the 1990s and the first decade of the 2000s. Its success has led other scholars to propose the idea that China is building a system of authoritarian resilience, as described above.[9] It is thus important to examine to what extent the administrative reform has been successful so as to develop a better understanding of China's possible future political trajectory.

Relations between the government and the people are, as in all countries, determined in part by people's experiences with the administrative bureaucracy and regulatory requirements imposed by the government. Since the early 1990s, administrative processes in China have changed significantly by: (1) cutting the number of regulations requiring government approvals for given activities; (2) changing the processes by which new regulations are promulgated; (3) enhancing government monitoring of administrative processes; and (4) increasing public transparency. Transparency, which goes well beyond the administrative realm, is addressed in detail in chapter 5. This chapter focuses on administrative streamlining and monitoring.

When pervasive administrative power, as practiced under the totalitarian conditions of the pre-reform period, proved to be disastrous, the leadership under Deng Xiaoping decided to reform. The first reform stage in the 1980s allowed initiatives by local authorities, by individual state-owned enterprises, and by private citizens. However, the party-state tried to maintain tight control, using its administrative power to check activities not initiated by the state. In the decade of the 1980s, every initiative, no matter how minor, needed official authorization. To get each of the required permissions involved dealing with dozens of administrative bodies and unclear procedures. As shown by the anecdotes at the beginning of this chapter, it was not uncommon that a private effort to develop a small enterprise needed to get more than 300 such permissions in the form of stamps, which meant seeking authorization from more than 300 different administrative offices at different levels, a process that could take months and even years. Newspapers, novels, movies, and television programs in the 1980s and 1990s reported on this burdensome bureaucracy and its devastating effects on efficiency, creating pressures for reform.

After 1992, when China introduced substantially enhanced market economy reforms to replace the planned economy (or command economy, to use Janos Kornai's term), private initiatives were not just allowed; they were encouraged and facilitated. This great shift of the fundamental nature of the desired economic institution provided strong momentum for the authorities to reform administrative processes. The contradiction between the extraordinary levels of red tape and the mushrooming of private initiatives became increasingly acute and had to be solved one way or the other: either initiatives would be suffocated by red tape and market reforms would fail, or the red tape would have to be cut to allow initiatives to flourish. But it took until the late 1990s for the call for streamlining administrative procedures to get the upper hand and lead to significant change.[10]

There are two discernible phases to the administrative reform process. The first phase, from 1997 through 2001, was characterized by local initiatives to simplify administrative procedures. The second phase, from 2002 to 2006, was characterized by a systematic and intense effort led by the central authority to reduce the number of required administrative approvals.[11]

Localities began the administrative reform process largely because of decentralization. With the growth of decentralization, local authorities were both forced to take responsibility for governance and given substantial power to undertake reform initiatives. After the reform and opening processes started in the late 1970s, economic growth rather than ideological loyalty became the single most important criterion for promoting cadres. Local authorities thus sought investments to boost economic development. The red tape inherited from the totalitarian period was obviously one hindrance to investment initiatives. If a project could only be carried out after years of procuring approval from hundreds of government agencies, few business people would be still interested in making investments. Potential investors complained about red tape, and the mass media ran numerous stories detailing cases and calling for reforms. Local as well as central officials understood the problem. But the bureaucrats stood their ground, insisting on retaining their approval powers. It was a prolonged stalemate, broken only in the late 1990s when a few localities broke through and started the streamlining.

Within a few years, these scattered local experiments were scaled up by the central authorities into a national campaign. Catalyzed by China's accession to the World Trade Organization in 2002, the central government instituted five rounds of reform, cutting more than a thousand items that needed administrative approvals and transferring the approval power for other items to localities or government-sponsored nongovernmental organizations.[12] The center's sustained effort to streamline the administrative approvals process sent an unequivocal message to all levels of government across the country that the number of administrative approvals should be reduced, the more the better. The State Council's efforts led to a nationwide campaign. Since the mid-1990s, governments at all levels across China have been abolishing thousands of requirements for administrative approval.

The streamlining campaign has not been a linear process of steady improvement. Few officials were willing to give up power voluntarily. Many of the abolished approval requirements were surreptitiously reintroduced under a different name. Some officials followed the orders from the center half-heartedly. But once the resistance to administrative streamlining in a particular region led to slower economic growth than other regions, the major decisionmakers in that region again began to push for streamlining reform. It is very much a game of three steps forward, two steps back. But overall, the requirements for administrative approval in China have been significantly diminished.

As we will see in subsequent chapters, this pattern of local experimentation followed by a national campaign has become a common approach to governance reform in China. In the 1990s local governments frequently took the lead in searching out new ways of governing. Many politically important initiatives, not just the administrative reforms but also initiatives related to transparency, civil society, and even elections, began as local efforts to address local problems without advance permission or even the knowledge of the center. Some reforms were still led from the center, but in many cases it was the localities that started the reform. In those instances, the role of the center has been to facilitate or to hinder the change that was initiated by the localities.

The first efforts to streamline administrative processes began in 1997 at the local level. Shenzhen municipality was one of the first localities to initiate the reform.[13] The indicative event is the circulation of the report "Yi Qingli he Chongding Xingzheng Shenpi Xiangmu Wei Zhongdian, Shixian Zhuanbian Zhengfu Zhineng Gaige De Jianyi" (Advice for Redefining Administrative Approval to Bring about Reforms and Change the Function of Government). It was written by Zhang Siping, then director of the Office of Economic Institutional Reform of Shenzhen prefecture, and presented to the prefecture leadership. The prefecture leadership accepted the report and ordered administrative bodies to take measures accordingly.[14]

The basic idea of the reform was to streamline the administrative approval requirements for private sector initiatives. Complicated procedures were greatly simplified. Administrative bodies scattered in different places were asked to move their offices to a one-stop administrative service center to save the applicants time. Procedures were required to be posted on boards and later on the Internet.

Following the administrative reform, there was a mushrooming of economic investment in Shenzhen prefecture. Localities across the country learned about the reform in Shenzhen and its impact. In the absence of any clear directives from the center, they took it upon themselves to implement similar reforms in order to promote economic initiatives and activities. Their zeal for economic growth through enhancing efficiency was driven by the fact that an official's performance in promoting economic development was the main criterion for his or her promotion to a higher rank.[15]

The second stage of administrative reforms started in late 2001. This effort was initiated by the center in the name of harmonizing domestic regulations (which were still largely derived from the planned economy

Table 2-1. *Administrative Reforms*

Year	Issuing authority	File number	Number of administrative approvals abolished	Number of administrative approvals transferred to localities
2002	State Council	国发[2002]24号	789	0
2003	State Council	国发[2003]5号	406	82
2004	State Council	国发[2004]16号	409	86
2007	State Council	国发[2007]33号	128	58
2010	State Council	国发[2010]21号	113	71

Sources: Compiled by the authors based on orders by the State Council for abolishing and transferring administrative approvals. Orders are available on the website of the central government of China. The complete text of each order is available at the following links:

www.gov.cn/gongbao/content/2002/content_61829.htm;
www.gov.cn/zwgk/2005-09/06/content_29621.htm;
www.gov.cn/gongbao/content/2004/content_62767.htm;
www.gov.cn/zwgk/2007-10/12/content_775186.htm;
www.gov.cn/zwgk/2010-07/09/content_1650088.htm.

system) with WTO regulations, which were based on market institutions and practices. The State Council established the Leadership Team on Reforming Approval Granting to push that reform in 2001.[16] Starting in 2002, the State Council issued five rounds of orders to cut administrative approvals. Table 2-1 shows the details of those rounds.

These administrative overhauls have involved all ministries and a wide range of issues. For example, approvals are no longer required to carry out any investment project in agriculture, forestry, irrigation, transportation, or machinery, provided the project does not involve government funds, is not a state-planned major project, and is not something that has been specifically forbidden by the government. Also, it is no longer necessary to get prior approvals to organize commercial exhibitions, as long as the exhibition does not include anything owned by foreigners. Universities now do not have to seek prior approvals from the ministry of education to name foreigners as honorary professors or employ them as visiting professors.

The reduction of red tape has continued in multiple rounds. The fifth, launched in July 2010, allowed domestic welfare organizations (charity funds) to develop joint projects with their foreign counterparts and foreign tourist agencies to establish branches in China. International nonbanking financial organizations can now establish branches in China without prior approval from the China Banking Regulatory Commission. Joint ventures in the field of health care are also now free of prior approval requirements.

After these efforts to streamline administrative approval processes, small and medium-sized initiatives in most sectors face many fewer administrative hurdles, and sometimes none at all. But the government still retains important administrative authority over large-scale initiatives, especially those in strategically important sectors, including finance, energy, telecommunications, and education.

Responses to the State Council's edicts varied by province, with local authorities making different efforts to reduce administrative power. Although some cut less than the center, others were more radical. For example, the government of Chengdu prefecture (in Sichuan province) cut 90 percent of its approval requirements, keeping 107 of the previously mandatory 1,166.[17]

Not everyone has been happy about directives abolishing administrative approvals. There are bureaucrats who want to keep the requirements in place, and some have succeeded in restoring some requirements. Thus there is a battle between those who want to cut red tape and those who want to keep it in place.

Another crucial dimension of the reform was regulating the power to determine which items would need approval and by what procedures. Before the turn of the twenty-first century, administrative bodies at different levels had almost unchecked power to impose regulatory requirements. They did not need the involvement of other government agencies at the same level or of their parent agencies at higher levels, or the involvement of any representative body or the general public, to establish approval requirements and procedures. In other words, government administrators had essentially free rein. Thus the administrative reforms that simplified application procedures significantly constrained the power of different administrative bodies. Now, when a government body wants to establish a regulation requiring citizens to seek administrative approval of any kind, that proposed regulation must usually be reviewed by local government, by the local people's congress, and by authorities at higher levels. The new regulation must be consistent with related laws. This change helps to put the administrative functions of government under the rule by law (if not yet the rule of law), thus helping to reduce the abuse of approval power. There is not, however, any equivalent of the public notice and comment period that U.S. administrative law requires for proposed regulations.

The third dimension of the reform was to enhance the monitoring of the approval granting process by other governmental organizations and even by the public. For example, Shenzhen prefecture (in Guangdong province) set up an electronic system to publicize the approval applications at all thirty-eight administrative offices on 239 issues in 2005, as we describe in detail below.[18]

Local Reforms: Starting in Shenzhen

Shenzhen prefecture was the first local government to embark on large-scale reforms of its administrative approval system. In 1980 the central authorities in China began to develop four Special Economic Zones, including Shenzhen. These were four islands opened to the world market economy during the original wave of economic reforms, in the sea of the planned and closed economy that existed throughout the rest of China at that time. The purpose of the Special Economic Zones was to experiment with new economic institutions and new interactions with the international economy. As one of the pioneer cities leading China's economic reform and development, Shenzhen's economic development had been hindered by the heavy administrative red tape. Beginning in 1997, Shenzhen implemented three rounds of reform to its administrative approval system, which aimed to simplify and downsize the administrative approval procedures and requirements, before experimenting with the Electronic Supervision System for Administrative Approval Procedures.

Shenzhen's reforms began in 1997 with self-reviews of all government departments and a series of meetings on procedural simplifications. That round resulted in a substantial reduction in Shenzhen City (42.44 percent of the original 1,109 items needing administrative approval were cut, leaving 628). The second major adjustment was made in 2001. This time, approval requirements were cut from 628 to 277, or nearly 38 percent. In 2003 the third round of reform was conducted against the background of China's accession to the WTO. This round of reform focused on improving the delivery and service quality of administrative approval, with standardization and clarification of requirements. These included the establishment of an Administrative Licensing and Approval Service Center; encouraging joint efforts between departments to cut the cost of applications; centralizing supervision and control instead of having fragmented supervision at the departmental level; setting up on-the-spot supervision to ensure the correct collection of fees; and improving the quality of service provided by the staff at the Service Center.[19]

The streamlining greatly facilitated individuals' pursuit of economic and social activities. Permission for an investment project that might have taken years to get can now be granted in a week or a month. Getting a passport used to take months but now only takes five working days. Previously, it was not uncommon for applicants to rent a house near the bureaucracies in order to live nearby during the weeks or months required to get the administrative approvals; that is no longer necessary. And because so many approval requirements were greatly simplified or abolished, the payment of petty bribes to officials decreased as well.

Shenzhen's administrative reforms helped improve the social and economic environment and became a model for the country. Officials from other provinces were sent to learn from Shenzhen's experience. Mudanjiang, on the border with Russia, undertook similar administrative streamlining some years after Shenzhen started its reform process. Before the reform, it had been impossible for villagers to export goods to Russia because the administrative approval requirements were so onerous. After the reform, which abolished some of the administrative approvals required for exports, villages were allowed to export vegetables to Russia. The villages bordering Russia managed to export US$2.8 million worth of tomatoes to Russia in the year after the reform was implemented.[20]

Keenly aware of the significance of the administrative reform, the central government formed a leadership committee in September 2001 promoting national reform of the administrative approval system. Despite these successes, there were also setbacks. Even after the reform, rent-seeking remained, and some regulations that had been removed or simplified crept back in. When the third round of reform began, Shenzhen's administrative approval system had 497 licensing or permit requirements, more than 200 of which had returned after the second reform.[21] For example, some regulations that had been canceled in the earlier round reappeared in new guises, such as ensuring food safety and protecting the environment.

Similar reforms undertaken by nearly a dozen other prefectures have included three elements:[22] (1) reducing the number of items that required licensing or permit approval (many prefecture governments managed to reduce these requirements by more than 40 percent); (2) establishing a central approval service system, usually called Administrative Approval Service Center (also called Administration Service System or Government Service Center")[23] to simplify the application process; (3) implementing e-services by providing these administrative services online and keeping the application process transparent and standardized. These measures have achieved substantial results within a short period of time.

Monitoring and Supervision

However, a gaping hole remained in these reform efforts. The behavior of the streamlined administration was not monitored sufficiently. It turned out that, contrary to the reformers' starting assumptions, government departments and civil servants did not necessarily behave with integrity simply because it was their duty to do so. Bureaucrats sitting in the administrative service center could still work slowly and prolong the approval process, even though the number of items needing their approval had been cut significantly. The lack of checks on the licensing process substantially reduced the impact of the administrative reform process. To fix this, the Shenzhen prefecture government tried another experiment: an electronic supervision system to oversee the process of granting licenses.

The Shenzhen Electronic Supervision System (Electronic Supervision System hereafter) was the first project funded by the prefecture's special fund established for the development of an electronic government (or e-government) service system. The project is the direct result of a joint research effort to improve discipline in China's public administration conducted by the Supervision Bureau of Shenzhen Prefecture and the United Nations Development Program (UNDP). Its objective was the same as that of the third administrative approval system reform: to establish a supervisory system to monitor the administrative approval process. As early as 2003, the prefecture's Supervision Office became one of the pilot places in the country's experiment with "constructing a clean public administration for China" and took up a study of "the effectiveness of supervisory bodies on public administration." In 2004, with encouragement from the central leadership and Supervision Ministry, which looked to Shenzhen as an experimental model for cleaning up China's massive corruption, the Shenzhen Supervision Bureau proposed the construction of the Electronic Supervision System and mapped the concept for the entire city's administrative approval system.

Planning for the system started in June 2004. It underwent a trial operation in November of that year, and it was officially launched on January 1, 2005, initially encompassing the services of thirty-one government departments for the 239 items that still required administrative approval and gradually expanding to include another twenty-eight government departments. The system employs information technology tools and video monitoring devices to supervise the actual processes of administrative approval (from receiving applications from the public, to processing, checking, and approval granting) and electronic monitoring of the process as it takes place in the administration hall. The system automatically issues warnings or alerts when administrative approval conditions or procedures are violated—for example, when approvals are not issued within the stipulated time frame or application fees are collected inappropriately.

Shenzhen's Electronic Supervision System consists of the electronic supervision interface, a video surveillance system, and an external network. The electronic supervision interface was the core of the Electronic Supervision System. It was installed in the government's local area network, which was not connected to the Internet to prevent acquisition of the data by outsiders, and included subsystems such as supervision of data collection, administrative approval performance evaluation, an integrated search function, statistical analysis, complaint handling, and system control and maintenance. This system enables the leadership to know the status of the administrative service provision and makes relevant information available to different actors upon request.

Video surveillance systems were installed at the prefecture government's administrative service hall, the Construction and Development Bureau, the Transportation Bureau, the Land and Resources Bureau, and the Public Security Bureau (the Police Department). These fixed-point surveillance mechanisms were connected to an integrated network to monitor the work, attitudes, and efficiency of the staff.

The website of the administrative approval service provided the interface with the Electronic Supervision System, which was accessible to the general public. The public can access the website directly to check the status and outcome of their applications for administrative approval, register complaints, interact with each other in an online forum, and/or submit a user satisfaction survey.

Shenzhen's Electronic Supervision System has helped control the arbitrary exercise of bureaucratic power. It has helped to sustain the reform of reducing administrative approval requirements by ensuring that administrative procedures are standardized, transparent, and efficient. If replicated widely across China, the system would reduce corruption, strengthen the government's administrative efficiency and effectiveness, and support continued economic growth—thus bolstering the system's legitimacy.

Prevention of Corruption. Administrative approval processes are necessary in any modern state and ideally are a core government function that serves the public. But such regulatory processes are also a breeding ground for corruption or abuse of authority. By drastically reducing regulatory requirements for licenses and approvals and by making the application process for approvals more transparent, corruption was reduced (at the same time that corruption in China in the field of developing infrastructure and in other fields skyrocketed). However, even with streamlined administrative approval processing, applications were processed by the staff arbitrarily, and corruption could still occur. Before the advent of the Electronic Supervision System, the public had often complained that authorities had used the approval granting process for "personal gain," and that they "operated in a black box." But such complaints have been reduced significantly. The increase in the number of re-registrations of "Internet bars" (or Internet cafes) in 2007 is one example of success. Of the 746 Internet bars whose licenses were renewed, the Supervision Bureau and Culture Department, only two filed complaints.

Strengthening of Efficiency. The Electronic Supervision System has raised civil servants' awareness of their responsibilities as well as their efficiency. Previously, lack of action and inefficiency were persistent problems. Applicants complained that it was "difficult to make the application be accepted, difficult to follow the processing, and difficult to get things done." Before the Electronic Supervision System was introduced,

Shenzhen prefecture administrators often delayed the granting of approvals, licenses, and permits. The rate of approvals granted within the stipulated deadline was less than 3 percent. Between January 2005 and December 2006, after the Electronic Supervision System was put into operation, of the 1,750,000 applications for administrative approval, only two exceeded the prescribed deadline. "Yellow card" warnings were issued in those two cases. Meanwhile, the number of approvals issued earlier than expected (at least one day before the deadline) reached as high as 80 percent on average, compared to 3 percent previously.

Promotion of Transparency. The Electronic Supervision System also promotes transparency in governmental administrative processes and legal enforcement, which in turn helps to consolidate the positive results of the administrative approval system reform. The system's implementation entails transparency and disclosure of information concerning the administrative approval processes of thirty-eight government departments. To improve the reform, the government carried out a series of investigations on governmental effectiveness and existing problems. In November 2007, the government announced that there were still fifteen problems with the administrative approval process mechanism. These included nonstandard assignment of duties and responsibilities for approval, absence of interdepartmental coordination, application fees not being collected in accordance with regulations, contradictory regulations for license approval, and inadequate information disclosure. The prefecture government had on twenty-five occasions announced publicly its evaluations of the efficiency of the Electronic Supervision System. It received 1,544 complaints and 1,385 instances of feedback from the public, and announced the results of follow-up action on 381 complaints and suggestions. Information disclosure and standardization of the administrative approval process also address the problem of asymmetrical information flow between the higher levels of administration and the supervising department, and prevents the approval system from being bogged down by excessive details.

Improvement of Administrative Management and Enhancement of Administration Service. In order to operate in accordance with the Electronic Supervision System, each governmental department is required to follow a strict set of procedures and to make the operating procedures known to the public. Its operation is monitored by the public through a supervisory mechanism. Before the introduction of the system, 40–50 percent of complaints were about the staff's service attitude and service quality. Since 2005, among the more than 1,500 complaints reported to the Electronic Supervision System, only a few were about the staff's attitude. Most complaints and appeals resulted from an inaccurate understanding of policies and a lack of coordination among legal provisions (a chronic problem given the contradictions embodied in China's rapidly evolving legal infrastructure—see chapter 5 on the contradictions between China's transparency regulations and secrecy laws). Some of the complaints were beyond the scope of the administrative approval system.

Development of Electronic Services. The use of the Electronic Supervision System allows government departments to perform some of their routine work "online" and to improve information sharing between government departments. Data were collected from thirty-one government departments. Seventeen departments established their own electronic information systems in the early stages of the system's operation. The use of information technology for the back-office components of the Electronic Supervision System has greatly facilitated the process of data collection. The other fourteen departments employed traditional manual operations or the administrative service hall management system for data collection. Those departments eventually incorporated information technology into their working system.

Asymmetric flow of information among different levels of governments was one source of the fragmented authoritarianism identified by Kenneth Lieberthal and Michel Oksenberg. Transparency and e-governance allow information to flow among different parts of the government more smoothly. Authority might still be fragmented, but much less so from information asymmetry. The achievements of the Electronic Supervision System have stimulated great interest within China and overseas. In April 2005 the Shenzhen Electronic Supervision System was awarded the national "Scientific Technology Advancement Prize." More than seven thousand national, provincial, and prefecture leaders visited the administrative approval center to learn about its operation. The China Central TV station, *People's Daily,* People's Network, Xinhua Network, Supervision Network, and other media covered the reform. The Central Committee of the Communist Party and the State Council held two conferences in Shenzhen to promote the Electronic Supervision System. At the National Conference on the Development of the Electronic Supervision

System for Administrative Approval in April 2006, Shenzhen municipality's Supervision Bureau offered the software used by its Electronic Supervision System free of charge to other provinces and cities. More than ten localities, including Guangdong, Inner Mongolia, Hubei, Fujian, Zhejiang, and Yunnan, have introduced the system with Shenzhen's help.

Officials from Hong Kong's Independent Commission against Corruption visited Shenzhen to observe and learn about the operation of the system. The Shenzhen City Supervision Bureau also participated in Transparency International's annual conference in 2005, the 5th Asia Pacific Regional Anti-Corruption Conference, and the Asia Pacific Economic Organization's Anti-Corruption Review Conference, to introduce its Electronic Supervision System.

Shopping for Services in Xiaguan

Another innovation was to move administrative services scattered in different bureaucracies to one place, to provide one-stop shopping.[24] Some localities call it a Governmental Affairs Supermarket. One such innovation took place at the county level in Xiaguan district within Nanjing prefecture in Jiangsu province.[25]

Xiaguan is one of the six districts in Nanjing municipality, capital of Jiangsu province, about 150 miles northwest of Shanghai. It covers an area of thirty-one square kilometers, and has six community offices that serve a population of 370,000 residents.

In the 1990s, Xiaguan district's economic and social development had lagged behind those of most other districts and counties in Nanjing municipality. Xiaguan, like most localities in China, did not have the encouragement and pressures facing Shenzhen, which as a Special Economic Zone received special attention from China's leadership. Xiaguan faced the more typical motives of districts throughout the country—the need to catch up with the neighbors in other districts.

The leadership of Xiaguan district, under pressure to achieve more rapid economic growth, decided to address its lagging performance by enhancing the efficiency of governance and went looking for solutions. In early 2000, some specific measures were taken. In June 2000, Xiaguan invited scholars from the United States, Japan, Hong Kong, Taiwan, and other areas to a seminar titled "Overseas Experience of Developing Communities." In September, major officials of the six subdistricts were sent to Shanghai for a study tour. In October 2000, the South Rehe Road and Xiaoshi communities began to pilot their own Governmental Affairs Supermarket.

In the Xiaguan Governmental Affairs Supermarket, more than forty administrative services, which had been housed in different office buildings in various locations, were brought together to provide public access to administrative services in one location and improve governance efficiency. After a couple of piloting months, all the communities adopted the model.

The Governmental Affairs Supermarket provides more than fifty types of public services: city planning, employment assistance, social security, legal aid, help with business licenses and tax assessments, and dozens more. Overlapping and parallel services have also been merged and restructured, in order to provide faster service. One important change is the disclosure to the public of what services are available. Previously, the public had no way to know exactly what services were offered, which departments were in charge of what, what the offices' business hours were, the names of the officials in charge, or how an inquiry should be handled. Very often, when people needed help from an official, they didn't know where to go and whom to turn to. In the Xiaguan Governmental Affairs Supermarket, members of the public work with a single staff member until the issue is resolved to the client's satisfaction.

Impact of the Governmental Affairs Supermarket

The switch to providing one-stop services has increased efficiencies in three dimensions:

—*Downsizing administrative staff:* Previously, there were eight offices with twenty-five to thirty-five staff in each community branch of the agency. With the creation of the Governmental Affairs Supermarket, community level services were brought together in one location with five to seven counters. Each counter has two staff to handle the services previously supplied by a whole office. Table 2-2 shows which agencies delegated which works to the offices at the Governmental Affairs Supermarket.

—*Reducing shirking of responsibilities:* With all governmental departments (offices) together, and a clear allocation of staff and responsibilities, instances of responsibility-shirking, buck-passing, and denials have been greatly reduced.

Table 2-2. *Services Delegated to the Governmental Affairs Supermarket*
by Relevant Departments of District Government

Department	Service
Bureau of Civil Affairs	Audits and approvals of small funds for disaster relief Audits and approvals of funds to those below minimum standards of living
Family Planning Commission	Processing of certificates to one-child family and benefit package to one-child family
Bureau of Cultural Affairs	Processing of applications to open bookstores
Supervisory Team for Urban Construction	Collaborating with communities to investigate violations of construction regulations
Bureau of City Planning	Collaborating with communities to process approvals for outdoor advertisements and posters
Bureau of Labor	Processing "Employment Registration of Township Unemployed Personnel"

—*Reducing time needed for processing paperwork:* What used to take days, even months, for the government to complete now takes minutes in the Governmental Affairs Supermarkets. Since their establishment, Governmental Affairs Supermarkets have handled more than 21,000 public inquiries and individual applications. Increased efficiency not only saves the people's time, but also improves relations between civil servants and the public.

Governmental Affairs Supermarkets have also helped to increase transparency in the administrative process:

—The public was empowered with a form of the "right to know" and now has access to policies, office hours, and procedures. The transparent working procedures curtailed arbitrary acts and nepotism and prevented civil servants from building their own patronage networks. Importantly, the increased transparency reduced the pervasive corruption in the administrative approval process.

—Public scrutiny of the administrative process was enhanced in two additional ways. First, the Governmental Affairs Supermarket now solicits feedback and evaluations from the citizens. Second, counter services (work attitudes, adherence to regulations) are regularly evaluated by officials and supervisors.

Administrative Reform as a Work in Progress?

For reasons both minor and major, administrative reforms like those described above have not yet transformed China's government into a fully modern and responsive state. The Governmental Affairs Supermarket approach, for example, despite its popularity in governing circles in China, remains very much a work in progress. The evaluation that led to the Xiaguan experiment's being awarded a prize as one of the best local governance innovations in China noted that its service system still needs substantial improvement. In particular, the decisionmaking power of front-line officials at the windows and counters is too limited. Many decisions still must be made by more senior officials. Often the communication between the counter and window service staff and their superiors takes too long. In addition, many administrative services need to improve their coordination with other departments at the same level.

A larger question is whether such administrative reforms are likely to go far enough to resolve the broader problems of creating a sustainable governing system for a rapidly modernizing China. As this chapter has shown, China's bureaucrats have much less power than they once did over the country's economy and its citizens. Systematic efforts to streamline bureaucratic and administrative processes have been made both by the localities and by the center since the late 1990s. Such reforms were initiated at local levels for the practical purpose of promoting investment and economic growth, and spread to other localities for the same reasons.

Pressures for administrative reforms accelerated with China's accession to the World Trade Organization. In order to meet the standard set by the WTO, the Chinese central authorities systematically examined the bureaucratic processes and power that hindered economic and social activities and lifted thousands of administrative barriers, particularly for private initiatives. In Shenzhen and Xiaguan local governments at different levels made serious efforts to reduce the government's administrative power over the people and to increase administrative efficiency and transparency. These efforts have dramatically cut red tape and increased efficiency, and in political terms have made the government less powerful relative to society and more accessible to the people. They have also helped to reduce corruption.

Despite such improvements, which have been replicated in numerous localities, the administration in China is far from fully responsive to its citizens. Regulators still have too much power from the perspective of a market economy and a free society. Reforms notwithstanding, far too many initiatives still require permission from the government through cumbersome and opaque procedures. It is proving very hard to reform bureaucracies that were entrenched in the command economy and had been operating for almost thirty years before China began moving away from totalitarianism in the late 1970s. During the first twenty years of the reform era, the administration did little to reform itself. Serious administrative reforms in the direction of bigger society and smaller government, and toward providing services to the society rather than maintaining control over it, have been carried out for only a little more than a decade.

In short, in some ways the administrative reform process has been quite successful. Red tape in China has decreased dramatically, albeit from an extraordinarily high level. Efficiency has been boosted. Economic initiatives from different sectors of the society have mushroomed, leading to a sustained level of economic growth never before seen. Politically, economic growth that increases living standards lends enormous legitimacy to the current political system, to such an extent that some people even think that administrative reform alone will be sufficient to sustain the political system long into the future.

Yet problems persist. Administrative powers have been substantially cut, but the administrative bureaucracy remains dominant. One indicator of the persistence of the state bureaucracy is the increasing number of staff. In the late 1970s and early 1980s, the number of staff in government agencies across China was below 6 million. After 2005, it exceeded 12 million.[26]

It seems questionable whether or to what extent streamlining the bureaucracy in itself would succeed in the long run without reform in other aspects of the political system. Mere administrative reform, although it can support high levels of economic growth as China moves from poverty to middle-income status, may fall short of providing the accountability, participation, and transparency mechanisms needed to govern China's increasingly complex economy and society. Despite impressive economic growth, more and more citizens are taking to the streets to protest government policies and misbehavior. According to official data, the number of demonstrations (in official Chinese terminology they are called *quntixing shijiang*—literally, mass incidents or group incidents) amounted to 87,000 in 2005; the number was 8,709 in 1997.[27] And despite scattered successes in controlling corruption, the problem is broadly perceived to be getting worse. Obviously, there is major public discontent with the government, which threatens the sustainability of the present political system.

One final aspect of the administrative reforms is worth mentioning. The reforms will likely have a spillover effect, although one that is hard to measure quantitatively or demonstrate conclusively. By reducing the government's dominance, the reforms make the government less like a ruler and more like a service provider. A system that requires approvals and permissions from the government is associated with totalitarianism and authoritarianism. A system that permits individuals to do many things without government approval fosters a new political culture of individuality and autonomy. This new attitude might never be internalized by the older generation. But it seems likely to become part of the values held by the younger generations.

3

The Evolution of Voting Mechanisms

A direct and competitive election for the mayor of a township called Buyun in Sichuan province was reported in the Chinese newspaper *Nanfang Zhoumo* (Southern Weekend) on January 15, 1999.[1] The report caused a sensation across the nation as well as among the international community of China-watchers, because competitive elections for any local authority higher than the village level had not happened since the revolution of 1949.

Thousands of websites, not just popular commercial websites such as sina.com and sohu.com, but also government-owned websites such as people.com.cn and xinhuanet.com, reprinted the news. The Buyun story has been posted by thousands of bloggers. It also became one of the most researched cases in studies of politics in China. According to the biggest data bank on research projects in China, www.cnki.net, at least 237 scholars across the country have written papers discussing the Buyun case. The story also quickly spread to the outside world. The U.S.-China Policy Foundation published an article about it in its academic journal.[2] One of the earliest academic assessments of the case available to the outside world was published in 2002, three years after the election.[3] Since then, around the world, hundreds of papers about politics in China have referred to this case.

The Buyun election was notable not only for the fact that it happened at all, but for where and why it happened and how it became known. Sichuan province, in China's hinterland, is far less economically developed than its thriving coastal counterparts and far more politically volatile, as the authorities have fewer economic resources available to placate dissatisfied citizens. The authorities responsible for Buyun township were looking for ways to engage a particularly recalcitrant citizenry. Madam Zhang Jinming, the county party secretary who decided to hold the election in Buyun township, told one of the present authors at a café in early 2002 in Suining prefecture that she saw the innovation as a possible way out of the difficult situation in which local residents were refusing to cooperate in any project launched by the township government. The appearance of the report in the weekly newspaper *Nanfang Zhoumo* was almost certainly not welcome news to the central authorities, who had no desire to encourage the spread of electoral processes at the township level and higher—but once the story was published, it spread like wildfire.

It is interesting to note how quickly this heady experiment in electioneering began to show signs of the gritty politicking familiar to any small-town American mayor. In the winter of 2001–2002, Buyun township held its second semi-competitive mayoral election. This time around the story made a much smaller media and academic splash. Luckily, though, one of the authors of this book, Lai Hairong, was in Buyun on that day, watching the voting, ballot counting, announcement of results, and the reactions of the candidates and the voters. He remembers vividly that the incumbent mayor was in a very bad mood, even though he won the election. The mayor (and the county officials who helped organize the election) had been very confident that he could win by at least a two-thirds majority, because his competitor was one of his subordinates and had not performed nearly as well as the mayor in the pre-election debate. Instead, the incumbent's margin of victory was less than 2 percent. County officials believed that a significant proportion of those who voted for the other candidate had done so in protest against the incumbent mayor's forceful way of doing things on a project carried out a number of months earlier. They predicted that this miserable victor would be more keen to listen as he served his second mayoral term.

Before the Buyun sensation, electoral competition for such a political post with meaningful state power was, if not taboo, at least very unlikely owing to the ruling party's clear position against any political competition. Political competition is a highly sensitive topic in China. The township election in Sichuan province and the news reports about it broke the quasi-taboo.

We call this and similar elections "semi-competitive" because voters had a choice among candidates; candidates were nominated by residents rather than by the party, but the competition among them was constrained in many ways. There were no candidate rallies, few posters, and no media advertisements; and naturally no organized opposition was allowed. The official Chinese term for this type of limited electoral competition is *gong tui gong xuan*—literally, "open recommendation and open election."[4]

The purpose of introducing the semi-competitive election was to improve the accountability of local officials to local residents. Officials in China have always been accused of being responsible to their superiors rather than to the public. It is widely perceived that the lack of official accountability to local citizens is the source of much of the misbehavior of the local officials and of the people's discontent with the political system. In addition, the decisionmakers recognize that competitive elections are an effective institution for holding local officials accountable to their constituents. But implementing competitive elections means giving up the power to appoint officials. Thus every decisionmaker must struggle to strike a balance between keeping power over local officials and holding local officials accountable to the people. The multiple experiments with semi-competitive elections in China, and the official resistance to their spread, underline this ongoing tension between the desire to hang on to a significant source of power—the power to appoint officials at the next lower level—and the need to institutionalize more meaningful forms of accountability in China's political system.

One of the structural factors making local experiments with semi-competitive elections possible was the extensive decentralization in China described in the previous chapters. Each level of the party-state hierarchy has a different revenue basis and is responsible for the operation of authority at that level, though there is also a scheme for sharing and transferring revenues between the center and the localities. The power of appointing cadres is decentralized in such a way that one level appoints the cadres of the immediate level below it, but not the levels below that. In other words, the center appoints the cadres at the provincial level but not at the prefecture, county, and township levels; the provincial authorities appoint the cadres at the prefecture level, but not at the county and township levels; the prefecture authorities appoint the cadres at the county level, but not at the township level; and the county authorities appoint the cadres at the township level. Authorities at higher levels set the rules for selecting and appointing cadres, but do not select and appoint cadres in operational terms at much lower grassroots levels such as the township. It is up to the county authority to decide how to select and appoint township cadres, as long as they do not violate the rules set by the center or provincial authorities. Usually the rules set by the center are general and allow for different interpretations, giving local decisionmakers flexibility in choosing lower-level officials if they want room for maneuver.[5] At the time of the Buyun story and thereafter, many local officials faced a difficult dilemma: an increasingly discontented public acting more and more against the government on the one hand and a lack of economic resources with which to appease them on the other. A few bold officials choose to experiment with new institutions that deviate to some extent from the dominant model, either to appease people or to rebuild the legitimacy of the state.[6]

The Evolving Electoral Scene: Government Posts

Voting in China is usually assumed to be a process in which citizens are forced to say yes to the only candidate nominated by the Communist Party. This was indeed the case before 1978. It is still the case for most of the "elections" today.[7] But the voting mechanism has been slowly and gradually changing. Elements of competition among candidates have emerged. In some cases, voters have choices.

The most visible competitive elections are those for state (that is, non-party and nonparliamentary) posts at the village and township levels. In these elections, the electorate is the general public (in contrast with elections in which only party members vote), and the positions to which the candidates aspire have executive powers. As noted above, these are semi-competitive elections in the sense that, although there is more than one candidate for each position, and more important, the Communist Party does not have a pre-selected candidate, the elections are not fully competitive in the Western sense because no opposition parties are permitted to contest in these elections and the campaigns are restricted. They are similar (but not identical) to the so-called multi-candidate elections that were held in some Eastern European countries under communism after the mid-1980s but before the fall of the Communist Parties in these

Table 3-1. *Semi-Competitive Elections for Administrative Posts, 1995–2009*

Level	First semi-competitive election	Number to 2009	Proportion of total (percent)	Provinces with the most semi-competitive elections
County	2004	13	0.5	Jiangsu, Hubei
Township	1995	>2,000	6	Sichuan, Yunan, Hubei, Jiangsu
Village	Late 1980s	240,000	60	Many across the country

Source: Hairong Lai, *Zhongguo Nongcun Zhengzhi Tizhi Gaige—Ban Jingzhengxing Xuanju zai Xiangzheng Yiji de Fazhan* (Political Restructuring in Rural China—The Spread of Semi-Competitive Elections at the Township Level) (Beijing: Central Compilation and Translation Press, 2009). Village-level data were supplemented by an interview with Weiming Shi on November 5, 2010.

countries in the period 1989–91.[8] In these multi-candidate elections, although no opposition parties were allowed to participate, individual citizens could be nominated as candidates without the endorsement of the party committees. In these semi-competitive elections, self-nominated candidates and candidates nominated by groups of citizens competed with one another. The competition could be among party members, or between party members and non-party members.

China introduced the term "multi-candidate elections" at the beginning of the "reform and opening" era in the late 1970s. But in practice, these multi-candidate elections were different from those in Eastern Europe and the former Soviet Union in that in China all the candidates were selected by the party.[9] Citizens had no access to the nomination process. In fact, to ensure that the person favored by the party would be safely elected, the party deliberately selected as competitors people who were unknown to the public or people obviously unqualified to hold the position. What we are focusing on in this chapter is a step forward from this kind of multi-candidate election: we examine cases in which most or all of the candidates were not pre-selected by the party.

These more meaningful semi-competitive elections were first introduced at the village level in the early 1990s, then spread to the township level later in that decade.[10] In the first decade of the twenty-first century, a few semi-competitive elections took place at the county level. But at this writing in 2011 there have been no semi-competitive elections for major positions at levels higher than the county (see table 3-1).

The table does not include the most recent years, for which systematic data are not available. However, anecdotal evidence makes clear both that such elections are continuing to occur, and that they continue to be controversial. For example, eleven semi-competitive township mayoral races were held in Shuyang county in Jiangsu province in October 2010,[11] and another dozen in Gushi county in Henan province.[12] Similarly, semi-competitive elections for township party secretaries continue, one in Shishan township in Meizhou prefecture in Guangdong province in November 2010,[13] and eighteen in Qujing prefecture in Yunnan province in October and November 2009.[14]

In all the semi-competitive elections listed in table 3-1, the general public (the head of family, head of an agriculture team, or member of the village council in votes for township mayor) rather than just party members took part in the vote. In the semi-competitive elections for township party secretaries, normally only party members voted, although occasionally a few non-party members were invited to vote. The weight of their votes is small. Nevertheless, there is some involvement of non-party members in the voting for township party leaders.

At the village level, where elections are held every three years, semi-competitive elections have been held systematically and repeatedly in many places, with some villages now having held as many as five. A considerable amount of research has been done on semi-competitive elections at the village level. Most studies have concluded that grassroots politics in China changed significantly with the introduction of semi-competitive elections.[15] But the impact on the Chinese political system as a whole has been limited, since most semi-competitive elections have been held at the village level.

At the township level, semi-competitive elections are much less institutionalized, and have received much less scholarly scrutiny. In 2004, the frequency of township elections was changed from every three years to every five years, and most of the townships that had held semi-competitive elections did not do so again. Only in Sichuan province and Northern Jiangsu province have some townships held semi-competitive elections more than once.

Most semi-competitive elections have been held in economically less developed regions, where social and political stability is difficult to maintain owing to the high level of discontent. Semi-competitive elections are in essence an effort to appease people by allowing them to select local cadres. Although the elections in themselves do not bring economic development, they seem to help calm a discontented local public, at least temporarily.

As discussed above, semi-competitive elections are initiated by local leaders. The center does not plan to hold or facilitate such elections—nor does it seem to have a plan in place to stop them. The center seems to take a position of observing, partly because these unconventional practices have been happening on the periphery of the political system, and partly because pressure to allow people to voice their opinions has been growing. The introduction of village-level elections with some degree of competition between candidates was a very important step in China's political development because of the deep linkage of the village councils to the party-state network.[16] However, since the legal status of a village council is a people's autonomous organization that does not have state coercive power, politically it plays a marginal role. The main responsibility of village committees is to distribute and redistribute collective property—arable land—among the villagers.

But an election with some elements of competition at the township level is politically much more significant, since the township is the basic cell of the state. What was demonstrated by the competitive election in Buyun township was that political competition of some sort had begun to spread to the official state apparatus.

As explained in chapter 1, there are five layers to the Chinese party-state hierarchy: the center, the province, the prefecture (or municipality), the county, and the township. Townships and counties are the lowest levels of legal authority in the Chinese political system, whereas village councils are "autonomous organizations of the masses."[17] In practice, township authorities have substantial power and responsibility over public safety, social and political stability, birth control, elementary education, infrastructure construction, taxation and fee collection, and the provision of other public goods.[18] Whereas the township authorities have coercive instruments, the village committees can only implement their programs through voluntary participation. Thus, elections for government posts at the level of the township and county are far more politically salient than village-level elections, with a potentially significant impact on the social and political lives of ordinary Chinese people. The withdrawal of full party control at the village level does not represent a significant challenge to overall party rule. To concede power to the people at the township level or higher, however, is a major step, one that the party-state has shown considerable caution in allowing. Nonetheless, some such innovations are occurring.

County Congresses

Electoral mechanisms are also popping up on the parliamentary side. Indeed, the first semi-competitive elections experienced in China were for members of county-level people's congresses—that is, for the equivalent of local (and largely disempowered) parliaments rather than the executive branch positions described above. The electorate in these elections consisted of ordinary citizens. According to the laws, representatives to township and county people's congresses are elected directly by township and county residents.

In the congress elections, it is not membership in the party per se that has distinguished which candidates run as independents from those backed by the party. Independent candidates can be party members, though most of them have not been. Candidates nominated by the party can be either party members or non-party members. Perhaps surprisingly, the party has nominated a considerable number of non-party members as candidates for election to the people's congresses. The difference between independent candidates and candidates nominated by the party is simply that that the latter were favored and supported by the party and the former were not.

In early 1980, eight citizens who were not nominated by the Communist Party were elected to the county people's congress in Beijing municipality.[19] The remainder of that decade saw several additional electoral victories by candidates that had not been nominated by the local CCP. After a three-year interruption due to the 1989 Tiananmen Square demonstrations and their aftermath, independent candidates—that is, candidates not nominated by the party—emerged again to run for election as representatives to county people's congresses.[20]

One of the most interesting cases was that of independent candidate Yao Lifa, who won an election and served as an important representative to the county congress for five years between 1998 and 2003 in Qianjiang county, Hubei province. During his term, he investigated the low-quality implementation of the village election law in Qianjiang county, helping village residents to appeal to the authorities at higher levels concerning their election rights. He investigated the investment projects initiated by the county government, disclosing waste and inefficiency. Not surprisingly, the local officials considered him a trouble-maker and succeeded in blocking his efforts to run for election again in 2003.[21] Another interesting case was that of Zeng Jianyu, in 1992 an independent candidate for representative to the county people's congress in Luzhou prefecture in Sichuan province, who won by disseminating leaflets and giving public speeches.[22] He won reelection, again as an independent, in 1997. During his nine years as a representative to the county people's congress, he voiced the concerns of ordinary people. After helping taxi drivers defend their rights against the local government, he was sued for allegedly receiving bribes of 4,000 Chinese yuan from some taxi drivers and sentenced to one year in jail.[23]

The stories of Yao Lifa and Zeng Jianyu were widely reported by the mass media in China and thus were known to a huge audience, from which they received considerable sympathy across the land. It is unclear whether this sympathy helped them in their specific localities. But their cases do reflect two key points: there is substantial public support for such figures nationwide, and the national authorities are at best tolerant of people who run for election as independent candidates.

The difficulties Yao Lifa and Zeng Jianyu endured did not deter other people from running for election as independent candidates. In 2003, in Shenzhen and Beijing, dozens of people ran for county congresses as independents, three of whom won. In Qianjiang county where Yao Lifa was once an independent representative to the people's congress, thirty-two people registered as independent candidates, although all lost, owing to local party and government manipulation. It was a fierce battle, though quiet. On the one hand, dozens of citizens were inspired by Yao Lifa's independent candidacy and wanted to emulate him. On the other hand, local authorities feared Yao Lifa and tried hard to prevent others like him from running.

At that moment in Qianjiang county, the local authorities clearly had the upper hand in the battle. But in other parts of China the struggle continued. In 2006–2007, according to reports in different provinces, the number of independent candidates running for election to the people's congress at the county level had increased significantly. Dozens of independent candidates won election in at least five provinces: Zhejiang,[24]

Qinghai,[25] Liaoning,[26] Yunnan,[27] and Shandong.[28] Although details on these elections and candidates are not available, what seems clear is that the possibility exists for independent candidates to run for election to county people's congress, and a very small but increasing number of citizens have done so.[29]

The relationship between the independent victors and the local governmental and party authorities is obviously frequently an unhappy one, if not always confrontational. Local officials have tried to stop independents from running and have created difficulties for them. But these independent figures enjoy sympathy across the country, and surprisingly garner extensive media coverage. Taking into consideration that most media are state owned, one can see how complex the picture is.

Another election for township and county people's congresses will take place in 2011–12. Scores of people in such prominent localities as Beijing, Shanghai, and Shenzhen have declared on their micro-blogs (the Chinese equivalent of Tweets) that they will seek nomination as independents. This time, the efforts of independent candidates caught the attention of the public and led to a wide debate on the Internet. The debate spread to such an extent that the Legal Commission of the National People's Congress was forced to respond. On June 8, 2011, the commission tried to pour cold water on the issue, announcing that legally speaking there is no such thing as an "independent candidate" because candidates are nominated by political parties, social organizations, or the jointly signed recommendations of ten or more citizens. This announcement merely served to fan the flames of the public debate (and ensured that the story was also picked up by the foreign press and reported overseas).[30]

The central authorities are playing down the sensation of "independent candidates," and it is almost certain that such candidates won't find it easy to win election to the local people's congress. But such pushback over the term "independence" is a familiar part of the reform terrain in China. Likewise, the term "unemployment" is officially rejected, although the existence of vast number of unemployed or laid-off workers has been evident since the early 1990s. The official term is "job-seeker" or "workers dropped from positions." But the rejection of the term doesn't prevent people from discussing unemployment issues in all media except the party newspaper. What is most important in the emergence of independent candidates for local people's congresses is that an increasing number of individuals are becoming politically active, and their activism is becoming well known to the public thanks to the Internet.

Voting within the Party

A striking step in China's use of voting mechanisms took place in 2007 at the top of the political system. On June 25, 2007, more than 400 high-ranking party officials (members and alternate members of the Central Committee of the Communist Party) voted to choose newcomers to the Politburo, the highest decisionmaking body in Chinese politics, from a list of 200 candidates.[31] Through this process, Xi Jinping emerged at the top of the list. Since the Chinese Communist Party came to power in 1949, members of the Politburo had always been selected from the top by the charismatic leaders (first Mao, and then Deng) rather than by their peers or subordinates. Thus 2007 witnessed one of the most consequential examples of the use of quasi-voting mechanisms in Chinese history.

There was no overt campaigning in this quasi-election. But there was indeed competition. Two hundred candidates competed for twelve to fifteen positions in the Politburo. The election was not reported in detail by the media, so exactly how the voting was conducted was unclear to the public. There are two likely reasons for the low profile of this important change. First, the party was experimenting with voting for the first time at the top level, and thus lacked experience and confidence in the practice. Second, because members of the Politburo select who will wield the top power in the country, reports that they had used an electoral mechanism would have set a sweeping example to all local authorities across the country about electing rather than appointing cadres. The party may not yet be ready to encourage wholesale emulation of this practice.

The Politburo quasi-election did not come as a bolt from the blue. Instead, as we will see below, the practice of having party officials selected by peers and subordinates through an electoral process, rather than being appointed by superiors, has been undertaken for a number of years for an increasing number of middle-level party (and state) positions. In 1995 the Central Committee of the Communist Party issued a directive entitled "The Temporary Regulation of Selecting and Appointing Party and State Cadres,"[32] encouraging local authorities to experiment with inviting cadres to vote for their peers and promoting those who won. In 2002, the temporary regulation was revised and became a formal regulation,[33] further encouraging appointment through voting. Since 1995, thousands of party-state positions at different levels across the country have experimented with voting—with the important caveat that the electorate in these cases is usually confined to party insiders, not the general public.

Yet the election at the Politburo level, even given the extremely limited electorate, may represent a significant step in the changing definition of how power is legitimated in China.[34] Achieving the highest levels of power now includes a quasi-electoral mechanism, even though the preferences of superiors are still an important factor. A more cynical interpretation is that the vote—widely referred to in reports as a straw poll—was an alternative way for elite factional politics to be played out.[35] In our view, however, the very introduction of the voting mechanism, regardless of motivation, reflects changing conceptions of how power transfers can best be managed peacefully and legitimately. This changing source of legitimacy may well have a far-reaching impact on political developments in the future, although its immediate influence is unclear.

The Local Experiments

We now turn to three local electoral experiments that have garnered attention in China in the early twenty-first century. None of the three took place in what citizens of fully democratic polities would recognize as key political contests, but in China such experiments touch at the heart of the political process. The first two involved elections for party posts. The third electoral experiment was conducted in a branch of the Women's Federation, one of the government-organized mass organizations (also known as GONGOs, or government-organized NGOs). As discussed in chapter 1, the party, the state apparatus, and the GONGOs are intermingled. The ruling party holds power over all the state organizations and all of the GONGOs. The state organizations (what in other countries would be known as government agencies in the executive branch) and the GONGOs are the implementation arms of the ruling party. Without some sort of democratization within the party, democratization of the governmental side will be seriously limited. And further democratization within the party is likely to make it much easier to bring about significant changes in the governmental power structures.

It is interesting to note that China's political evolution nearly took a very different direction in the 1980s, one that would have drastically changed the party's role. In 1988, the 13th Party Congress passed a reform package requiring the abolition of party organs in government agencies and mass organizations. But this reform package was short-lived because of the demonstrations of 1989 and the crackdown that ensued. Had that broad reform been instituted, we would not now be focusing so much attention on the political evolution of the party itself.

But as things turned out, the party has remained the paramount political institution. It is the party that makes decisions. The state apparatus exists to implement party policy. A high-ranking party official is surely simultaneously occupying a high-ranking state position, but the converse is not necessarily true—a high-ranking state official, although almost certainly a party member, may or may not simultaneously occupy a top post in the party committees that make the most important decisions. For example, at the county level, the executive committee of a county party committee is the most important decisionmaking body. It is usually composed of eleven to fifteen county party officials. The head of the department of education is an important state official in the county government, but in very rare instances he or she is a member of the executive committee of the county party committee.

Here lies one of the biggest differences between China and most countries in the world. Elsewhere, a political party is a mechanism for bringing together people with broadly shared political views and getting them elected. It is important only when it is able to win elections, through which it get its members into government positions (either via parliamentary seats, as in the British parliamentary system, or directly into executive branch positions as in the U.S. presidential and gubernatorial system). And once the winners take office, state affairs rather than party affairs become (at least in theory) the most important considerations.

In China, the ruling party is the mentor and controller of the state. Party positions are the key governing posts, with government jobs decidedly of secondary importance. A change in the state power structure does not necessarily mean that the party power structure changes too. But a change in the party power structure will definitely change the power structure of the state. Therefore, intra-party semi-competitive elections are actually more important than semi-competitive elections for township mayor or for representatives to township or county people's congresses, at least at the current stage of political evolution in China.

Intra-Party Democratic Reform in Rushan City

We start our exploration of local experiments in intra-party democracy in the small eastern county of Rushan, on the eastern Shandong Peninsula facing the East China Sea.[36] Its population of 580,000 (of whom some 43,000 are party members) is divided into fifteen townships that are further subdivided in 601 administrative villages. Rushan (which confusingly is a county that has been granted "city" status) is a top performer in China's economic growth sweepstakes. In 2004 the city first entered the ranks of China's top 100 counties for overall economic development, and it has continued to soar, ranking fifty-fourth in 2006 and thirty-fifth in 2007.

Rushan's reforms were "local" in the sense that their precise form was not set by the central authorities. But those reforms did directly reflect a central party policy shift stemming from the party leadership transfer that took place in 2002, when Hu Jintao became president of China and Wen Jiabao became premier at the 16th Party Congress. The new party leadership appeared more interested than its predecessors in strengthening the party system by promoting intra-Party democracy. Intra-party democracy was one of the most frequently mentioned (although vaguely defined) political terms in the following years in the mass media. This green light from the top gave local officials room to experiment with new ideas.

Starting in 2003, Rushan's party leaders set out to respond by regularizing the meetings of the local party congress to increase the participation of party members in the political process and by introducing direct and competitive elections for township party secretaries and county party committee members.

Before these reforms, as everywhere in China, the Rushan local party congresses were convened only once every five years. In the long gaps between party congresses, the local party leadership did not have to report to the local party members in any formal or institutionalized way. Unsurprisingly, the party congress was an institution with low participation, and the local party leadership had every incentive to concern itself far more with pleasing party superiors at higher levels than with interacting with its ostensible constituency of local party members. Thus, simply increasing the frequency of the meetings of the county party congress to annual sessions and requiring the party leadership to report on its work to the party representatives, subject to their discussions and comments, constituted a meaningful reform. Starting in 2004, annual meetings of the local party congress in Rushan county at both the county level and the township level were organized, boosting the participation of party representatives in the local political process.

To give teeth to this experiment in accountability, the reform made each leader's report subject to a secret vote at the annual party congress. Those who did not receive enough favorable votes would have to improve their performance significantly or face dismissal. Under the new rules, a leader with less than an 80 percent yes vote cannot be promoted; one with less than a 60 percent yes vote will be transferred to another position; one with less than a 50 percent yes vote will be issued a warning; and anyone receiving less than a 50 percent yes vote in two consecutive years will be dismissed from his or her leadership position.

Such criteria placed unaccustomed pressure on township party leaders. In a case study describing the Rushan experiments, the Xujia township Party secretary, Wang Wei, was quoted as saying, "We have to work very hard because we are subjected to the work appraisal and deliberation at the congress every year. . . . previously, both of our eyes looked up toward the higher authorities; now at least one eye must look downward."[37]

For the other half of the experiment, which changed the way in which representatives to the county party congress would be chosen, three of Rushan's townships (Fengjia township, Kou township, and Xujia township) were picked to introduce semi-competitive elections for the township party congresses. Until then, candidates for party congresses had been nominated by party committees at higher levels. That is, a Rushan county–level party committee would have picked the candidates for the fifteen townships in the county. The township party members would then duly vote yes to the list, although they might not actually know anything about those candidates. Under the new initiative, the nomination process was opened up. In most electoral units, there was more than one candidate. All candidates were required to present themselves in front of the meeting of the township party members before the voting, which was by secret ballot. In March 2004, in these three towns, 507 party members nominated themselves as candidates to be representatives to their respective party congress. After the campaign, 284 were elected as representatives.

As Rushan county regularized the meetings of the party congresses, turning those more frequent sessions into more meaningful tools for intra-party accountability, and introduced semi-competitive elections for the representatives to the party congresses, it also promoted direct elections for the village and township party secretary posts and party committee memberships that are the core of party power at each level. Once again, the experiment aimed at moving away from the existing nonparticipatory method of selecting these leaders, in which the county party secretary would select township party leaders from among people he personally knew, and those township leaders in turn would select the village party secretaries. There would then be a vote in the party congress, but it was to confirm the single candidate rather than to make a choice. The Rushan county party set out to increase the participation of party members in selecting their leaders.

Under the new Rushan county initiative, elections for township party secretary and other party committee members were conducted as follows. First, the county party committee did not nominate candidates. Instead, it set rules and determined which vacant positions would be open for election. It was the party congress representatives who would later elect the secretary, vice secretary, and other party committee members. The county party committee publicized the rules and encouraged all party members to take part in the elections.

Second, preliminary candidates nominated themselves or were nominated by the township party congress representatives. In Fengjia township, thirty-three party members were nominated as preliminary candidates. In Rushankou township, twenty-eight party members were nominated as preliminary candidates.

Third, the qualification of the preliminary candidates was checked by the county party committee. In Fengjia township, fourteen of the thirty-three passed the check. In Rushankou township, sixteen passed the check. And in Xujia township, three candidates competed for the position of the township party secretary, seven for the position of the vice secretary, and nine for the other committee member positions.

The fourth stage was the actual electoral competition and the vote by secret ballot. Each candidate was required to develop an electoral platform and present it in front of the party congress. This gave all candidates an opportunity to present themselves publicly, and the congress representatives a chance to learn about the candidates and their programs. After that, the congress representatives voted for the township party secretary and other positions of the party committee.

Incorporating the Private Sector. Members of the party committee at all levels were without exception full-time officials working in the committee establishment. Rushan county experimented with the practice of introducing two "part-time members" to each party committee (the committees usually have nine members) at the township level. These part-time members are party members who work in the private sector. They were elected also on a competitive basis by the party congress. This reform thus served a dual purpose: broadening the number of positions to which elections applied, and incorporating the perspective of the private sector into the key decisionmaking body at the township level.

For example, Liu Fangyou was a general manager of Hua Long (Rushan) Food Company Private Limited, a food enterprise in Xujia township with foreign investors. He was elected as one of the part-time township party committee members. Among others, he provided a series of valuable views and ideas for the development of Xujia township's new industrial area.

The introduction of party members in the private sector to the local party committee was a striking change by the Communist Party. Private entrepreneurship was the ideological enemy of socialist China before 1978. After the private sector was allowed to develop following the reforms initiated in 1978, and especially after China moved decisively in 1992 to encourage the emergence of a private sector, private entrepreneurs became one of the new salient social forces. But they were not allowed to join the party. A decree (known as the Number Nine Document) issued by the Central Committee of the CCP in 1989 specifically forbade recruiting party members who were private entrepreneurs.[38] However, things kept changing. Following years of discussions among high-ranking party decisionmakers in the 1990s, in the year 2000 General Secretary Jiang Zemin proposed the concept of "three representations," which says that the party should represent the advanced productive forces, the advanced culture, and the interests of the vast majority of the people—quite a change for a party that had long based its identity on

its claim to represent workers and peasants. Jiang included private entrepreneurs as part of the advanced productive forces, thus paving the way
for an ideological legitimization of allowing private entrepreneurs to join
the Party. Jiang reiterated his concept of "three representations" in his
speech commemorating the eightieth anniversary of the founding of the
Chinese Communist Party. The concept of "three representations" was
later written into the party prospectus in 2002, formally opening the door
for recruiting private entrepreneurs into the Communist Party.[39]

Since the early 2000s, an increasing number of private entrepreneurs
have been recruited to the CCP. But none of these party members were
appointed or elected to any decisionmaking body in the party committee.
Rushan seems to have been the first case in which private businessmen
became members of local party committees.

Bringing in the People. Starting in the early 1980s, the party began
permitting, even encouraging, direct semi-competitive elections in China's
660,000 villages, home to some 700 million of China's 1.3 billion people.
These elections served to select village committees (which are not party
committees), and these elections have been increasingly competitive and
open, covering some 60 percent of all villages. But the village party secretary was still appointed by the township party committee. The different
source of power of the two positions, top-down in the case of the party
secretary and bottom-up in the case of the head of the village council, led
to conflict between these two positions. Different localities experimented
with different ways to solve the problem. Rushan county was one of the
first places to try involving non-party member residents in selecting the
village Party secretary.

In 2004, Rushan county selected 120 villages, or 20 percent of the villages, to experiment with the new practice. The innovation involved con-
ducting an opinion poll before the township party committee nominated
a candidate for village party secretary. It polled the non-party member
residents (usually 90–95 percent of the villagers) about the popularity
of each party member in the village. The township party committee then
chose those whose popularity exceeded a certain threshold, say 30 percent
or 50 percent, to be candidates. Then the village's party members would
vote to select a party secretary from this list of popular candidates. This
practice was intended to lead to better coordination between the village
party secretary and the head of the village council by giving the full village

population some say, while keeping ultimate control of this key party post in party hands. In 2007, 50 percent of the villages in Rushan county implemented this new mechanism for electing the village party secretary.

The Ya'an Prefecture Story

Far from coastal Rushan City, deep in China's interior in Sichuan province, the Ya'an prefecture leaders confronted similar concerns about how to make the party system more effective and responsive.[40] The organization department of the Ya'an prefecture party committee selected two counties within the prefecture to conduct pilot experiments in 2003: Yucheng district (county) and Yingjing county.[41]

Ya'an prefecture was chosen as a pilot location for regularizing the role of the local party congress as a more important institution partly because Ya'an had been a pilot location for introducing semi-competitive elections to the township level in previous years. In Ya'an prefecture in 2001, semi-competitive elections were held in 174 towns and 1,110 villages. In those elections, 64 incumbent cadres in townships, 181 incumbent village party secretaries, and 215 incumbent heads of village councils lost the elections, replaced by younger candidates who enjoyed more popular support. These changes nurtured an atmosphere for accepting more changes in the prefecture. This is very similar to what happened in Rushan City, in the sense that the introduction of some semi-competitive elections led to demands that the same practice be introduced to higher positions and to better acceptance of the new practice among the party-state officials and ordinary citizens.

As in Rushan and everywhere else in China, the county party congresses within Ya'an prefecture, which were supposed to review the work of the county party leadership, were convened only once every five years. And the representatives to the county party congresses were usually selected or appointed by the county party committee (the leading body), and often simply by the county party secretary together with two or three of his or her close colleagues. The new experiment was to introduce direct and semi-competitive elections for representatives to the county party congresses, and to increase the frequency of the party congress meetings.

Under the new practice, the nomination process was open to ordinary party members. A party member could be nominated as a preliminary candidate via one of the following three methods: (1) he could nominate himself; (2) he could be nominated by the signed recommendation of more than ten party members; or (3) he could be nominated by the organization department of the county party committee, which is the traditional centralized way of making nominations.

There were 13,677 party members in Yucheng County. The whole county was divided into 82 electoral districts. Of the 1,380 party members nominated as preliminary candidates, 764 were self-nominated, 376 were nominated by the joint recommendation of more than ten party members, and 240 were nominated by the organization department of the county party committee. The proportion of candidates in the electoral districts who had nominated themselves varied from 25 percent to 45 percent.

According to the "Procedures for the Electing Party Representatives," incumbent party cadres no longer enjoyed "privileged treatment." Each candidate was required to present himself in front of the party rally, according to the candidate list arranged by family name. Some people suggested that the township party secretary and mayor should be exempted from these practices and that their names should be at the top of the list instead of being listed with other candidates. These proposals were rejected, and incumbents enjoyed no special treatment in the elections.

In Yingjing county there were 5,456 party members; 736 candidates were nominated as preliminary candidates in the same three ways. Preliminary candidates were elected by secret vote. In Yucheng county 242 candidates were elected from the preliminary candidates. Competition was intense. At the Bureau of Education there were 374 party members, 348 of whom voted in the election. They elected five candidates from a list of twelve preliminary candidates. At the Bureau of Health there were 129 party members; 126 party members voted and elected three formal candidates from the seven preliminary candidates. In different townships candidates representing the regions were elected in the same way. In Yingjing county 241 formal candidates were elected.

In a second departure from previous practice, detailed information about each candidate was publicized. Previously, the public did not know much about the people selected as representatives to the party congress, and were certainly not invited to comment on their qualifications.

One candidate, the party secretary of Miaogang township in Yingjing county, was the subject of numerous complaints from other party members. People complained that he did things too bureaucratically and forcefully and thus was not qualified to represent the party members. The electoral commission reviewed the complaints and, on the basis that the selection of the secretary as a party representative should be decided by all the party members, put him on the list of candidates for the party members to vote on. It was a direct election via secret ballot, in which all party members voted. According to the rules, only candidates who received more than 50 percent yes votes could be representatives to the party congress. Each candidate was required to give a speech in front of the voters. Even the county party secretary, who previously would have automatically been a representative, had to meet his constituents and go through the election process. He was probably the first county party secretary in China since 1949 who had to compete for a seat in the county party congress.

The result was that six incumbent leaders lost the election, including the unpopular party secretary of Miaogang township, the vice party secretary of Yaoqiao township in Yucheng county, the mayor of Shaping township, the vice party secretary of Xicheng township, the director of the Food Bureau, and the director of the Family Planning Bureau. The election was a new experience for both the party officials and the party members. It was said that the party secretary of Miaogang township cried after losing the election. For him and other losers who had been the senior officials in the locality and had enjoyed great privileges, it was a stunning blow. According to the rules, if a cadre in a leadership position such as the township mayor or the party secretary lost the election, he would be given an observation seat in the county party congress and half a year to improve his performance, at which time the Organization Department of the county party committee would organize a review of his performance in his electoral district. Those who received less than two-thirds yes votes in the review would be fired on the spot.

In July 2004, a follow-up study revealed that, half a year after losing his election, the Miaogong township party secretary did not receive enough yes votes in the review and was thus dismissed from the position.

Going GONGO: Voting for the Leaders of the Women's Association in Qianxi County, Hebei Province

Our third case takes us out of the realm of direct party politics and into the world of the mass organizations, or GONGOs.[42] The crucial background to this story starts with China's extraordinary pace of urban industrialization. The huge demand for labor has driven workers, in particular male laborers, from rural to urban areas, leaving behind a countryside populated primarily by women, the elderly, and children. In a county called Qianxi in the northeastern part of Hebei province, close to Beijing, women are doing at least 60 percent of the agricultural work, most of which had formerly been done by men. In some villages, apart from the village cadres hardly any men remained. The agricultural workforce thus came to be dominated by women.

Nonetheless, female participation in village committees was low and declining sharply. In the 4th Qianxi County Village Council (in 1997) only 70 percent of the female population voted, and only 12 percent of the members elected to the Village Council were women. In 1998, a new law, the Village Committee Organization Act, had instituted semi-competitive elections for village councils. In the process, it eliminated quotas for the number of female representatives in village committees, instead merely indicating that "there should be an adequate number of female representatives in each village." Because the largely marginalized (if numerically dominant) rural women were unable (and perhaps unwilling) to compete, there had been a precipitous decline in the number of women elected. The Ministry of Civil Affairs issued an emergency notification regarding the need to maintain a sufficient quota of women representatives on the village councils. Most people believed that without enhancing women's capacity and willingness to take part in politics, the low representation of women would be hard to change.

This created an opportunity for the largely moribund county branch of the Women's Federation to find new life by reinventing itself as a mechanism for women's political empowerment. The Women's Federation is part government organization, organized by and receiving funding from the government, but more closely resembles civil society organizations, with its lack of executive or administrative authority. Such "quasi-government" bodies had previously answered primarily to party and government cadres at higher levels, rather than to the people whose interests these organizations were ostensibly created to serve. The Qianxi Women's Federation in the 1990s was no exception.

In response to the growing problem of the lack of female candidates for village councils, the Qianxi Women's Congress invited the government's

Civil Affairs Bureau to discuss how to overcome not only the entrenched sexism common in rural areas, but also the female candidates' own lack of competitiveness. At the time, the rules requiring that elections to the Women's Congress be held every three years were widely ignored, with the party branch secretary of each village simply appointing representatives. With life tenure, these directors had little incentive to engage with villagers, but nonetheless dominated women's access to political participation. Thus, the federation decided that the solution was to change the processes by which women became involved in the Women's Congresses, and to set up direct elections. These elections, which under existing rules were supposed to be held concurrently with or after elections to the village committees, would instead be held a month in advance of the village committee elections, enabling successful candidates for the Women's Congress to stand as competitive candidates in the village committee elections.

With that decision made, the federation set out to transform women's political participation in Qianxi. With support from a task force that included representatives from the county people's congress, the county government, the Civil Affairs Bureau, and the party, which provided guidance in the interim period leading up to the election of the new Women's Congress, the federation undertook a program of publicity and education to identify and train new candidates for political office. Multiple training sessions were held throughout the county during the summer of 1999 (a relatively quiet period for agricultural labor), with 100 of the more impressive participants selected for further training in October. A trial election was held in December in Qianpo village, with 360 of the village's female population of 363 in attendance to hear seven candidates' speeches (and some 200 male villagers looking on). Similar elections held in another fifty villages also saw high turnouts and multiple candidacies.

The elections transformed the Qianxi Women's Congress, making it a far younger, more educated, and more vibrant organization with stronger ties to the village communities the federation is meant to serve. The victor in that first trial election went on to be elected to replace the previous director of the Qianxi Women's Congress, and was also elected to her village committee. Overall voter turnout for elections increased from 70 percent to 96 percent, and the number of women elected to village committees increased from 12 percent to 26 percent. By 2002, the Qianxi County Women's Federation managed to promote the direct and competitive election for village women's associations in 417 administrative villages at seventeen towns in the county.

In short, the innovation opened up new avenues for a broad range of women to enter politics. In making this possible, the Qianxi Women's Federation demonstrated a substantial change in thinking about how marginalized communities should be addressed. Rather than relying on appointed representatives within a monolithic political system, as the Women's Federation was established to do, the reform empowers members of that community to engage directly in political contestation.

Conclusion

Electoral competition, in however marginalized a part of the party-state, is usually thought to be the last thing that a traditional Communist regime wants to allow. After the case of the direct semi-competitive election for the mayor of Buyun township in Sichuan province was reported by *Nanfang Zhoumo* in January 1999 and reprinted by numerous media outlets across the country, an article published in a newspaper edited in Beijing criticized the innovation. *Fazhi Ribao* (Legal Daily) claimed that the semi-competitive election violated a constitutional provision requiring that township mayors be elected by the township people's congress rather than township residents.[43] Subsequently, rumors abounded that central authorities had more than once ordered local authorities to carry out elections in line with the law.

This opposition from the top meant semi-competitive elections (other than intra-party votes) could not spread swiftly across China. But there is one point worth noting about the nature of that opposition. The language of the accusation over the semi-competitive election was not the type of dramatic political or ideological charge of counter-revolutionary or capitalist practice that was typically used before the 1990s in similar cases. The objections were based on technical issues such as articles in the law, which in the Chinese context means that the problems were discussable. The neat result of this critique was that in later cases of semi-competitive elections at the township level it was the *candidate* for township mayor who was semi-competitively elected by the residents. Once the residents had voted to select someone as a candidate, the township people's congress would then vote for whomever the residents had chosen. In this way, the terms of the law stipulating that a township mayor be elected by the township people's congress were met, but in practice the mayor had the legitimacy of having been chosen by the township residents as a whole.

It is not just ideological hostility against competitive elections and the concerns expressed by the center that deter local officials from imitating the experiments described above. The practical reason they do not do so is obvious. By introducing semi-competitive elections, the local party secretary would give up the important power to appoint local officials. Voluntarily renouncing an important source of power is not what ambitious—or corrupt—officials normally do anywhere.

Still, semi-competitive elections have continued to spread to more villages, and upward to the township and county levels, although at a very slow pace. The major reason why local party secretaries have been willing to share their power is that they have to do so in order to appease increasingly independent, and in many cases discontented, local residents.[44] Not all local party secretaries facing the same changed public choose the semi-competitive election as a solution. Most seem to rely more on traditional instruments: the stick of coercive state power and the carrot of economic benefits. Only in those localities running out of economic resources, and that also have an open-minded party secretary, would the semi-competitive election be likely. Thus one has to note two things about semi-competitive elections in China: (1) they are spreading; and (2) they are spreading very slowly.

There is one dimension of semi-competitive elections that seems not to have yet been realized by the CCP: the party turns out to be rather good at managing competitive elections such that its preferred candidate often wins even when the election is free and fair. Thus on the one hand, most of the winners of semi-competitive elections are party members. On the other hand, the center and those localities that have not experimented with semi-competitive election worried about the failure of the party candidates. This worry, rather than ideological considerations, is often the real source of concern about or hostility to competitive elections.

But in most of the thousands of semi-competitive elections across the land in the past two decades, the party has demonstrated its capacity to organize meaningful ones. And the party is clearly good at promoting its own candidates. With the likelihood of more semi-competitive elections being implemented in the future, the party may become more comfortable with competition and confident in its ability to win fairly.

Yet party confidence is clearly much greater in elections to party posts than in those involving the general public. Intra-party democracy might not be sufficient to promote democratization in the wider society. But it does seem likely both to transform the traditionally vertical power structure of the party into one that is more broadly accountable and to familiarize the party with competitive elections.

While the party is cautiously experimenting with semi-competitive elections here and there, the broader society shows enthusiasm for competitive elections. The media, especially the new media, cover them heavily. Independent representatives who strove to check the behavior of local officials, thus provoking the dislike of and even retaliation by those local officials, have received considerable sympathetic media coverage. Not every case of this kind succeeded in receiving such media attention or public discussion. But people do see a considerable number of such cases being reported and discussed openly, demonstrating a dynamism that was not seen before in China.

Many China watchers are skeptical about the significance of these electoral experiments. They tend to emphasize the degree to which the party retains firm control over key appointments and strongly guides the selection process. They also note that the party, although it debates whether elections beyond the village level are needed for legitimacy reasons, generally comes down against elections even at the relatively low level of the township. All this is true. However, localities and the party itself are still experimenting, and the more they experiment, the more citizens are exposed to the ideals and mechanisms of electoral processes. The question is not whether the party is about to adopt wholesale electoral reform, but whether the groundwork is being laid for more far-reaching change in the future.

4 | *Civil Society*

While on a trip to China in 2010, *Philadelphia Inquirer* foreign affairs columnist Trudy Rubin filed the following story:

> Late last year, HIV-AIDS activist Thomas Cai was suddenly summoned to appear the next day at a mysterious meeting in Beijing.
>
> Cai is the founder and director of the well-known nongovernmental organization AIDS Care China—one of the first civil society groups to provide support for AIDS sufferers and their families. But he had no idea whom he would be meeting in the Chinese capital. To his total surprise, he and eleven other scientists were ushered in to meet with President Hu Jintao.
>
> "We were not instructed before what to say," Cai recalls, referring to the normal practice when meeting with top Chinese officials. Instead, the president told Cai "not to say good things, but to talk straight" about the HIV-AIDS problem. For three hours, Hu listened to frank details about grassroots health problems in China.
>
> Yet even though this AIDS activist was invited to meet the highest leadership, Chinese officialdom has not let AIDS Care China register officially as an NGO. "We're getting lots of recognition, but we are still not recognized," says Cai.[1]

As Rubin notes, China's government is conflicted. The authorities know that the country needs organizations like AIDS Care China to focus on China's enormous social and environmental problems and to deliver services the state no longer provides (or never did provide), but fear their potential capacity to organize politically in opposition to the existing system. As a result, social organizing is simultaneously permitted and constrained. The rules, and the ways they are implemented, leave much room for confusion. As Thomas Cai found, it is possible to be endorsed at the highest levels but still shunned locally.

Nonetheless, huge numbers of myriad types of social organizations are sprouting throughout the country. Many are legally registered and working closely with local authorities. Many others avoid the complex requirements of becoming a legally recognized NGO and instead register as for-profit businesses, or fail to register at all. Local authorities are trying out all sorts of variations on the rules, trying to get groups of citizens to take on some of the burden of providing social services without risking too much in the way of independent organizing. Even the existing "mass" organizations, like the All-China Federation of Trade Unions or the Women's Federation we discussed in chapter 3, which were all that China had in the way of social organizations under Mao, are experimenting with ways of connecting with their ostensible constituencies.

The "society" side of the state-society relationship is complex, confusing, and crucial to China's political trajectory. Society is organizing itself apace, from chambers of commerce to environmental advocacy groups to the reemergence of traditional clan-based bodies. There is no doubt that the trend in social organizing in China is exponentially upward. Since the reforms began in the late 1970s, the withdrawal of the party-state from more and more realms has created space for citizens to form associations in pursuit of their own interests and left gaps in meeting social needs. Thousands and perhaps millions of organizations have sprung up.

Such societal organizing is key to understanding China's political future. How it develops will help to determine whether China develops the building blocks that could make a meaningful democracy function well. Centuries of experience have made clear that it takes far more than elections to make democracy work. At its heart, democracy is a system that requires citizenship—people within the polity who are engaged, informed, and above all able and willing to work together to solve their common problems. That capacity for collective engagement does not arise automatically as part of the process of democratization. Instead, the causal arrow may run in the other direction: it is when a society already knows how to work together in what is called "civil society" that effective democracy is likely to emerge. The vibrancy of that associational life, with the social capital and organizational skills it encapsulates, is a powerful indicator of how readily democratic institutions could take root.

But the evolution of civil society in China is by no means smooth. A century of war, revolution, decades of deliberate repression of all independent civic groups, and social chaos capped off by the Cultural Revolution has undermined the preexisting social bonds. The gaps are highly visible, represented vividly in the tens of thousands of sometimes-violent protests every year. And because the party-state is deeply conflicted about the degree to which it wants civil society to develop, it does its best to keep tight limits on the size and scope of all such groups, and repeatedly cracks down hard on anything that looks as if it could be a challenge to the party's authority.

Civil society is everywhere a confusing and contested concept—more or less a catchall for all the myriad forms of social organization above the level of the family that are neither profit-seeking nor governmental. It includes everything from bird-watching clubs to homeowners associations, trade unions, chambers of commerce, professional associations, and human rights groups. In China, the picture is further complicated by the rapidly evolving nature of the occupants of the associational space— the existing mass organizations, the formally registered NGOs, the vast numbers of unregistered grassroots organizations—and their relationship to the party and the government. Despite the complexity, there are patterns that hint at how civil society is developing and where its many parts might fit into the tapestry of China's politics. Woven into the story are key questions about the loss of central control and the growing capacity of localities (including both predatory elites and potential reformers) to interpret center policies as they wish.

The Meaning and Importance of "Civil Society"

Civil society is commonly defined as the "third sector" in social organization beyond the family, defined by what it is not—not government, not profit-seeking business. Instead, it is the "everything else" category, all the organizations and affiliations beyond family in which people organize themselves to achieve collective goals. The scope can be large or small— a national political party or a local choir. The purpose can be good or evil—humanitarian rescue or terrorism. All that is required to be counted in the category of civil society groups is that people come together to act collectively in pursuit of a common goal, in the absence of government's coercive capacity or business's profit motive.

The term has been used in something like that form for centuries, dating back to the conceptualization during the eighteenth-century Scottish Enlightenment of civil society as "a realm of solidarity held together by the force of moral sentiments and natural affections" sufficiently strong to knit people together in groups that could act collectively for sustained periods.[2] (Even at the time, not everyone saw this growing third sector as an unmitigated good, pointing to the potential for conflicts between such groups or the danger that individual interests would overshadow the good of the group.)

It was a nineteenth-century Frenchman, Alexis de Tocqueville, who most vividly called attention to the connection between representative government and civil society. Tocqueville analyzed the nineteenth-century United States as a country of joiners enjoying an abundance of voluntary associations in which citizens could develop democratic skills and norms.[3] Twentieth-century social scientists came to agree, arguing that democracy needs a "civic culture," with attitudes and habits conducive to political participation, particularly the belief that citizens are capable of influencing government. To form those attitudes and habits, experience can come not only from direct political engagement, but also from experience in a wide variety of groups that serve as "channels of political socialization."[4] A culture rich in such channels not only gives people ways to articulate their shared interests; it also teaches them to form coalitions and to compromise—the basics of democratic governance. By participating in voluntary associations, people learn how to organize groups, vote, develop agreed rules, persuade others to act collectively, and accept disagreement and defeat within the context of a larger shared endeavor. Since then, democracy theorists have regularly asserted the importance of associational life as a bulwark against state authority in democracies and a mechanism for democratizing authoritarian states.[5]

Such thinking put the notion of "civil society" in the global spotlight in the aftermath of the collapse of the Warsaw Pact governments in the late 1980s. The new governments and their citizens faced the daunting prospect of creating instant market economies and democratic politics, in societies where the state had dominated to the exclusion of virtually all other social actors. Suddenly, these countries needed new ways to provide services, amalgamate interests, provide means for debating the public good, and form building blocks for political contestation by bringing together people with similar views and interests. Western, and especially American, funders assumed that the creation of vigorous independent civil society organizations was a crucial means of solving the dilemma, and pumped substantial international aid to new NGOs throughout the region.[6] Autonomous civil society organizations were considered vital not just for their role in bringing down authoritarian regimes, à la Solidarity in Poland or Charter 77 in Czechoslovakia, but also as the basis for building up a more responsive and democratic system.

Since then, thinking about the connection between democracy and civil society has been strengthened by the notion of "social capital." The notion of "social capital" is both simple and surprisingly powerful in explaining why superficially similar societies can experience diverse patterns of economic and political development, and in particular why, in the words of a leading scholar, "some democratic institutions succeed and others fail."[7] Social capital refers to the social networks created by the various associations that criss-cross societies, bringing people together in an interlocking web of connections.

Those networks have value well beyond the immediate goals they set out to accomplish. In a society with an abundance of social networks, people interact repeatedly and thus know that doing someone a good turn now may be repaid by that person in the future (the "shadow of the future"). The density of interactions also increases what could be called the "shadow of the neighborhood." Your interaction today with someone in a community sports league may cause a third member of the league to make a comment about you to a friend in a church group, who happens to be a partner in a business from which you are seeking a donation for your NGO. Based on that indirect connection, the business partner may be more inclined to trust that you will use the money for its intended purpose. The denser the web of such associations, the more likely it is that members of the polity will assume that others are trustworthy and behave accordingly. Such trust, and trustworthiness, turns out to be key to the successful performance of democratic institutions.

We can illustrate the connection of social capital to China's prospects for democratization with a brief detour to a very different country: Italy. Making democracy work has been the theme of thousands of debates and studies, and among the best of them is the groundbreaking book of that title by Harvard professor Robert Putnam. Over more than two decades of rigorous empirical research and deep analysis, Putnam and colleagues set out to figure out why the economies and politics of northern and southern Italy have persistently, over centuries, diverged dramatically. On virtually every measure, life in the north of Italy is better than life in the south. Putnam and his colleagues set out to understand why.

What they found was startling to social scientists accustomed to thinking that successful democracy emerges when societies reach an adequate level of economic achievement. Certainly, the correlation between democracy and high levels of per capita GDP is strong. Indeed, one reason that China's political trajectory is now such a crucial topic is that China is approaching the middle-income level at which countries generally experience strong pressures for democratization. Yet democracy is not an automatic consequence of increasing modernity. By digging deeper into the local variations in democratic performance even at a given level of economic performance, Putnam found that the level of social capital—the density of social networks within a given community—strongly predicts how well governing institutions perform. For reasons dating back centuries, when the north of the country was governed by small republics while the south had a centralized empire, northern Italy continues to have a much stronger associational life than does the south. Now, northern Italy, with its much denser network of associations, is richer, better governed, more law-abiding, even happier than southern Italy.[8]

Essentially, a rich array of social networks allows people to trust one another on a much wider scale. Because so many people are themselves members of organizations, they develop positive attitudes toward collaboration and the skills needed to maintain and further develop such collaboration. With a dense and overlapping network of associations, people are far more likely to be at least indirectly connected to one another. Social capital makes governance based on rules of law far easier to accomplish. Rule of law can be had with a relatively light government touch in the northern Italian types of high social capital settings, while in the southern

Italian low social capital environments, authorities have a much harder time. As Putnam puts it:

> Collective life in the civic regions [with strong social networks] is eased by the expectation that others will probably follow the rules. Knowing that others will, *you* are more likely to go along too, thus fulfilling *their* expectations. In the less civic regions nearly everyone expects everyone else to violate the rules. It seems foolish to obey the traffic laws or the tax code or the welfare rules, if you expect everyone else to cheat.[9]

Putnam's work, and the enormous literature on social capital it helped to spark, has had a huge impact on intellectual debates in China. As one leading group of scholars noted, it "provided a new vocabulary with which to discuss the functions of civic groups in the West and in China," a vocabulary that was quickly employed as an argument for lifting restrictions on Chinese associations on the grounds that "civic groups can be functional to social development without necessarily posing a threat to the state."[10] The concept has sparked research into what is actually happening on the ground, which turns out to be quite a lot. As Qiusha Ma finds in her pioneering study of voluntary grassroots groups ranging from environmental NGOs to Peking Opera fan clubs, "The grassroots associations are nourishing and reawakening the trust, reciprocity, spirit of cooperation and collective actions initiated by people that were destroyed by the CCCP's coercive government prior to the reforms."[11]

Civil Society with Chinese Characteristics?

There appears to be a growing understanding that the success of China's efforts to introduce rule of law, control corruption, and rein in the localities' predatory elites will depend at least in part on the vibrancy of the country's associational life—its civil society. But what forms do and will that associational life take in a country under such extraordinary stress, where so many organizations are not counted in the official statistics?

The one indisputable truth about social organizing in China is that it is large and growing fast. Figures from the Ministry of Civil Affairs indicate that, as of late 2010, there were 243,000 registered social organizations (usually membership groups), 195,000 civil nonenterprise institutions (usually service providers rather than membership organizations), and 2,168 foundations.[12] These numbers can give a broad sense that associational life has become significant, but the official figures tell us little about how significant. The official rules under which NGOs and other associational forms operate are so restrictive that they have sparked a strong tendency to operate outside the formal rules—often with official tolerance, as long as the groups are serving approved purposes or, more cynically, are serving the purposes of particular officials.

Certainly the usual Western model of independent, autonomous social organizations does not appear to be quite what China's party-state has in mind. The central authorities seem to be thinking more along the lines of what social scientists call a "state corporatist" model, one in which the state allows hierarchically ordered and controlled associations to play limited roles as a way of reconciling large numbers of divergent interests.[13] As the party-state loosened its stranglehold on the economy, the developing market economy began creating those large numbers of divergent interests. In many cases, China's authorities responded to the needs for new intermediary trade associations by simply transforming governmental industrial bureaus directly into "nongovernmental" trade associations.[14] As China evolved away from the "iron rice bowl" that had provided social services entirely through the workplace, the party-state has actively encouraged the growth of service-provision groups to serve the needs of vast newly marginalized populations. And as we discuss below, the handful of existing "mass organizations," which had previously been the only ostensibly "nongovernmental" form of social organization allowed, have begun to evolve but still, for the most part, do the party-state's bidding rather than represent their members' interests. Yet at the same time, China has also seen an explosion of (often unregistered) grassroots organizations of all kinds, and an increasing number of groups that use the Western terminology "NGO" and often have relationships with international NGOs.

But given the peculiarities of China's governance structure and economic system, neither the "independent autonomous civil society" model nor the "state corporatist" model quite tells us what is now happening in the social organizing realm, much less what that organizing implies for China's future. China does not just have a state; it has a party-state system that for decades suppressed all independent social organization and that continues to intrude deeply into its citizens' efforts to pursue group interests. The central authorities are trying to combine a Leninist, all-pervasive party model with a partially market-based economy, under conditions of extremely rapid economic growth and the ensuing dislocations that modernizing societies always endure.[15] This puts quite a dent in the political space available to social groups to organize in ways that could provide a counterweight to state power. At the same time, China has a very strong, if often unregistered and hard to assess, private sector, but state-owned enterprises (SOEs) continue to dominate huge swaths of the economy.[16] With such unusual features in the other two sectors, the "third sector" may not resemble those found elsewhere.[17]

Understanding China's civil society is even more complicated by the obvious, yet often ignored, reality that "China" is not one single coherent entity. While many parts of the government may find civil society groups annoying or threatening, others, such as the Ministry of Environmental Protection, may find them useful allies in intragovernmental power struggles. Moreover, the post-1978 reforms have emphasized decentralization. Now, while central authorities may want to see civil society develop in particular directions, it is usually local governments that determine which groups get to do what.

And China, like virtually all countries, is increasingly porous externally. As much as the country's leaders want to maintain political control and social stability, for the past several decades they have pursued a deliberate strategy of opening China up to the world. China has benefited enormously from the resulting economic integration, and China cares deeply about being seen as a responsible power. As part of this opening to the world, China has allowed international NGOs (INGOs) and international funders such as the Ford Foundation to become important actors in the development of China's civil society. Foreign funding has been crucial both for the relatively small number of advocacy organizations within the country, which are often dependent on outsiders for most or all of their funding, and for the development of the horizontal links between civil society groups that China's regulations discourage. One notable example is the China NPO Network, established in 1998 in Beijing by the heads of a number of Chinese NGOs to foster communications among them. Lacking government approval or funding, the network faced serious resource constraints. Backing came from the World Bank, the Ford Foundation, and various INGOs—support that has contributed considerably to the development of horizontal links across China's burgeoning civil society.[18]

All this complexity raises many questions that are key to understanding China's political trajectory. Are associations of citizens arising that do, or may eventually, provide a counterweight to the state? If so, how extensive? What can be said about the formation and scope of social capital, as reflected in civil society? How do civil society and existing authority structures interact, and what does their interaction portend? Can the party-state control the explosion of citizen self-organizing to take advantage of its economic and social benefits without bringing about a fundamental change in the relationship between state and society?

From Mao to NGO? The Evolution of China's Associational Life

Social organizing is not new to China. Clan groups, of course, have been around for millennia, but such kinship-based connections are not usually included in the categories of voluntary association of interest to us here. Traditional groups such as flower clubs, incense clubs, and temple clubs have played major roles in promoting social integration in some areas for many decades, remaining active even after the 1949 revolution, although temporarily forced into abeyance by the 1966–1976 Cultural Revolution.[19] The first nonkinship civic associations appeared as the Qing dynasty was breathing its last in the late 1800s, with the short-lived reformist group known as the Qiangxue Society. When the Qing dynasty banned the society in 1896, scarcely five months after its founding, a wave of voluntary groups streamed forth, with another wave emerging after the 1911 overthrow of the Qing dynasty and the founding of the Republic of China. The latter wave included hundreds of political organizations and even more chambers of commerce. The May Fourth movement of 1919 spurred yet more. During the long struggle for control over post-dynastic China, the KMT and the Communist Party established hundreds of trade unions and thousands of peasant associations.[20]

But from the time Mao consolidated power in the 1950s until the start of the Cultural Revolution in 1966, virtually all social organizing was subsumed under a handful of party-controlled mass organizations. Their task was to help the party run the country, rather than to respond to the interests of citizens. During the ten chaotic years of the Cultural Revolution, social organizations essentially stopped functioning.[21] No figures were kept for most of the first several decades of the People's Republic after 1949, but available estimates indicate that few new associations were established until the post-1978 reforms.[22]

Following a brief period in which open debate was allowed, from 1979 to 1981 (the "Democracy Wall" time), the 1980s saw both widespread economic reform and intra-elite debate over political reform. The withdrawal of the state from more and more arenas created economic and social space for new groups and new ways of thinking about who should do what within society. Outside intellectuals worked closely with party-based believers in political reform, creating journals and think tanks and holding conferences and discussions about possible political trajectories. But by the end of the decade, as increasingly painful economic reform measures sparked inflation, unemployment, and the disintegration of the iron rice bowl system of social security, social upheavals developed into massive student-led protests that ended only with the party-state's June 1989 violent crackdown. Since then, the authorities have responded harshly to anything that hinted of a resurgence of a widespread social movement. In the 1990s, civil society organizing had to take place within the context of a system hell-bent on two and only two goals: economic growth, and maintenance of the party's position as sole authority.[23]

But the government soon found that it could not deal with the country's enormous social and environmental problems on its own. The policies meant to foster rapid economic growth, it turned out, also engendered massive social dislocation and extraordinary environmental degradation. Recognizing that it needed help, the government looked to new ways to involve the growing numbers of social organizations. In the late 1990s it launched a "societalizing social welfare" campaign aimed at involving both for-profit and nonprofit private actors in providing social services of all kinds and expanded the range and scope of NGOs.[24] To keep things on the party-state's terms, this expansion was accompanied by a tightening of controls, including the promulgation of strict regulations in 1998 and a requirement for "re-registration" that some social organizations did not survive.[25]

And China's decision to open itself to foreign influences necessarily brought with it foreign ideas about the roles of civil society groups. Also crucial to the development of Chinese social organizing was an international conference: the Fourth World Conference on Women, held in Beijing in 1995. The conference itself was an intergovernmental affair sponsored by the United Nations, but like all such UN mega-conferences it was accompanied by a parallel massive NGO forum. Although the Chinese authorities exiled the NGO component to Huairou, thirty-five miles away (much to the fury of the 30,000 or so participants), the NGO forum nonetheless provided a powerful introduction for thousands of Chinese to notions about what NGOs are and what they can do. In addition to the experience of the conference itself, China's preparations did much to spread awareness about NGOs. The All-China Women's Federation (ACWF), one of the mass organizations developed under Mao, sponsored more than 8,000 training workshops and seminars around the country that reached some 2 million women in advance of the summit, creating a surge in Chinese women's organizations and introducing the term "NGO" widely.[26]

Since President Hu Jintao and Premier Wen Jiabao rose to the country's top positions in 2002, the party-state has struggled to find ways to engage the power of social organizing for what it defines as the collective good, while vigilantly opposing any organizing that could lead to threats to the party's grip on power. Their new emphasis on "harmonious society," in sharp contrast to the previous focus on economic growth at all costs, brought with it even greater attention to the need to provide services in welfare, medical care, education, and all the usual arenas of a modernized country. As China experts Yongnian Zheng and Joseph Fewsmith have noted, the new policies have created new possibilities for the development of civil society organizations:

> In the economic sphere, the government has attempted to reduce its direct management role by establishing intermediary organizations such as trade associations and Chambers of Commerce to perform sectoral coordination and regulatory functions. In the social welfare sphere, the government wants to foster NGOs onto which it can offload some of the burden of service provision. In the social development sphere, the government wants NGOs to mobilize societal resources to supplement its own spending.[27]

But what would seem on the surface to be a relatively congenial atmosphere for the development of social organizing masks considerable tensions. There continue to be periodic crackdowns on the space for associational life.

In 2005, for example, the authorities launched a national campaign investigating associations with foreign funding or contacts, a response to the "color revolutions" in Georgia, Kyrgyzstan, Serbia, and Ukraine that the party-state saw as significantly influenced by Western support to local NGOs. David Shambaugh's fascinating assessment of the evolution of the party quotes numerous Chinese analysts who contend that American foundations, think tanks, and NGOs are subversive entities working in China on behalf of U.S. government agencies, including U.S. intelligence agencies:

> [They] disseminate propaganda about democracy and freedom, so as to foster pro-Western political forces and train the backbones for anti-governmental activities [and] take advantage of their experiences from subversive activities abroad to provide local anti-government forces with a package of political guidance from formulation of policies to schemes of specific action plans. . . . All that the NGOs have done [has] played a crucial role in both the start and final success of the "Color Revolutions."[28]

Yet in 2008, China and the world saw signs of how far social capital and nongovernmental organizational capacity have come. In the aftermath of a devastating earthquake in Sichuan province, millions of Chinese citizens rallied to provide aid and assistance of all kinds, some acting individually or in spontaneously formed networks, others through hundreds of NGOs and scores of foundations.[29]

By 2010–2011, in the run-up to the leadership transition scheduled for 2012, the authorities appeared to be engaged in a nearly schizophrenic effort to simultaneously restrict and foster development of civil society. Film star Jet Li's One Foundation was permitted to register with the Shenzhen Civil Affairs Bureau as the first private foundation allowed to seek public donations. Such major municipalities as Beijing and Shanghai ramped up their procurement of social services from NGOs, with Beijing announcing in March 2011 that it would procure 300 more service projects from NGOs that year. The need to find ways to address widespread discontent over widening inequality, soaring inflation (especially food prices), and rampant official corruption led Premier Wen Jiabao to pledge more resources and benefits such as tax breaks for NGOs.[30]

At the same time, however, the party-state remains deeply wary of the "third sector." The 12th Five-Year Plan on Economic and Social Development, adopted by the National People's Congress in March 2011, shows the central authorities as more concerned with maintaining stability and order (especially in the wake of the "jasmine revolutions" sweeping the Arab world) than with liberalizing the rules for social organizing, with a budget that allocated more funding for "upholding stability" via internal security measures than for the People's Liberation Army.[31] Along with its call for an increased role for social organizations in providing social services, the plan urges party and government departments to "institute a set of codes of practices and criteria for social organizations' activities and to raise the effectiveness of government supervision."[32]

As is so often the case with such messages in China, the implications of the plan's messages seem to be unclear even to experts within China. The *South China Morning Post* interviewed several of them shortly after the plan was released. Guo Yushan of the NGO Transition Institute saw the new push as intended to reinvigorate the semi-official, traditional Communist Party or government-affiliated social organizations such as the Women's Federation, trade associations, and workers' unions. Wang Ming of Tsinghua University's NGO Research Centre and a Chinese People's Political Consultative Conference delegate, was more optimistic, expecting that at a minimum, NGO registration requirements would be eased.[33]

The emergence of modern NGOs and accompanying formal regulations, however, is mostly an urban phenomenon. In the countryside, associational life is strong, and traditional groups can even work in informal ways to exert accountability pressures on government officials. In one study involving 316 villages and a set of case studies, Lily Tsai finds that moral standing within the community can be a strong incentive for officials in providing public goods.[34] This informal channel of accountability works particularly when officials are full members of groups that are open to everyone in the jurisdiction, such as village temples. While levels of social trust and degrees of NGO autonomy are no doubt important factors in the development of a robust civil society, Tsai's study provides a reminder that in China's state of transitional authoritarianism one can find social capital and accountability working in unusual and unexpected ways.

Supply and Demand

One way to get a handle on this extraordinarily complex picture is to think in terms of supply and demand for social organizing. On the demand side, the dismantling of the iron rice bowl has created enormous new, or newly unmet, needs: health care, care of the skyrocketing number of elderly, access to expensive higher education, cultural preservation. In particular, the vast scale of internal migration within China has left millions of workers living far from their official residences and thus unable to access residency-based social services. And the rise of a market economy has created all the usual disruptions experienced when societies undergo the "great transformation" of capitalist modernization, multiplied by the pace and scale of everything Chinese.[35] New firms and other market actors act to protect their new economic interests, while society fights back over everything from environmental protection to labor practices.

On the supply side, China now has virtually all of the conditions usually associated with a vibrant associational life. It has a large middle class of people with economic resources and increasing autonomy in setting their own agenda. The size and nature of that middle class is hard to measure and hotly contested.[36] Even more contested are the political implications of that middle class, with hot debate over whether China's middle class will follow the Western model of supporting democracy as a way of protecting its own interests, or pay greater deference to the state as long as the state continues to deliver the economic goods.[37] But without a doubt it is the middle class that has the leisure time and education needed to organize groups to act effectively on their own behalf, or on behalf of the greater social good as they define it.

The other crucial supply-side fact is communications capacity, which enables interest groups to find and talk to one another. China's soaring Internet capacity now has roughly a third of the population online.[38] And an astonishing 755 million of China's population of 1.3 billion have mobile phones.[39] Organizations, formal and informal, do much of their work online, using the Internet to communicate and to run issues campaigns.[40]

In short, in China we see powerful push and pull factors leading to an explosion of civil society organizing. And to an uncertain, confusing, but nonetheless important degree, they exist in the context of some amount of political "space" in which the party-state allows associations to operate.

But that political system is still a one-party authoritarian state in which the authorities are simultaneously attempting to reinvigorate Leninist pervasive party control. We now turn to a crucial question: How exactly are those authorities trying to keep control?

Governing Civil Society

The developing legal framework governing associational life reflects the party-state's dilemma. It wants to foster the development of a sector that can help to fill enormous social needs, but simultaneously to ensure that the evolution of the sector does not lay the groundwork for political activities that could challenge the party's ultimate control. In the nuanced language of the International Center for Not-for-Profit Law (ICNL), "management of the emerging civil society sector by Communist Party and state agencies remains exceptionally robust."[41]

The degree of robustness varies considerably depending on the type and purpose of civil society groups. Social service providers and similar unthreatening groups experience less governmental intrusiveness, while advocacy and policy groups are much more carefully scrutinized and managed. When the party imposed tighter controls after the uprisings of 1989, eliminating some foreign-supported groups seen as tools of the West, it classified types of associations based on the degree to which they were seen as having latent political power that could challenge the CCP. Independent labor unions, residence and community committees, and religious groups all fell into the "high latent political power" category, whereas sectoral associations, chambers of commerce, government-organized NGOs, and grassroots associations were seen as less politically salient.[42]

Chinese laws refer to social organizations (*shehui tuanti*), foundations (*jijinhui*),[43] civil nonenterprise institutions (*minban fei qiye danwei*),[44] and quasi-governmental public institutions (*shiye danwei*).[45] The "social organizations" category includes most of what Westerners would recognize as membership NGOs, while civil nonenterprise institutions do not have members.[46] As noted above, as of 2010, according to the Ministry of Civil Affairs, there were 243,000 registered social organizations, 195,000 civil nonenterprise institutions, and 2,168 foundations.[47]

Each category is governed by different laws, particularly with regard to the requirements for registration—the sine qua non of legal existence.

For most social organizations, legal registration is no easy task. Under the 1989 Regulation on the Registration and Management of Social Organizations (amended 1998), only one social organization of a given type is allowed to register within any one administrative region. To become that one favored entity, under what is known as the system of "dual registration," organizations are required to first find a sponsor—known colloquially as a "mother-in-law"—in the form of a relevant government ministry or agency at the appropriate level of government and then seek approval from the local Civil Affairs Bureau.[48] Ambiguities in the Ministry of Civil Affairs' classifications can make it difficult for associations to find appropriate sponsors, and government agencies are not necessarily eager to take on the burden, and dangers, of responsibility for the activities of outside groups.

Once a sponsoring government agency is found, that body can influence everything from leadership appointments to activities to financing to daily operations.[49] Once registered, organizations remain permanently answerable to both the sponsoring agency and the Civil Affairs Bureau. Officials have great discretion to deny permission to register, to intervene in internal management and decisions, to demand access to information, and to limit speech and activities.[50]

International NGOs face a more confusing scene. For most, there are no clear regulations to say what is permissible and what is not. Foreign chambers of commerce are required to register with the Ministry of Foreign Economic Relations and Trade, which simply grants approval and does not have supervisory "mother-in-law" authority. But all other international civil society groups function in a kind of legal limbo that can make life in China challenging. They have shown considerable ingenuity in finding ways to operate legally, basing themselves in Hong Kong or Macau or in localities whose bureaus of civil affairs are willing to register them, or working through Chinese NGO or government partners. The Ford Foundation, in an unusual case that had approval from the very highest levels of Chinese authority, managed to procure a Chinese government sponsor, the Chinese Academy of Social Sciences.[51]

In March 2010, China cracked down on the connections between foreign institutions and domestic NGOs. It began implementing new regulations further constraining the capacity of independently organized NGOs to raise funds from abroad, with provisions requiring special bank accounts and notarized agreements and allowing the authorities ample room to decide whether donations are politically or morally acceptable.[52] Given the unclear tax rules that in practice provide few tax advantages to indigenous Chinese donors and the lack of a culture of philanthropy of the kind that led to the establishment of the major American charitable foundations, China's civil society has depended heavily on outside sources of funding.[53] It is not clear what the new rules will do to the funding available for existing groups or to the development of civil society more broadly.

Legal registration matters for both practical and political reasons. Practically, without legal status there is no entity that can open a bank account or get a phone line. Politically, groups that don't formally exist can be easily disrupted. Yet these onerous requirements lead many civil society groups to look for easier ways to function, and those social organizations that do register as such tend to be those with larger-than-normal social and financial resources and connections.[54] Some claim business status, which can be credible if they offer goods or services (such as training) for a fee. The China NPO Network, for example, ended up registering as a for-profit agency under the aegis of the Bureau of Trade and Industry for lack of a willing mother-in-law.[55]

Because the regulations consider groups operating as part of existing entities to be "internal" organizations that need not register, many become *gua kao*—"patronized groups"—sheltered by existing units of governments, private firms, mass organizations, or social organizations that have succeeded in registering.[56] That gets around the one-entity-per-place requirement and avoids the mother-in-law intrusiveness, but leaves the groups dependent on the goodwill and political protection of the patron. In 2010, the prominent Center for Women's Law and Legal Services, which had been affiliated for fifteen years with Peking University, found itself out in the cold when the university severed the connection after the center refused to follow instructions to back away from sensitive women's rights cases.[57]

Even within the legally registered universe, the tight regulatory approach is running into problems of erratic enforcement. Local officials charged with implementing the laws have other incentives—maintaining economic growth and social stability are higher priorities than enforcing regulations. At the same time, local predatory elites, which may be targets of NGOs, have multiple ways to constrain those NGOs, even if the NGOs are providing the services and problem-solving the center wants. And in some cases, local officials create their own NGOs as covers for graft and mechanisms for agency slush funds.[58]

Overall, the rules aim to make civil society groups function as subordinate bodies extending the reach of the party-state. The rules prohibit establishment of regional NGO branches, so national organizations can only be in Beijing, and local ones can operate only in one place.[59] Such rules are designed to prevent horizontal ties across localities that could articulate and aggregate social interests on a larger scale. Clearly, the party wants to be the sole occupant of that space and does not allow strong independent networks across regions. Thus social capital is constricted in scale, with relatively little in the way of networks that can build bridges between localities. And even within local areas, the rules do not encourage the development of a strong associational life. Where the sector has nonetheless emerged, both national rules and local governance experiments strive to maintain party-state control while reaping the benefits of voluntary associations.

Walking the Tightrope: Experiments in Regulating Civil Society

These rules and practices add up to quite a tricky balancing act, and one that lends itself to numerous experiments in governance. As is so often the case in China, fluidity and rigidity co-exist, with a wide range of national legislative and regulatory initiatives in process and significant local experiments under way.

One local example of the party-state's efforts to guide and control the third sector is found in a subdistrict of wealthy and bustling Shanghai, where the Changzhou Road Municipal Office of Putuo district won a "Chinese Local Governance Innovation Award" in 2008 for establishing a municipal NGO Service Center.[60] Changzhou is typical of such municipal subdistricts, with 126,000 people crowded into an area of less than four square kilometers, undergoing all the stresses and strains of rapid modernization and economic growth, and with a booming civil society sector. Of the 288 NGOs identified as active in the subdistrict, only 95 were officially registered, and nearly 200 "public leagues" (mostly sports clubs and cultural groups) were also not registered.

The local authorities faced pressures to "guide" the nongovernmental sector to ensure that it would meet escalating demands for social services and relieve the burden on the state without becoming unduly independent. Their solution was to create a municipal NGO Service Center as a nonprofit, nonenterprise institution run by nongovernmental employees (although some recruits were full-time party staff), which would provide services and assistance to NGOs and from which the government could purchase services. The director is the general secretary of the local party branch, and funding and office space are provided by the subdistrict. Nonetheless, the Changzhou Service Center is deemed to be an NGO, duly registered under both the Subdistrict Office and the Putuo district Civil Affairs Bureau.

Legally registered NGOs in the subdistrict receive a variety of forms of assistance from the Changzhou Service Center. The Service Center organizes road shows to inform the community about NGO services, issues special licenses that allow NGOs to enter communities, residences, and commercial buildings, and holds meetings to bring together NGOs to share information and develop cooperative activities. It also brokers the sale of NGO services to the government, essentially allowing the government to subcontract to NGOs a host of service-provision roles, such as services for the elderly, vocational training, culture and art enrichment, preschool education, and even matchmaking services.

Yet the Service Center also plays an overtly political role. Among its key functions are to graft party branches onto NGOs, to register public leagues, and to build a "precautionary network" of party members and the public to "defend legal NGOs and combat illegal ones in a bid to maintain social stability."[61]

At the same time, another wealthy and bustling municipality is trying a very different experiment, with what appears to be the blessing of higher authorities. In 2009 the Ministry of Civil Affairs and the municipal government of Shenzhen put forward a Cooperative Agreement on Advancing Integrated Reforms in Civil Affairs. Shenzhen, which as China's first Special Economic Zone grew from a village of 30,000 in 1980 to a thriving metropolis of over 14 million in 2010, has been selected as the site for a new set of experiments in the management of social organizations. Under the new rules, organizations will be allowed to dispense with the requirement to find a sponsoring agency when registering with the Shenzhen Civil Affairs Bureau—a notable reform of a requirement that has hindered development of a large-scale, legally recognized citizen sector. Shenzhen will also take over regulatory jurisdiction of domestic and foreign foundations and develop a range of other reform measures up to 2015, all subject to continuous government assessment and consideration of expanding successful reforms to other parts of the country.[62] The province of Jiangsu is also experimenting with subnational regulation of philanthropic foundations and charitable activities, which, as in Shenzhen, is being assessed by the national authorities as a potential model for other regions.[63]

Mass Organizations and GONGOs

One set of associations escapes all these rules and regulations, with official blessing. Until recently, official "mass organizations" such as the All-China Federation of Trade Unions (ACFTU) and the Women's Association filled the available space for interest group representation (without necessarily representing the interests of those groups). Now, as political space has opened to a degree, and as government support (particularly financial support) is withdrawn, these mass organizations are being driven in new directions. Some local components of the mass organizations are trying to take on more normal representative roles, developing social capital and organizational skills that stretch more widely than independent NGOs would be allowed to do (although they remain far from becoming autonomous bodies). Thus, these often disregarded holdovers of the Maoist era are worth a closer look.

Probably the most important are trade unions, as exemplars of both how China's civil society has been organized in the past via government fiat and how that system is evolving as the party-state's dominance has weakened. Trade unions are key civil society organizations in most liberal democracies, organizing large swaths of the population into politically active constituencies with strong shared interests. When China's economy was entirely state-controlled, trade unions served merely as a way of extending the party-state's reach into the workplace. Rather than representing the interests of workers vis-à-vis their employers, under central planning—when the state was the employer—unions primarily served as agents of the state, serving workers only to the degree that the state's definition of workers' interests required.[64] All were bound together under the All-China Federation of Trade Unions, which remains a vast network with thirty-one provincial trade union federations, ten national industrial unions, and over a million "grassroots" trade union organizations with a total membership on the order of 170 million.[65] The notion of the union as a mechanism by which workers could collectively bargain with their employers did not exist.

Once China's post-1979 reforms began promoting the development of a more market-oriented economy, both the party-state and the unions themselves faced pressures to reconsider the roles of unions.[66] China's ongoing economic reforms, involving massive job losses at formerly state-owned but now privatized firms, pension and welfare reforms, and escalating inequalities, have made labor a crucial node of social contention, especially since the early 1990s.[67] After 1992, when the political system began to recover from the trauma of Tiananmen Square and Deng Xiaoping launched a new round of market-oriented economic reforms, workers became employees subject to being hired or fired and with the right to choose their place of employment.[68] Firms (including state-owned enterprises as well as private entities) began to be evaluated on the basis of their economic productivity and the tax revenue they generate for the state, rather than for their capacity to implement the party-state's plans, maintain social order, and provide social services. Because of the extraordinarily high emphasis on rapid economic growth, neither the party-state nor the enterprises showed great interest in protecting workers' rights—particularly for the many millions of rural migrant workers, who have faced massive discrimination and exploitation with little capacity to organize in their own defense.

Now, however, the evolution of the market economy and the huge scale of migrant labor is putting trade unions under intense pressures to develop into bodies that meaningfully represent the interests of their members. As conflicts became more frequent and more violent, the authorities faced growing incentives to allow unions to more meaningfully represent the interests of their worker members, thus gaining their trust and positioning themselves to ease conflicts between capital and labor. At the same time, unions found they needed greater capacity to reflect worker interests if they wished to attract and retain members.

Yet despite multiple reforms of the Trade Union Law and the evolving nature of declarations from the governing body of the All-China Federation of Trade Unions, there was no question of allowing truly independent unions that could become large-scale political actors on the model of Poland's Solidarity.[69] The government continues to pay for union staff and administration, although not for the unions' activities.

To a considerable extent, unions have failed to rise to the challenge, instead confining themselves to relatively minor roles such as distributing partial benefits on behalf of the state and enterprise, and/or organizing leisure, cultural, and recreational activities for employees. Local government officials, whose careers depend overwhelmingly on successful short-term economic growth, often push unions to favor the interests of capital over those of labor. This is true even, or perhaps particularly, in the richer, faster-growing coastal regions, whose spectacular economic performance has depended on very low labor costs and tight profit margins within highly competitive global supply chains.

Yet there is considerable variation across localities. In some cases, existing unions are evolving to take on new roles. In others, new organizations are arising to represent worker interests. The complexities are compounded by the extraordinarily high rate of internal migration of the labor force. On labor issues, the party is supposed to represent worker interests, so the formation of associations claiming to do the same can be seen as an inherent challenge to party legitimacy. On internal migration, the vast army of internal migrants fall through the cracks of China's rudimentary social welfare provisions, often unable to obtain legal residency under China's restrictive system of residency permits, enroll their children in local schools, or access normal government services.

The transformations sweeping China are cascading through even its officially organized unions, as the case of the Quanzhou City Federation of Trade Unions in Fujian province reveals.[70]

Quanzhou City has the best-developed private economy in Fujian province, with capital flowing in from local sources and from Taiwan and the Chinese diaspora in Southeast Asia. The region's business enterprises focus mainly on labor-intensive manufacturing, producing such goods as clothes, shoes, caps, electronic products, and building materials. In 2005, the city had a GDP of 180.4 billion RMB, with 90 percent of it coming from non-public sectors of the economy. The city has over 20,000 nonpublic enterprises, more than 90,000 privately or individually owned businesses, and almost 2 million employees. Local workers, however, constitute a small proportion, and 80 percent of the employees come from other regions of Fujian province, Hunan province, Anhui province, and Sichuan province. Migrant workers constitute almost one-sixth of the city's total population.

After the turn of the century, a combination of factors pushed the local authorities to look to unions as a way of managing growing tensions. Many of the local enterprises, especially those in labor-intensive industries, were small and medium-sized businesses that paid their employees no more than the minimum wage (350 RMB), frequently neglected concerns about working conditions, and did not pay required overtime.[71] Complaints about wage arrears and work-related injuries became common.[72] The resulting tensions led to violence in which workers blocked and locked up or burned down their factories, along with a soaring crime rate, which together got the attention of the local government.

Starting in 2003, however, the southeastern coastal regions, including Quanzhou City, began experiencing shortages in the labor market, as the central government attempted to rebalance the increasingly unequal rates of economic growth across China's regions by expanding investments in rural areas and agriculture.[73] By 2003–2004, critical shortages of workers were limiting or even halting production in a number of the city's enterprises, and others moved their production lines out of the city in search of labor.

At the same time, the city saw increasing development of "civil trade unions"—essentially clan associations and other networks based on geography or kinship that posed a challenge to the official trade union's authoritative status as defender of workers' rights and interests.[74] These clan associations set out to help workers claim back wages and seek compensations for injuries, but their existence outside the official system raised fears within the party-state of the emergence of new, independent actors.

Facing all these pressures—dissatisfied workers, labor shortages, and institutional competition—the Quanzhou municipal trade union took steps to reach out to private sector workers. From the early 1990s the authorities had been establishing trade unions in the city's villages and townships. By 2005, the overwhelming majority of workers in private enterprises had joined up, with a total membership in the Quanzhou Municipal Federation of Trade Unions of 1.3 million, of which over 1 million were workers in private enterprises. The federation also established twenty-eight industry-specific trade unions (such as those for garment, petrochemical, and tourism workers) intended to perform such roles as negotiating for equal treatment within industries, formulating labor standards for each industry, signing labor contracts (since many enterprises had avoided signing written contracts with their employees), and collective agreements and collective wage negotiations. In 2005, the total number of business enterprises in the city that had signed labor contracts reached 35,200; of the 1.19 million workers who signed labor contracts, 75 percent worked in nonstate-owned enterprises. More than 30,000 enterprises established collective agreements covering 1.4 million workers. Collective wage agreements were inked in the tourism and garment industries, and regional wage agreements were signed in the economic and technical development zones where workers were concentrated.

The federation also took on the role of lobbying the party and the government on behalf of worker interests, forwarding numerous recommendations to the party municipal committee and municipal government, proposing legislation to the people's congresses and the municipal Chinese People's Political Consultative Conference (CPPCC), and brokering annual conferences between unions and government officials at the city and county levels. It established a legal association for protection of workers' rights. Courts at both the city and the county level have established labor arbitration tribunals.

The Quanzhou unions are also aiming to increase a form of migrant worker political participation, recommending workers to participate in the election of national model workers and to serve as representatives on local CPPCC committees and in people's congresses. In what might be seen as the beginnings of European-style corporatism, for several years the Quanzhou people's congress and government have allowed workers to sit in on meetings of the standing committee of the people's congress and the plenary committee of the CPPCC, and have also elected rural migrant workers to be representatives of the people's congress and CPPCC at various levels.

The Quanzhou City trade unions have also received the government's financial support and are thus better equipped to protect the rights and interests of workers. The city's rules require that enterprises with established trade unions contribute only 0.8 percent of total wages of staff and workers to support trade unions, while enterprises without trade unions should contribute 2.5 percent of total wages. In 2002, Quanzhou City entrusted the local taxation department to collect funds for trade unions from enterprises that were obligated to contribute, thereby improving the efficiency and effectiveness of fund collection. The unions are using the resulting funding to disburse cash to needy workers and for other activities. Within three years, the funds of the trade unions in the city quadrupled. Since 2004, the Quanzhou municipal government provided trade unions with an annual fund of 500,000 RMB, to help them protect the rights of their employees. This yearly financial assistance has become a system itself. Every year before the lunar festival, workers are told: "Needy workers who require cash for the festival, please seek help from trade unions." Such workers are eligible to receive up to 300–500 RMB. In the system's first year of implementation, more than US$100,000 were offered as "festival incentives."

Yiwu City (a prefecture in wealthy and fast-growing Zhejiang province) tried another experiment that initially ran into strong local resistance, but ended up earning the praise of the country's top leadership.[75] Until the late 1990s, like most state-based trade unions, Yiwu City's did little if anything to represent workers. The city's approval in July 2000 of the Yiwu City Legal Rights Defense Association as a nonprofit association within the union initially appeared to be an ambitious and unusual initiative, creating the first labor union legal rights defense body in the country. The plan was to create an "integrated" rights defense system, which would work closely with government and party. One of the association's first moves was to assign two politically influential senior staff to be registered at the Zhejiang Jingzhen law firm, which in turn appointed lawyers to work at an office in the association who could undertake legal action on labor disputes.

There was initially quite a fight at the local level, with local authorities whose interests were threatened resisting the changes. Within weeks, the new association faced a challenge from a government department demanding the association scale down its work scope and change its name to the Yiwu City *Workers'* Legal Rights Defense Association. Shortly thereafter, under pressure from the Legal Bureau, the law firm pulled out its resident lawyers, and the association was forced to downgrade its name further to the Yiwu City Legal Assistance Center, Workers' Section, with considerable constraints on its functions.

Then, in late 2004, a reporter published an exposé on the Yiwu situation, which caught the attention of China's highest-level officials. China's top leader, President and Party Secretary Hu Jintao, was widely quoted as saying that it was important to study the Yiwu experience, to develop and improve rights defense mechanisms under the leadership of the trade unions, and to strengthen the function of the trade unions and serve the workers.[76] Other leaders weighed in in support of the Yiwu model's "integrated" approach to labor rights, which featured close collaboration with government departments, industry organizations, intermediary social organizations, and other actors in a markedly nonadversarial approach.

This story is revealing on many fronts. The initial effective resistance by the entrenched local elite, a resistance commonly faced by unions and NGOs trying to assist workers with legal recourse, was overcome only by direct intervention from the very top of the Chinese hierarchy. That intervention was forthcoming partly because of media coverage, and because the Yiwu innovators went to great lengths to design an "integrated" approach that appealed to the party's deep concern with retaining overall control. And the central authorities have a policy favoring legal aid provided by trade unions as a means of dealing with labor problems.[77]

But addressing pay issues and other workplace rights is only a partial solution to the many problems of migrant workers, whose needs extend far beyond the workplace, as the southern island province of Hainan has found. Since 1988 the island has been a provincial Special Economic Zone, and has attracted an enormous influx of migrant workers.[78] Most of these are relatively uneducated young single men from the less economically developed central and western regions of China. Within Hainan province, Haikou City found itself with nearly a third of the migrant labor population, and within Haikou City, the central urban area of Longhua district—the economic, cultural, and traffic hub of the city—had the highest concentration, with a migrant population of some 50,000.

In 2004 the Longhua district in Hainan province was one of the Local Governance Innovation Award winners for its establishment in 2003 of the Longhua Migrant Workers' Management Association, an unusual example of a local government initiative that developed into a legally independent nongovernmental organization, albeit one that retained ties to government bodies. Starting in the mid-1990s, the district government and party committee, struggling to manage escalating crime rates and public health issues attributed to the influx of migrants, set up a series of Migrant Workers' Homes to address the migrants' two most pressing problems: housing and jobs. Taking advantage of large swaths of uncompleted real estate residential construction, in 1997 the District Political and Legal Committee, with support from the municipal committee and government, opened the first of a series of Migrant Workers' Homes that combined dormitory housing and stalls and/or stores, which the migrants could rent at a fraction of the market rate to operate small businesses. In essence, these became what in other places would be called "social enterprises"— small businesses that combine for-profit and charitable models to meet social needs in what is intended to be a financially sustainable manner.

The first Migrant Workers' Home was set up on a downtown site that had been abandoned by its owner, remodeled to provide dorms along with 212 stalls and twenty stores, and then rented to migrants to operate wholesale flower businesses. Also onsite were services that included an employment consultation center, access to help with government departments, and what was called a "defense team for the protection of migrant workers." In 2002, two more homes were set up, and in 2004, the model was expanded to include produce markets and other business types.

In addition to providing housing and stall rentals at below-market prices, the homes took on the full range of government responsibilities for managing migrant populations—safety, rights, cultural needs, and family planning. The government allocated the land, contributed resources, provided service centers, and stationed district defense officers in each Migrant Workers' Home. The deputy secretary of the committee's Department of Public Security and Integrated Management had overall responsibility for overseeing management of the homes. One innovation was a clever tool to protect migrants from other government departments. The district government pledged to pay all fines imposed by government departments on businesses based in the homes, which proved to be an effective means of combating the unreasonable fines often imposed on vulnerable migrants. As the case study notes, "A natural consequence of this measure is that cases of tax abuse in the Migrant Workers' Homes have completely vanished."

Each home was established as a legally independent entity, meant to be for-profit but with access to government assistance and private donations to keep rentals and services affordable for the migrants. Although each home specializes in a different business (flowers, car repair, etc.), and the model has been diffused into a number of experiments in the district, all have to abide by common rules and management guidelines.

Although the homes appear to have succeeded at providing their inhabitants with a range of economic opportunities and social services, the district quickly ran into a problem of scale. Homes could handle only a few hundred migrants each, but with more than 50,000 migrants already in the district (many of whom were employed in such mobile jobs as construction or domestic service that are not well suited to the homes model), and more migrants being drawn to the district as word of the new approach spread, it became clear that something more would be needed. In the face of these challenges, the relatively limited scale at which social enterprises generally operate was just not enough.

This led the Longhua District Political and Legal Committee in 2002 to take steps toward the creation of a Longhua District Migrant Workers' Association. The initial proposal, submitted to the Haikou City Office of Civil Affairs, quickly ran afoul of the central government's regulation banning the formation of such groups. Under the 1999 "Notification on Enhancing the Management of Non-Governmental Organizations by the General Office of the CPC Central Committee and the General Office of the State Council":

> Civil departments at all levels should exercise firm control over the nongovernmental organizations that cover overly broad domains and function with ambiguous identities, and are to prohibit the establishment of non-governmental organizations concerning Qigong, special populations (veterans, laid-off workers, and job-bers), and religions, which are harmful to national unity and go against national constitutions and regulations.

With a quick name change and submission of a "report Regarding the Change in Name and Constitution of the Longhua Migrant Workers'

Association," the newly renamed Longhua District Migrant Workers' Management Association (MWMA)—the first autonomous association for migrant workers in China—was born.

As is generally the case in China, however, autonomy is a relative concept. Like all registered NGOs, the MWMA has a government body as supervisor, in this case the Longhua District Public Security Integrated Management Commission. Although it describes itself as a nongovernmental organization "formed voluntarily by migrant workers," its first chairman was Yang Laiqing, the former deputy secretary of the Political and Legal Committee that developed the Migrant Workers' Homes concept, who was explicitly tasked with representing the government.

Yet clearly the MWMA represents a significant move toward greater scope for independent action on the part of the district's migrant workers. Unlike the Migrant Workers' Homes, which had a for-profit (if limited-profit) model, the MWMA's purpose is what in other countries would be seen as traditional service delivery for this self-defined group: "to improve interactions and relations among migrant workers, to protect the legal rights of migrant workers, to improve the economic status of migrant workers, and to more effectively provide services for migrant workers." Any migrant worker can join or leave at will, and relevant organizations (including the individual Migrants Workers' Homes) are also formal members. Both individuals and organizations pay dues, which provide the bulk of the funding for the eleven paid staff (the rest comes from the district government).

As soon as it was up and running, the MWMA began looking to expand within the township. It set out to create a migrant workers' network through affiliates in subdistricts at the township level, reached out to community residents' commissions at the village level, and undertook publicity campaigns. It spread not just geographically but also substantively, establishing a Legal Rights Defense Department and over time making the defense of migrant rights its top priority.

One final award-winning experiment is worth a brief mention in this discussion of trade unions and labor. The Sichuan provincial trade union and the municipal trade union of the provincial capital, Chengdu, together won one of the Local Governance Innovation Best Practice Awards in January 2010 for a set of initiatives to help migrant workers defend their rights.[79] Migrant workers both to and from the province often encountered the usual problems—hopelessly delayed wage payments, lack of compensation for injury, and so on—and the usual lack of recourse. The provincial trade union reached out to help them. It was one of the first to recruit migrant workers into the trade union (before 2004, trade union law did not cover private sector workers). From 2006 to 2009, the union helped defend 1,211 cases in which the rights of migrant workers had been infringed, helped migrant workers receive payments of more than 36 million yuan, and helped them receive injury compensation and other payments of more than 6 million yuan.

So far, this seems like nothing out of the ordinary. But most important from the perspective of building social capital and social networks, Sichuan trade union officials reached mutual help agreements with their counterparts in other provinces, a crucial step in coordinating talks between migrant workers—who by definition have moved across local boundaries—and employers. By the end of 2009, eighteen of thirty-one provincial trade unions had reached mutual help agreements. At that time, the Sichuan agreements covered 8.2 million migrant workers from Sichuan to other provinces, some 73 percent of the total number of Sichuan workers that had migrated to all other provinces.

Environmental NGOs

Trade unions and other civil society groups focused on workers and labor issues have to deal with a context in which state-based organizations are overwhelmingly dominant. It is a very different story, however, for groups focused on environmental issues, to which pre-reform China paid little attention. This tabula rasa has attracted an increasingly robust ecosystem of environmental NGOs, or ENGOs. In North America and Europe, environmental groups play a major role directly in policymaking and in highly visible and often highly confrontational public campaigns, sometimes at the same time. In China, the nascent environmental movement's civil society groups face all the constraints described in this chapter—legal restrictions, resource constraints, and the realities of political life in the party-state system; nonetheless, environmental protection is the arena in which social activism appears to be advancing most rapidly.

Although activists began campaigning around environmental issues in the 1980s, particularly against the construction of the Three Gorges Dam, such campaigning screeched to a halt with the 1989 crackdown and in the tense years that followed. Thereafter, as China's mounting environmental damage provoked growing concern, a UN-sponsored international conference once again helped to spur organizing within China, although this one was held in far-off Brazil. The 1992 Rio Conference on Environment and Development and the resulting Rio Declaration helped to inspire the establishment of national ENGOs in China.[80] The next year saw the establishment of Friends of Nature (FON), a national grassroots environmental NGO (although set up as an affiliate of the Department of Culture in the Beijing municipal government). Over the next decade or so, FON was quickly followed by more ENGOs, many of which were created by staff splitting off from existing organizations.

The rise of China's ENGOs paralleled, and interacted with, the take-off in Internet use, particularly through the bulletin board system (BBS) forums that have become a pervasive component of Chinese associational life. Greener Beijing and Green-Web, for example, both started online and grew to encompass volunteers who organized community environmental activities and campaigns.[81]

These ENGOs have had several things going for them. On the political front, environmental issues are increasingly seen, at least by the central authorities, as relatively free of political sensitivities, a pattern reminiscent of developments in central and eastern Europe before the fall of the Berlin Wall. At the same time, official concern over the catastrophic scale of China's environmental degradation and lack of official capacity to respond effectively to it has made some officials more willing to reach out to activists outside government. China's relatively weak national Ministry of Environmental Protection, and its counterparts at the provincial, municipal, and county levels, have little authority over other government agencies and lack the capacity to rein in rapacious patterns of economic growth.[82] To them, ENGOS can be natural allies. Foreign funders and environmental activists have poured into the country, supporting the development of ENGOs with funding, technical assistance, and networking with the global environmental movement. And because environmental issues only really appeared on the Chinese agenda in the 1990s, the sector does not have large and entrenched government-organized NGOs (GONGOs) of the All-China Federation of Trade Unions ilk. Environmental GONGOs such as the China Environmental Protection Foundation and the All-China Environment Federation are no older than the ENGOs themselves.

Despite all this, environmental NGOs must still take care not to provoke undue official antagonism and often must play games to get around registration rules and obstacles.[83] They remain mostly quite small, youthful, and poorly resourced. Their impact on policy processes is largely limited to personal networks that happen to link ENGO members to officials, partly because environmental policymaking processes themselves are poorly developed. Nonetheless, civil society's role in environmental activism is strikingly different from the processes involving labor and workers.

Conclusion

Two plausible scenarios emerge from the convoluted story of China's evolving civil society. In one, the party-state recaptures effective control of China's associational life, embedding party structures deeply within all important forms of social organization and preventing the widespread development of strong and broad ties that can escape the party's control. That is a scenario in which a reasonably vibrant associational life may bolster authoritarian resilience via its positive effect on economic performance, but one in which civil society will do little more than provide services (such as official trade unions) and enable people to enjoy hobbies together.

In the other scenario, Chinese society develops a strong capacity to organize and carry out collective action in search of social goals, with social organizations and networks that can articulate, aggregate, and represent the multifarious interests of this increasingly complex society. This could be a scenario that sees political liberalization thanks to society's increased capacity to form interest-based groups able to act in defense of their interests.

Social organization is undoubtedly growing rapidly in China, in part with the blessing and support of the party-state, and in part under severe constraints. The space for associations that can serve as autonomous counterweights to state authority or pose challenges to the party's position through advocacy and criticism is extremely limited, although such associations do exist. Much more common are civil society organizations that provide social services, and GONGOs that are increasingly caught between their traditional role as arms of the state and the pressures they face to serve the interests of their ostensible members. Both are seen by the party-state as *extenders* of a system that keeps the party's political control front and center.

But even what appear to be unthreatening roles carry with them potential for political significance. Service providers often morph into advocates and rights defenders, as the Longhua district experiment with housing migrant workers shows, as they come to see the larger systemic causes of the problems they are trying to ameliorate. And beyond this, the habits of effective collective action die hard—the skills and norms learned in a homeowners association can transfer to organizations with quite different goals.

But neither local nor central authorities have yet shown signs of willingness to substantially loosen controls on social organization to the degree that would be needed to support the evolution of a rich, dense, and overlapping set of networks that reach across the country. The CCP both fears and needs civil society organizations. It needs them to help with the task of governing a huge, rapidly changing country that is beset with a vast array of enormous problems, and to bolster the development of the social capital that is a fundamental requirement of all economies that have moved into the club of wealthy countries. It fears them as potential sources of conflict and especially as potential sources of challenges to its authority.

In such a complex environment, how does one know what to look for to understand the roles of civil society organizations in China's political trajectory? The legal structure and the officially approved experiments described here say a good deal about what roles the central authorities would *like* such organizations to play, but not about whether it actually is possible to walk this tightrope. The dual registration system for NGOs is clearly designed to subordinate social organizations to the party-state, but its awkwardness makes it difficult for China to foster the service providers and other types of organizations that the party-state needs to help manage China's enormous problems. Similarly, the new restrictions on foreign funding may be seen as helping to protect the existing structures from possible foreign political influence, but in the absence of a well-developed culture of philanthropy in China, the restrictions may prove counterproductive. And the tight constraints on the formation of social bridges spanning localities and regions facilitate the party-state's vertical control, but also deprive China of potential channels of social resilience that may be badly needed in the face of what will undoubtedly be enormous economic, social, and environmental strains in the coming years.

But the organizational capacity, scope, and resilience of China's civil society is not up to the party-state alone. Despite thirty years of difficult conditions, China's citizens have developed an extraordinary array of grassroots groups, professional networks, and registered organizations whose strength cannot be directly measured but was hinted at in the aftermath of the Sichuan earthquake in 2008. Even the officially formed mass organizations like the trade unions and women's federation show signs of evolving into something that may help respond to the interests of China's citizens, as we saw both in this chapter and in the elections chapter. The authorities are not leading the way; they are scrambling to keep up with an increasingly dynamic third sector.

5

From Local Experiments to National Rules: China Lets the Sunshine In

In February 2009, Premier Wen Jiabao held his first online chat with Chinese netizens, offering an unprecedented opportunity for ordinary citizens to directly raise their concerns with top leadership. During the online conversation, Premier Wen said, "I have always believed that the public has the right to know what its government is doing and thinking about, and the right to criticize and make comments on government policies."[1] He has since held two more online chats, in 2010 and 2011, responding on issues from rising consumer and housing prices to corruption and access to health care and rural education.[2] These events show how the Party is attempting to adapt to changing conditions created by information technology, and how the top leadership is trying to demonstrate a changed attitude on the nature of the relationship between individual citizens and the state.

In today's China, information increasingly flows through cross-cutting social networks, rather than being rationed vertically through layers of the bureaucracy. Social issues rise to the surface through Internet chat rooms, cell phone text messages, and the blogosphere. These communications are sometimes allowed by central authorities—such as when they involve local abuses of power—and are sometimes stamped out, such as when they touch on politically sensitive issues like Tibet or Tiananmen Square. At the same time, not only are Chinese leaders such as Wen going online to engage citizens, government agencies are increasingly putting out more information proactively through websites and press releases, and appointing spokespersons to interface with the public. Most dramatically, China recently jumped on the bandwagon of a burgeoning global trend with the adoption of regulations that are contemporary China's version of a freedom-of-information act.

What drives a formerly totalitarian state, in a country whose history comprises thousands of years of centralized governmental opacity, to move down the path of increasing government transparency? The short answer is the same one that has driven the reforms discussed in previous chapters: necessity. It is widely recognized both within and outside the country that governance in China suffers from far too much secrecy and far too little accountability. The government's monitoring capabilities have not kept up with the multiplying complexities of a rapidly "informa-tionizing" economy and society, to use the best available English equiva-lent of the Chinese term. The decentralized structure of the bureaucracy means that central authorities are not fully informed about the true size and costs of government at other levels. Within the party-state structure, the decentralization of administrative and fiscal responsibilities without the corresponding building of vertical accountability mechanisms has compromised the ability of central ministries to enforce national policies and to hold local governments to account. Government agencies do not readily share information with one another in the same locality, nor do higher levels get the complete and unvarnished truth from their inferiors. Ordinary citizens, for whom access to information about the govern-ment and party would provide a minimal step toward enabling them to protect their rights and hold their officials accountable, learn the least of all. Indeed, Minxin Pei's argument that China's political evolution has become trapped is based in large part on the extent of such information asymmetries in the absence of meaningful accountability mechanisms.

Yet the move to more transparent governance is driven by more power-ful and specific forces than simply a recognition that China has a secrecy problem. Those include:

Information Technology. One major driver is the positive interaction between market forces and information technology. As China's economic reform and global integration deepened, so too did the need to shift from information systems based on hoarding and selective vertical dissemina-tion to ones based on freer flows determined by demand and supply, not just for firms, but also for government. At the same time, advances in information technology made the move to new information systems much easier. The Chinese government started adopting computing and Internet technologies in the 1980s, and set up a Leading Group on National Informatization in 1999, as well as a State Council Information Office to carry out policies set out by the Leading Group. This corresponded to greater use of the Internet by citizens as well, and growing demand for more government information to be available via the Internet.[3]

WTO Accession. China's accession to the World Trade Organization in December 2001 came with requirements for greater transparency in its trade-related rules and regulations. These obligations were taken seriously because WTO review mechanisms would regularly monitor China's implementation efforts in this area. As part of the extensive legal, regulatory, and administrative changes brought about by accession, China agreed not just to publish its trade-related laws and regulations, but also to allow for public comment before the implementation of regulations, and conducted widespread training and research on international approaches to transparency.[4]

Fighting Corruption. As mentioned in chapter 2, China's fiscal and administrative decentralization has led to major monitoring and enforcement problems. The government is therefore searching out new tools for bureaucratic control in two ways. First, the central government needs access to better and more timely information about the behavior of local governments so as to impose more discipline. Second, greater disclosure of government-held information allows other segments of society to also hold local governments to account and reduce corruption. The 2004 Fourth Plenum of the 16th Party Central Committee, for example, called for the government to strengthen its governance capability and described the issue of fighting corruption as an "issue of life or death for the Party."[5]

State-Society Mediation. A final motivation is the growing need to provide channels for an increasingly connected and complex society to voice its grievances. Traditionally, the *xingfang* system, which allows citizens to send petitions regarding official misconduct to the Office of Letters and Calls, has been the main official channel through which grievances are dealt with. Advances in modern communication and transport, along with the multiplying social problems brought by rapid socioeconomic changes, mean that "the system is overwhelmed and the government spends more energy trying to dissuade people from petitioning than it does trying to resolve their problems."[6] A more open government could work to provide more channels for resolving social issues and thereby strengthen state-society accountability and state legitimacy.

Regulating Openness

For all these reasons, China's governance innovations have included the promulgation of a version of a freedom-of-information rule. In 2007, the State Council issued a set of regulations on Open Government Information (OGI), requiring all administrative arms of the state to proactively release information related to their work, and allowing citizens to request information held by the agencies (as well as providing administrative and legal channels to appeal rejections to these requests). One year was set aside for government agencies to make the necessary preparations for implementation, and the regulations came into force in May 2008.

The national rules came about after several years of experimentation with transparency systems at lower levels, as well as a concerted effort to glean lessons from freedom-of-information acts and right-to-information laws around the world. China is not alone in experiencing these pressures and in attempting to respond. Its OGI rules are part of a powerful global trend toward rules that promise more open and transparent government.[7] This chapter thus tells three interwoven stories: about the importance of the transparency measures themselves for China's political future; about how the regulations evolved as they moved from the local to the national level and what that reveals about the prospects for China's experimentalist approach; and about how that evolution compares to similar laws and regulations in the rest of the world, particularly other major emerging powers and their standards of best transparency practices.[8]

The transparency trend started in China at the village level in the 1980s in the "open village affairs" movement, and grew to include municipalities and provinces in the early 2000s. Plans for a national OGI regulation started in May 2002 with the formation of a research group at the Chinese Academy of Social Sciences. While a draft was submitted to the State Council in July 2002, the government did not implement the guidelines immediately, but instead built up experience by allowing cities to experiment and issue their own Open Government Information guidelines.[9] Guangzhou's OGI provisions came into force in January 2003, followed by Shantou municipality in Guangdong province's Special

Economic Zone. Shanghai issued its OGI provisions in January 2004, followed closely in the next month by the business hub of Shenzhen. Similar experiments continued across the country. In 2004 alone, over twenty-four municipalities and provinces adopted some kind of OGI legislation. By mid-2006, the number had increased to more than thirty.[10] (See box 5-1 for a chronology of OGI in China.)

These transparency regulations represented significant shifts in governance, reflecting the blow that new communication technology, in particular the Internet, has dealt to traditional approaches, and the government's rising awareness of the need to transform the role of the state in China.[11] The proactive release of information for public consumption overturns the established system in which information is hoarded and rationed to increase bargaining power within the bureaucracy, and channeled vertically upward through successive layers of the bureaucracy. And the very notion of transparency and the granting of permission to citizens to request information subverts existing mind-sets that the state "owns" the information pertaining to its activities and that secrecy should be the accepted norm of operation.

But like all regulations and laws that purport to open governments up to public scrutiny, China's OGI regulations reflect a series of balancing acts between legitimate needs for the protection of some kinds of information, the power of vested interests to protect their secrets, and the public interest in greater disclosure. China's experimentalist approach allowed different localities to try different balances. When the center established national rules to supersede the local experiments, the changes in where the balances were struck reveal a good deal about the challenges of national-scale governance reforms.

The OGI Regulations—from Local to National

Transparency laws encompass several broad concerns: underlying principles, scope, context, and processes. With regard to underlying principles, China's regulations underwent considerable change as they moved from local to national. Both Shanghai and Guangzhou's OGI provisions explicitly state the "right to know" as part of the guiding principles.[12] This is generally considered to be the most fundamental element of transparency laws and rules around the world—the principle that citizens are entitled to have access to government-held information. In

---

Box 5-1. *Chronology of Open Government Information (OGI) in China*

March 1988 The Second Plenum of the 13th Central Committee of the Communist Party of China calls for openness of work systems as an important component of honest government, and approves experiments in open government affairs.

September 1997 General Secretary and President Jiang Zemin calls for "open government affairs" in his report to the 15th National Communist Party Congress.

November 1998 The Organic Law of the People's Republic of China on Villagers Committees institutionalizes village-level self-governance and the "open village affairs" system, especially for fiscal transparency.

December 2000 "Notice of the General Offices of the Central Committee of the Communist Party of China and the State Council on Comprehensive Implementation of an Open Government Affairs System in Organs of Political Power at the Town and Township Level Throughout the Country" calls for promoting "open government affairs" at the town and township level, and for preparations to implement "open government affairs" at the county (city) level and above.

December 2001 China joins the World Trade Organization and signs on to certain international transparency commitments.

November 2002 Guangzhou City in Guangdong Province adopts China's first local OGI provisions, effective January 1, 2003, which established a clear presumption of disclosure and for the first time in Chinese history requires government organs to proactively disseminate government information and gives "natural persons" the right to request information from the Guangzhou government.

Excerpt of chronology prepared by Freedominfo.org contributor Jamie Horsley, deputy director of the China Law Center, Yale University, Senior Research Scholar and Lecturer in Law, Yale Law School. The full chronology can be viewed at www.freedominfo.org/regions/east-asia/china/.

---

contrast, Article 1 of the OGI steers away from such explicit statements on the right to know. Instead, it states that the objectives of the regulations are to "enhance transparency of the work of government, promote administration in accordance with the law, and bring into full play the role of government information in serving the people's production and livelihood and their economic and social activities."[13] The change in language is highly revealing, as it shifts the very basis of these transparency

January 2003 Shanghai Municipality adopts China's first provincial-level OGI provisions, effective May 1, 2004, establishing a comprehensive structure for implementing and reporting on the OGI system.

March 2004 China's State Council issues the "Outline on Implementing the Comprehensive Promotion of Administration in Accordance with the Law," which sets administrative transparency and promoting OGI as nationwide governmental objectives.

March 24, 2005 The "Opinions of the General Offices of the Central Committee of the Communist Party of China and the State Council on Further Promoting Open Government Affairs" articulated Party and central government policy to encourage greater administrative transparency and called for formulating national OGI regulations.

January 2007 China's State Council adopts the "Regulations of the People's Republic of China," nationwide administrative measures that were published April 2007 and called for institutionalizing information disclosure systems throughout the government at all levels down to the town and township.

August 4, 2007 The "Notice of the General Office of the State Council on Preparing Well for Implementing the Regulations of the People's Republic of China on Open Government Information" set timelines for government organs to prepare required catalogues of and guides to requesting government information.

April 29, 2008 The "Opinions of the General Office of the State Council on Various Issues of Implementing the Open Government Information Regulations of the People's Republic of China" provided some useful guidance, including that classified information can be redacted to permit disclosure of at least portions of the record, but also specified that, if requested information does not relate to the requester's "special needs" as mentioned in Article 13 of the OGI regulations, the government organ may decline to release the information.

May 1, 2008 The OGI regulations take effect on the International Labor Day holiday.

regulations from being founded on citizen rights to being driven by more technocratic objectives of good governance.

The shift also shows up in the varying assumptions about whether disclosure should be the norm, with secrecy the exception, as the Shanghai and Guangzhou rules indicated.[14] In contrast, the OGI regulations place specific restrictions on the limits and conditions of disclosure. For example, Article 8 states that "[t]he government information disclosed by administrative agencies may not endanger state security, public security, economic security, and social stability." Without further specification, the article provides wide scope for officials to withhold information and great uncertainty about what might be taken to entail the endangerment of security and stability.[15]

Another contrast emerges with regard to who is allowed to ask for government information. Local transparency provisions had provided fairly broad scope for citizens and organizations to request information, in that no prior conditions needed to be met.[16] In contrast, Article 13 of the OGI regulations only allows citizens, legal persons, or other organizations to make requests for information "based on the special needs of such matters as their own production, livelihood, and scientific and technological research."

Such differences in the transformation of local transparency experiments into national reform reveal the tensions and varying priorities that can exist between local and central authorities. While Shanghai and Guangzhou led the way in testing the effectiveness and boundaries of governance via transparency, the national regulation was not only scaled back in its scope, but reflected significantly different values: efficient governance, rather than the right to know; and secrecy as the norm and disclosure the exception, rather than the reverse. These important differences aside, the OGI regulations in general match the standards set by Shanghai and Guangzhou in terms of the bureaucratic processes to be followed in organizing and releasing information.[17]

The International Comparison

China's OGI can be compared not only to its own internal experience, but to the broader trends elsewhere. For example, international practice about which parts of the government are covered by transparency rules varies enormously. In the United States, for example, the Freedom of Information Act (FOIA) applies only to federal agencies, although most states have their own similar laws. India's more recent and sweeping Right to Information Law, by contrast, covers all levels and branches of government and extends into the private sector to the degree that such information is relevant. In China, Article 2 indicates that the OGI covers "information made or obtained by administrative agencies in the course of exercising their responsibilities and recorded and stored in a given form," but political agencies, such as people's congresses, and judiciary agencies, are not formally covered by the regulations. Given that the trend has been toward more broadly applicable laws, China's focus on bringing transparency to administrative rather than political affairs further underscores the practical motivations behind the state's move toward greater transparency: the end goal is to improve governance efficiency.

Transparency in the China Context

In theory, the national OGI regulations could reduce information asymmetries and strengthen accountability relations through multiple channels. First, the proactive disclosure of information from township to provincial levels could greatly reduce monitoring costs for central agencies, increase the efficiency of government operations, and reduce opportunities for corruption. Second, the measures could be used to strengthen state-business accountability. Despite the transition from planned economy and the introduction of market forces in China, ties between government and enterprises have arguably gotten closer over time, particularly at subprovincial levels. These close and opaque relations typically suit local government interests, given the overwhelming national priority on economic growth. The trade-off, however, is a lack of regulation on enterprise behavior, and a tendency to protect enterprises at the cost of other social goals such as health and the environment. With the introduction of transparency regulations, governments facing requirements to disclose economic, administrative, and other types of information might feel more pressure to enforce regulations on the private sector than they do to promote economic growth. Third, citizens could access more information about the activities of government, thereby using the information to hold the state to account or to request information about issues of concern. Fourth, NGOs might be able to use the regulations to carry out a range of functions, from monitoring state and enterprise behavior to serving as interpreters and transmitters of information to raise public awareness on pertinent social issues.

Each one of these different effects could affect the governance system in a different way. The first and second channels, by strengthening efficiency, reducing corruption, and tightening enterprise regulation, could

Box 5-2. *Transparency Laws and Practices around the World*

It is easy to dismiss comparisons of China's OGI regulations and practices with Freedom of Information Acts in established democracies such as the United States or Sweden (and Chinese official frequently do so), given their very different economic and political circumstances. But the global trend toward greater government transparency is no longer limited to wealthy democracies. Three large developing countries stand out as particularly useful sources of lessons for China: Mexico, South Africa, and India.

Mexico had experienced more than seventy years of one-party rule under the Institutional Revolutionary Party (PRI), undergoing a gradual process of democratization in the last quarter of the twentieth century that culminated in the election of the first non-PRI president in 2000.[a] Along the way, government transparency was a much-debated topic, with a growing consensus that access to government-held information should be afforded as a basic right in a democratic society. Civil society groups led the charge, linking up with international counterparts and academics both to learn about how to draft, enact, and enforce appropriate laws, and to develop external allies who could help push Mexico toward greater transparency. Mexico's new president, Vicente Fox, had run on a platform that included a call for government openness, and the candidate was true to his word: in 2002, thanks to both the civil society groups and the new president's leadership, Mexico enacted the Federal Access to Information Law.

The Mexican case shows the importance of both civil society participation (domestic and foreign) and government leadership in getting a meaningful law enacted. The implementation in this case is even more interesting. To institutionalize open government, Mexico established the Federal Access to Information Institute, known by its Spanish initials IFAI, as an autonomous body headed by five or six independent commissioners. IFAI ensures that government agencies comply with the law, reviewing appeals from people whose requests for information have been rejected, and maintaining a strong track record of ruling in favor of such requests. Mexico also set up an electronic system called Infomax to send information requests to federal agencies and to allow the public to review requests and responses. Because the 2002 law applied only to the federal level of government, each state in Mexico has enacted its own law and established its own state institution following the federal example. While no freedom-of-information law is perfect, and Mexico's is no exception, it seems to have made a difference in how Mexico treats government-held information. Since its implementation in 2004, more than 300,000 requests have been received, some leading to major discoveries of corruption.

But implementation in the absence of such factors has proven more difficult elsewhere. South Africa attempted a similar move after the end of apartheid. But its broader effort to institutionalize protection of the human rights that had been so badly violated in the previous regime took priority. Although the 1996 Constitution (Section 32) provides a right of access to information, four years went by before enabling legislation was adopted: the Promotion of Access to Information Act (PAIA).[b] And its implementation has been much criticized. An assessment of several countries' implementation records by the Open Society Institute's Justice Initiative found that South Africa fared particularly poorly, with agencies simply ignoring the majority of properly prepared requests.[c]

The most remarkable of all the major emerging country stories, however, is clearly India's sweeping transparency law, the result of a sustained and extremely widespread campaign carried out by a vast network of civil society groups across the country. Although most campaigns for access-to-information laws are led by middle-class professionals (lawyers, academics, and the like), India's had a much broader base. The story started in the dusty rural villages of the Indian state of Rajasthan, where workers and farmers fed up with being exploited got themselves organized in the early 1990s. The triggers were cases in which day laborers on government-funded rural development projects, such as school construction or road-building, would ask for their wages, only to be told that their names were not on the roster of employees. People began coming together, organizing sit-ins to demand not their money, but access to the rosters (which local officials were refusing to share). Under intense pressure, local officials eventually gave in, leading to some highly entertaining public readings of rosters that were found to be littered with the names of dead people and of people who had no idea that they had supposedly been employed and paid. To cut a very long and complex story short, over the next few years Rajasthan and several other Indian states enacted right-to-information laws. These grassroots campaigns came together in the National Campaign for People's Right to Know. After the Congress Party was returned to power in 2005, it honored a campaign pledge to establish a right-to-know law, turning to people involved in the campaign to help with the drafting. Among the more noteworthy provisions of the resulting law is one that holds individual government officials personally liable for compliance with the act's tight deadlines for responding to requests for information. Failure to respond appropriately can lead to individual officials' being fined for each day of delay.

a. For detailed information on the Mexican case and its ongoing saga, see www.freedominfo. org/regions/latin-america/mexico/.

b. Dale T. McKinley, "The State of Access to Information in South Africa," prepared for the Centre for the Study of Violence and Reconciliation, Johannesburg, 2004.

c. Laura Neuman and Richard Calland, "Making the Law Work," in *The Right to Know: Transparency for an Open World,* Ann Florini, ed. (Columbia University Press, 2007), p. 183.

enhance both the governing capabilities and the legitimacy of the ruling party and thus strengthen the sustainability of the regime. The third and fourth channels, by empowering citizens and enhancing civil society activities, could generate more democratic space in the system.

However, transparency policies vary widely from country to country, and the effectiveness of the OGI regulations should be considered within the circumstances specific to China. As described earlier, unlike transparency laws in other countries, including Mexico, South Korea, India, and the United States, which are based on the right to know, China's OGI regulations are circumscribed in both spirit and substance. In spirit, the regulations are motivated not by notions of freedom of information or the right to know as an end or a principle in itself, but by the instrumental goal of improving governance. Since the regulations do not apply to the CCP, the judiciary, or the legislature, major political decisions—which are made within the Party—are not subject to the same requirements of transparency.[18] However, as we will see later in this chapter, the Party and the judiciary have nonetheless been making cautious moves toward greater openness.

Second, the fact that the OGI regulations are State Council regulations rather than a law passed by the National People's Congress means that the OGI regulations fall short of a legal requirement on the government.[19] There is therefore a legal inequality between openness and secrecy, since the restriction of information is governed by the State Secrets Law and the Archives Law, and there remains a lack of clarity over how these laws interact with the OGI regulations. Indeed, the earlier analysis of the text of the OGI regulations suggests that the spirit of the policy is that secrecy is the norm and disclosure the exception, rather than the other way around as embraced by freedom-of-information or right-to-know laws.[20]

For all of these reasons, plus the fact that the regulations are nested within China's system of single-party rule, we cannot assume that the accountability shifts that are often assumed to accompany effective transparency policies apply in the same way.

It is not clear whether the regulations will have even the limited effect intended. Approximately three hundred laws have been passed in China in the past thirty years, and in the opinion of one academic, many have suffered from poor and uneven implementation.[21] The first major challenge, as described in the introductory chapter, is that the bureaucracy is highly fragmented, both horizontally across functional issues, and vertically in authority and reporting structure. Local governments—from the provincial level downward—operate under highly decentralized conditions, such that as central regulations are channeled through the layers of the state, the policy intent becomes diluted and distorted. The second challenge is that a high degree of informality persists through the system (particularly at lower levels), with decisions being made on the basis of informal social norms and personal ties rather than policy considerations and requirements. The result is that the implementation and enforcement of new regulations are negotiated in uneven and idiosyncratic ways.

Third, international experience makes it abundantly clear that the most successful transparency regulations are those that are embedded within the decisionmaking processes and choices of a range of social actors—from the media and businesses to citizens and NGOs—actively requesting information, interpreting it for a wider audience, and using it to advocate for their interests. India's powerful Right to Information Act, which arose out of a nationwide grassroots campaign that itself grew out of scores of local campaigns, is effective in large part because so many citizens and civil society groups are prepared to use it, and keep using it. In the United States, the media-savvy National Security Archive (a nonprofit not to be confused with the official National Archives) has had extraordinary success in using U.S. FOIA requests to generate major international coverage of stories ranging from the Cuban missile crisis to the Osama bin Laden file.[22] In China, however, where even relatively independent media must do a careful dance with the authorities, while citizens are fairly disempowered and NGOs have to operate with care, demand is far more limited.

With the regulations in force only since 2008, it is too soon to judge their success or failure. We can, however, see positive developments beginning to happen, along with a host of persistent remaining challenges. To see what is happening, we look at national changes as well as those at the local level.

In China's decentralized structure, national policies are implemented only if there are vested interests and powerful agents pushing for change at the local level. We start on the positive side with local governments, drawing from the examples of the Beijing municipal and Hunan provincial governments. These two cases demonstrate the scope of what can be accomplished when national rules are implemented vigorously at local levels.

Within the State—Changing Mind-Sets

One notable development is a growing shift in official mind-sets toward embracing openness as a mode of governance. One expert on the OGI regulations has noted that, increasingly, government officials are less skeptical about transparency, recognizing that it is a growing trend and that the government needs to be more open.[23] More and more central ministries are proactively releasing information about their activities, reducing the gap between the requirements of the policy and actual implementation. Increasingly, government websites include columns devoted to open government information, chat room functions for discussion, and mailboxes for engaging with government officials.[24] The change in mind-set implies new approaches on how citizens and the state can and ought to engage with each other and the government's self-conception of its role in governance, as reflected in new official slogans such as "transparent government," "accountable government," and "law-abiding government."[25]

This type of adjustment is often not easy for officials. In interviews, government officials described the difficulty of shifting from the old mind-set that "the government regulates people" to the new one under the OGI that "people regulate the government."[26] The challenges of transition show up in daily government operations. The General Affairs Office of the Hunan provincial government, for example, only dealt with other government agencies in the past, but with the implementation of the OGI regulations found itself having to interact with the public for the first time.[27] Beijing municipality found that training helped the transition process a little, but another important factor in changing mind-sets was the positive feedback that government personnel received as they engaged with the public and with each other. For example, personnel dealing with requests from the public were touched by the personal stories of the citizens and were therefore motivated to go back and learn more about the OGI regulations. The interactive process led to what was described as a transformation in government culture, from one that was unwilling to release information, fearful of releasing information, and ignorant of how to release information to one that is much more accepting of the value of openness.[28] In Beijing municipality's experience, the change in mindset helped in the end to improve the quality of government services.[29] The sharing of experiences within the bureaucracy was another source of positive feedback. In Beijing's Xicheng district, an internal document is circulated monthly among relevant agencies to share examples of cases with positive outcomes and to update the latest developments in OGI. Such practices help both to disseminate knowledge and to build the norm of transparency as part and parcel of the government profession.

Within the State—Streamlining and Organizing the Bureaucracy

The implementation of the OGI regulations involves organizing vast amounts of information, setting new guidelines for responsibilities and specific procedures to be followed, and cleaning up old and contradictory guidelines. This process itself has the effect of making government processes clearer and the exercise of authority more disciplined within the state. However, successful implementation requires substantial financial and human resources, given the amount of information that needs to be reviewed, organized, streamlined, and published. This means that poorer regions with more cash-strapped governments will face more obstacles in implementation.

For example, in the first year of implementing the OGI regulations, the Beijing municipal government invalidated 52 approval processes, revised 76 approval processes, and consolidated 275 approval processes.[30] As a reflection of the commitment to implementation, government resources were channeled toward the task of transparency, with OGI offices established at the municipal, district, and county levels, and over 2,000 government staff trained at the municipal level and 24,000 at the district (that is, submunicipal) level. Staff resources were allocated to OGI matters, an internal coordination committee was established, and rules and regulations were drawn up to guide the implementation.[31] Beijing's Xicheng district government also set up a coordination agency to evaluate the work of the functional agencies and planned to conduct a public evaluation involving 10,000 households.[32] In Hunan province, implementation activities included declassifying vast amounts of government information, establishing websites and gazettes to release information, and validating and canceling various government administrative procedures.[33]

The broad scope of the OGI regulations leaves substantial room for interpretation and government discretion, unless individual local governments attempt to clarify specifics through additional guidelines. The General Affairs Office (GAO) and Legislative Affairs Office (LAO) worked to create implementing specifications that went above the level of detail required by national guidelines. For example, while the national regulations generally prohibit the release of information that involves state secrets, Article 9 of the Hunan Implementing Measures clarifies that "government information whose general content requires public awareness or participation but which contains content that involves state secrets should be released only after undergoing legally prescribed procedures of declassification or redaction of the classified content."[34] Such details reduce the scope of discretion available to authorities to reject disclosing information based on the state secrets law. In Hunan's Yuhua district, local government officials have formulated specific rules and regulations to clarify the process of OGI implementation, setting out clear institutional responsibilities on OGI and establishing a joint committee and an expert evaluation group. In addition to the categorization, organization, and release of information via the Internet, local government staff were also trained on what the OGI and the accompanying Administrative Procedural Regulations (APR) required from them in terms of implementation. The Yuhua government further launched publicity efforts to raise citizen awareness of these changes.[35]

All these activities in Beijing and Hunan show an active effort to delineate the roles of local authorities, and to move toward greater state-society accountability. Implementation guidelines such as the APR drawn up by the Hunan government represent an attempt to regularize and systematize the process of using power, and to define how state power should be wielded. These guidelines therefore move the government closer to a rule-based system, reducing the scope for arbitrary decisionmaking and providing stricter demands for government openness.[36] These specific examples are a significant achievement, considering that the lack of political will is often the single largest obstacle to success in the implementation and sustainability of transparency regulations.[37] Officials interviewed in Hunan province who were directly in charge of OGI implementation cited the personal attention by then-governor Zhou Qiang as one key driver of the provincial government's progress.[38] The Beijing municipal government, as well, emphasized the direction of the top leadership for China to move toward responsible, accountable, transparent, open, and law-based government as a motivating factor in implementation efforts.[39]

Between State and Society

Transparency measures are often thought to strengthen citizens' ability to hold the state to account. In China's one-party system, where the OGI focuses on the state apparatus but bypasses the party component of the state-party system, it is not clear if the same dynamics play out. One sign that the OGI measures are providing a channel for citizen participation is the large increase in requests for information in Beijing, from just over 300 in the 2008–2009 period to over 4,000 in the 2009–2010 period. Some of the citizens requesting information are, as one would expect, from the social elite, such as lawyers, professionals, and university professors. However, others are also making requests, including, according to one report, a range of people from retired workers to artists and displaced homeowners.[40]

The type of information being requested also reveals the top concerns of the citizens. Most requests are about the politically and socially important issue of land requisition.[41] For years, cash-strapped local governments have resorted to illegal seizures of land for development in order to boost their budgets. Citizens whose land has been seized have found few channels for recourse or redress.[42] In addition, the requests also cover a big range of other concerns, from retirement benefits to education fees, budget information, and the use of fees collected for the construction of public infrastructure.[43]

The active use of the OGI regulations has also led to changes in public policy that mirror trends elsewhere. Government budget transparency has become a particularly strong concern of good governance advocates. Budgets, after all, are the center of government power, where decisions about social priorities are operationalized and where choices about how to spend the citizens' tax dollars are made.[44] A series of high-profile, nationally publicized cases of citizens (lawyers, professors, professionals) requesting information related to government expenditure generated a nationwide debate that led the Ministry of Finance to release details about the 2009 approved national budget and stimulus plan. In March 2010 the Budgetary Affairs Commission of the National People's Congress (NPC) Standing Committee announced that local government budgets submitted to the NPC, as well as ministry and State Council department budgets approved by the NPC, would be disclosed to the public. Guangdong and Shanghai governments also disclosed their budgets, where such information had earlier been deemed to be a state secret. Other government ministries have since followed suit.[45]

Indeed the greater social space allowed by these regulations may have encouraged the growth of forces to boost the implementation process. In 2009, Beijing University Law School's Center for Public Participation Studies and Support and Yale Law School's China Law Center launched the Open Government Information Watch Alliance (OGIWA) project to assess the progress of OGI implementation across forty-three agencies under the State Council, thirty provinces, and ninety-seven administrative units at the prefectural and city levels in six provinces. (Details of their findings are presented later in this chapter.) The publication of results in turn keeps pressure on governments to abide by the regulations, and influences public discourse by raising awareness of government transparency as a social issue.

Between State and Civil Society

Two of the governance reforms we address in this book are tightly connected: those about transparency, and those about civil society. Around the world, transparency measures work only when there is sustained demand for government-held information. While some individuals will actively seek access to government records of personal concern, it is through civil society organizations that demands are sustained and built on over time, and through which government disclosures are widely disseminated and translated into pressures for governmental change.

A number of NGOs are seizing the opportunity, using the OGI to demand information relevant to their missions. Their use of the OGI regulations keeps pressure on the bureaucracy to sustain implementation efforts and raises the costs of inaction for laggard agencies. Around the world, disclosure mechanisms are being developed particularly rapidly in the environmental arena, with government agencies and domestic and foreign NGOs all involved.[46] The Ministry of Environmental Protection, which as we saw in chapter 4 has an unusually positive relationship with civil society, has been a strong advocate of government transparency, establishing Open Environmental Information (OEI) measures in 2008 that set out specific responsibilities of information disclosure for Environmental Protection Bureaus (EPBs) at all levels of government. One NGO, the Institute of Public and Environmental Affairs (IPE), used the increasing availability of information on polluting enterprises to strengthen its online air and water pollution database, enabling multinational companies to check whether their local suppliers in China have been complying with pollution standards. Companies such as Walmart and Nike, for example, use the database to check supplier behavior and ask violators to improve their pollution management procedures, which are then verified by a third-party auditor and an alliance of environmental NGOs called Green Choice Audit. Only after the alliance determines that the polluting firm has taken corrective action and has received a satisfactory audit report is the polluting firm taken off the pollution database and the report, including information on corrective action, published on the Internet.[47]

In 2008, IPE partnered with an American-based environmental NGO long active in China, the Natural Resources Defense Council (NRDC), to establish the Pollution Information Transparency Index (PITI), which ranks over a hundred municipal governments on environmental disclosure. The 2009 PITI results showed a low level of compliance overall, with some good performers but highly uneven progress in implementation across regions, highlighting the large gap between the OEI requirements and actual implementation. The 2010 PITI saw an increase in the average score, but also a fair number of cities having their scores drop either overall or in specific categories, highlighting the challenges of sustaining reform.

Other international and national NGOs have also used the OEI measures to conduct their own assessments. Greenpeace, for example, published a report in 2010 detailing the environmental disclosure performance of eight multinational companies listed in the 2008 Fortune Global 500, and ten Chinese companies listed in the 2008 Fortune China 100, all of which had been listed by Chinese environment agencies as having exceeded pollution discharge standards. The NGO found that none of the twenty-five factories belonging to these eighteen companies disclosed their environmental information within the required time period after being listed as pollution standards violators. Two of the factories had been found to be using or discharging excess amounts of hazardous chemicals. Four factories belonging to three companies eventually disclosed some, but very limited, information.[48] In a setting where state enforcement of environmental regulation is often selective and based on informal bargaining,[49] additional pressure on enterprises from nonstate sources can bolster the effectiveness of these transparency regulations. The Center for Legal Assistance to Pollution Victims (CLAPV) published a citizen manual on how to use the OEI measures and conducted training for local NGOs, as well as an assessment of how well seven municipalities complied with the OEI measures.

The strong NGO role is not limited to environmental issues, however. An HIV/AIDS organization, Aizhixing, was also able to use the OGI regulations to request and obtain information regarding government policies on the protection and care of HIV/AIDS patients. The release of information, however, was not automatic, and the NGO had to file administrative appeals as well as litigation, with mixed success.[50]

The NGO activities outlined here emphasize the lessons of chapter 4 about the evolution of state and civil society relations. Rather than government and NGOs interacting with each other as monolithic wholes, interest alignments arising from these transparency regulations reveal divisions between the central government and local states, as well as between functional agencies. In environmental protection, for example, the Ministry of Environmental Protection (MEP) has been a stronger proponent of state-civil society cooperation than other functional agencies. In January 2011 the MEP issued "Guidelines on Cultivation and Guiding Orderly Development of Environmental Non-Government Organizations," which not only noted the importance of NGOs in environmental governance, but also exhorted localities to strengthen their engagement:

> Each province, autonomous region and municipality is required to do well the following work: developing the plan for cultivating and supporting development of environmental NGOs; expanding their space for activities and development; establishing the mechanism where government and environmental NGOs could communicate, coordinate and cooperate; rewarding excellent NGOs and individuals; strengthening the development of talents and carrying out comprehensive & multi-level training; strengthening guidance and facilitating self-discipline of environmental NGOs; facilitating international exchange & cooperation of environmental NGOs and so on.[51]

This proactive position could be due in part to the weaker bargaining position of the ministry within central decisionmaking structures in advancing the environmental agenda, stemming not just from China's focus on economic growth, but also the relative newness of the ministry (it was elevated from the State Environmental Protection Agency to a full ministry in 2008.) Another reason for the MEP's positive disposition toward NGOs is its lack of resources to monitor and influence local government dealings with polluting enterprises. The MEP thus has an incentive to encourage the development of NGOs and stronger engagement with governments at the subnational level.

Restraints on the State: The Judiciary

While the OGI measures do not apply to the judiciary, its evolution toward greater transparency could signal the spreading of the norm of transparency to other arms of the state. In the late 1990s, the Ministry of Public Safety, the Supreme Procuratorate, and the Supreme Court issued directives to their subordinate organizations across the country to increase operational transparency. Starting in 2002 local courts in urban areas began installing central television systems through which all court debates are recorded and which allow officials of higher courts to view any of the debates live. In 2010 the practice was elevated to the national level when China's Supreme Court ordered all local courts to install such systems.[52] Such scrutiny is important given that local courts report to their local governments, not to courts at higher administrative levels. The lack of separation between the judiciary and the Party-state means that court decisions are often less than independent.

Since the late 2000s, local courts have experimented with a wide range of mechanisms to boost transparency. In March 2010, for example, Henan province ran a live broadcast of a trial on rent dispute on the Internet via www.chinacourt.org, with the intention of providing more such broadcasts at the subprovincial level.[53] Liaoning province has also started experimenting with Internet broadcasts of trials, as well as uploading written records, and audio and video recordings of court trials onto government websites.[54] In the same year, Chongqing municipality launched the "Sunshine Online Grand Platform for Facilitating the People," which links the websites of the forty-fix procuratorates in the city. The system integrates information across administrative levels of the judiciary, and allows citizens to access information about individual cases, such as the names of the people involved, the main points of the case, and the prosecution process.[55] The city of Shanghai has also made advances in court transparency. Zhabei district court of Shanghai, for example, is not only broadcasting trials live, but also publicizing court procedures and information on the enforcement process, and encouraging the construction of digital archives.[56]

The OGI measures have also affected the judiciary directly, in the increase in administrative appeal and administrative litigation cases dealing with OGI matters. In Shanghai, for example, over 50 percent of administrative appeals are OGI-related. In 2008, Shanghai courts dealt with 283 lawsuits related to OGI. In addition, lawyers are using the OGI regulations to request information to build evidence for their cases.[57] In a move showing the interconnectedness of these issues, in November 2009 the Supreme People's Court not only drafted a set of guidelines for interpreting the OGI, but also published the draft for public comment.[58]

These efforts to make the courts more transparent interact with other developments in information technology to change the ways in which citizens can engage the judiciary. For instance, in 2010, Ningxiang county court in Hunan province published a verdict from a 2006 loan dispute. The media reported that the verdict quoted "Article 159" of the civil code, but the civil code itself only has 156 articles. This led to an investigation of the judges and aides involved in the case and the assembling of another team of judges to review the lawsuit.[59]

Restraints on the Party

There are nascent signs that norms of greater transparency may be spreading beyond the bureaucracy to affect arms of the CCP. In March 2009, the CCP selected three counties to pilot reforms toward greater party transparency: Cheng'an county in northern Hebei province, Suining in eastern Jiangsu province, and Wuhou in southwest Chengdu province. In Cheng'an, the photograph, résumé, and mobile and office telephone number of the chief of the Communist Party Committee (CPC) is publicly displayed on the bulletin board of the county government building, along with the same information for other senior officials. In addition, budget information pertaining to each government department and major projects was also displayed. The county went further to streamline and categorize its government functions and to more clearly delineate responsibilities between the Standing Committee, the Discipline Inspection Commission, and the full CPC. County Chief Zhang Chenliang was quoted as saying that "[b]y making their responsibilities public, residents will know who to turn to if there is a problem or complaint."

In November 2010, the Communist Party Central Committee's Discipline Inspection Commission and Organizational Department issued joint guidelines that expanded the pilot to more counties. The document noted the value of transparency as a tool to standardize the use of power and to improve supervision over the exercise of Party authority. The same article quoted Dai Yanjun, vice director of the Party Building Department of the Party School of the CCP Central Committee, as saying that the goal was to strengthen the balance between the Party's decisionmaking, executive, and supervisory powers, and in so doing strengthen intra-Party democracy.[60]

In a related development, the fourth plenary of the 17th CCP Central Committee in September 2009 proposed setting up a Party committee spokesperson system, to help release information on CCP affairs and allow for interviews. In December 2009, the State Council Information Office announced efforts to accelerate the setting up of spokesperson systems in CCP Central Committee departments and province-level CCP committees.[61] In July 2010, the Central Party School, where mid- to high-ranking Party officials are trained, opened itself up to sixty reporters, including forty-two from two dozen foreign media outlets.[62]

There is limited evidence on the social and political impact of such pilots on Party transparency and intra-Party checks and balances. However, the fact that these pilots are taking place, and the official pronouncements in recognition of the need for stronger Party accountability, reflect growing awareness within the CCP of the need for reform.

Challenges

Scope of Regulations: Tensions between Secrecy and Openness

The first challenge in implementation stems from the delicate balance that the government wishes to strike between improving governance and social stability by imposing greater bureaucratic discipline and the empowerment of nonstate actors on one hand, and retaining control and power on the other. This tension is revealed in the scope of the OGI regulations described at the start of this chapter.

The fact that the OGI regulations are State Council regulations and hence trumped by the State Secrets Law and Archives Law has a number of implications. First, there remains a lack of clarity over how these laws interact with the OGI regulations. As such, officials can easily cite either law as a reason for nondisclosure. Second, without the legal recognition of citizens' right to know, combined with the slow process of legal reform, it is difficult for citizens to appeal rejections of their requests for information. The ambiguous regulatory relationship between secrecy and transparency leaves authorities still with a wide scope for interpreting their obligations depending on circumstances and according to the immediate interests at hand.

The government's conflicted relationship between secrecy and openness is underscored by the fact that while major efforts have been put into improving transparency, the state has also been actively stepping up its censorship, making sure it retains control over the nature of information to be disclosed and the boundaries of permissible public discourse. In 2008, for example, major events in China drew intense international media attention. In March, unrest erupted in Tibet with hundreds of monks and nuns protesting against Chinese rule.[63] Two months later, in May, Sichuan province was rocked by a 7.9 magnitude earthquake that killed tens of thousands of people. In August, the world's attention turned to China once more as it hosted the Beijing Olympics. The government's inconsistent approach to media coverage of these events reveals the competing tensions within the state about how to deal with large-scale incidents and events, and its overriding concern with preserving stability.

Jonathan Watts of *The Guardian* and former president of the Foreign Correspondents' Club of China, recounts that during the Tibet unrest, except for one foreign journalist who happened to already have been in Tibet, "no foreign journalist was allowed there at all to actually see for themselves what was happening. . . . So it's sort of a lockout-blockout. It's the old way of doing things."[64] Censorship efforts were stepped up during this period, with the websites of Yahoo!, YouTube, and *The Guardian* affected, along with local feeds of broadcasts from BBC World and CNN.[65] After the Sichuan earthquake, Watts notes that "there it was not so much government policy. It was more an accident that we, the foreign media, were given amazing access. We weren't blocked out of the area. We were able to wander around freely, and I think this wasn't by choice, it was anarchy, you know—everything broken down." A few weeks into the aftermath of the earthquake, however, when stories of schools collapsing surfaced and questions over low-quality construction arose, "suddenly then foreign journalists were being blocked out of schools . . . and the parents who were complaining were being told to keep their mouths shut. And there was this going back to the crackdown [and] closed-up side of things. And the senior officials we spoke to were saying, well, transparency was good, transparency was very useful . . . [but] this has now become an issue of social stability, and so no, we cannot allow you to have all the information you want or go wherever you want."

Censorship and media control was also an issue during the Beijing Olympics, but some controls were lifted for foreign correspondents. For example, journalists were allowed to travel around the country without permission or supervision from the Foreign Ministry. They were also allowed to conduct interviews as long as the prior consent of individuals or organizations was sought, rather than having to apply to authorities for permission.[66]

Less than a year later, when conflict between Uighurs and Han Chinese broke out in Urumqi, the capital of western Xinjiang province, reporters found a changed media policy. Rather than blocking out foreign correspondents, Watts recounts that "the Foreign Ministry actually arranged a press center, and there were tours for foreign visiting foreign journalists. And they were really trying a different approach." At the same time, the content of news on the Internet continued to be censored, including information on the sources of Uighur discontent and Chinese assimilation policy in Xinjiang. This lighter touch of regulation reflected a more sophisticated approach that relied more on subtle spin tactics than on overt and blunt instruments of physical control.[67]

These cautious moves toward greater openness, however, were far from inevitable and can easily be reversed, particularly when events tap into national concerns over instability. In early 2011, popular revolts broke out across the Middle East against ruling autocratic regimes, starting in Tunisia and then spreading to Egypt, Libya, Bahrain, Syria, and Yemen. In China, online calls in February 2011 for a "Jasmine Revolution" were met with a strong show of force from the authorities, involving not just heightened efforts at censorship on the Internet, but also a crackdown on foreign journalists. Journalists were physically handled, detained, and delayed as they attempted to cover citizen responses to online calls.[68] That the responses were in fact quite limited and overshadowed by the massive police reaction reveals the deep-seated fear within the state about how information and new technology could feed into social instability and citizen mobilization.

It remains to be seen how this tension between openness and secrecy, and between loosening and tightening control, will evolve over time. Since the regulations apply only to the administrative arms of the government, greater accountability through OGI can directly affect the bureaucracy and the organization of government (for example, via the classification of certain information as state or personal, as sensitive or not), but any potential impact on the political system is far less straightforward.[69]

Marginal Impact

The impact of the OGI regulations is difficult to measure. For instance, as one official pointed out, a fall in requests for information may not reflect a fall in the use of the regulations, but rather that the needed information is now being proactively disclosed.[70] Visible change, when it has taken place, has been stark. However, the degree of change remains marginal to date. For example, of the millions of enterprises in China, only roughly 50,000 enterprise pollution violations have been recorded and published on IPE's website (as of November 2010). Of these, only about 300 violators responded to explain the source of their violations and measures taken to address the problems, and only 50 have submitted to third-party verification by the environmental alliance.[71] In IPE and NRDC's 2009 assessment of city-level compliance with the OEI measures, only 4 out of 113 cities assessed met the minimum compliance score of 60 points (out of 100 points). The 2010 assessment saw this number increase to 11, but also saw a fall in scores across 28 cities. The unevenness and low level of compliance reflects the major challenge of enforcement: there are few mechanisms the central government can rely on to ensure that policies on paper translate into actual changes in practices.

Citizen Awareness and Use

While the range of people who have requested information using the OGI is large, the majority of users tend to be the policy and social elite— such as lawyers in Shanghai and Beijing, investors in Shenzhen, and law professors at leading universities—and the small section of society that has already been engaging with the government through petitions.[72] For example, university students have used the OGI to request information about the use of public funds. Professors have filed requests for information about public revenue accruing from highway tolls. In Hunan, a legal aid center that could have provided assistance to citizens needing access to information found that there was no demand for their services on OGI issues even one year after the regulations came into force, as users of the OGI tended to be those who were already very knowledgeable and adept at navigating the legal and government systems.[73]

In Hunan's Yuhua district, despite the proactive steps by the government to disseminate awareness of the OGI and implement the regulation, there had yet to be any OGI requests one year after the regulations came into force.[74] In the environmental sphere, even after the OEI measures came into force, citizen requests for environment information remained low. The MEP received a mere seventy-two requests for information in 2009, while Guangzhou received seventeen requests in the same year, mostly from NGOs rather than individual citizens, underscoring how political will is necessary but insufficient for effective OGI implementation. One anecdote revealed that the Dalian city government in Liaoning province, in the face of a lack of public requests for information, took it upon itself to file requests with local agencies, in order to keep up the pressure for agencies to abide by the OGI regulation.[75]

Disconnect between Information Released and Information Requested

Disclosure is also highly uneven across types of information. Information disclosed by the government—such as the text of speeches and regulations—is not necessarily relevant or valuable to society. A study by the Chinese Academy of Social Sciences found that a large proportion of government websites are poorly organized and difficult to navigate.[76] Another assessment of seven municipal Environmental Protection Bureau (EPB) performances in OEI implementation found systematic differences in the degree of disclosure of different types of information. The EPBs performed best in disclosing standard, nonsensitive information such as the institutional setup of the organization, its duties, and contact information, and performed worst in disclosing the list of heavily polluting enterprises that had violated national or local emissions standards. The study also frequently found disclosed information to be incomplete or out of date. Information about the types and disposal of hazardous waste, as well as about discharge of pollutants and lists of heavily polluting enterprises, was the most difficult to obtain. The reluctance to reveal such information is not surprising, given the local focus on economic growth and typically close ties between government and business at the subprovincial levels. The unevenness in types of information disclosed and in the completeness and timeliness of disclosure partly reflects the massive administrative efforts required to implement transparency policies. In equal part, the uneven performance also stems from overly broad guidelines at the national level, leading to inconsistencies across regions and ministries.

And while the government's move to disclose its budget information in response to citizen pressure can be viewed as a big symbolic step forward in transparency, it is not clear that the actual disclosed information is of high substantive value. For example, the 2010 budget information was released well after the spending decisions had already been approved by the National People's Congress, so the disclosure had little impact on the allocation of funds and did not allow for citizen participation or deliberation. The categories of information were also often too broad to be meaningful, with revenue and expenditure figures organized in general categories such that the total information added up to only about a page.[77] Improvements in budget transparency in the future will depend very much on continued citizen pressure and political will within government agencies.

This disconnect between disclosed information and information that is of immediate use and value to society cuts across other areas. For example, to the extent that citizens have used the OGI, it has mainly been to address long-standing grievances that have not seen progress through other government channels. The OGI regulation has ended up becoming a second *xingfang* (petition) system, particularly in addressing land requisition issues.[78] This raises another challenge, as the land cases tend to be historical. In Hunan, the government found that almost all of the information requested was dated before 2005, with some from the 1980s and 1990s.[79] In Beijing, the government had only organized its information from 2003 onward, and did not necessarily have the administrative capacity to fully satisfy requests regarding cases before 2003.[80] On one level, there are basic organizational challenges to meeting these requests about historical information. At a deeper level, there remains significant reluctance on the part of government to release information that might present it in a bad light or threaten to undermine social stability.

One official talked about the conflict between abiding by the regulations while also adhering to the national priority of maintaining stability. Agencies working on land requisition cases in the past were not subject to transparency regulations, and many approvals were not handled according to the law. Release of records now would clearly show that the government did not act legally. Moreover, because the illegal actions were taken by past generations of officials rather than the current generation, current agencies should not be held responsible. Since the practice of administration according to law started only a few years ago, the reasoning went, it would not do any good to expose the wrongdoing of past officials and would only cause unrest. Now, however, with the OGI regulations in place, each and every approval in the land requisition process is done according to law and put up on the website, so of course no OGI requests on these cases are made.[81]

The land issue is particularly difficult to deal with because it brings tension to China's focus on economic expansion. One official opined that it is difficult for local government to sacrifice what it sees as efficiency in development for the sake of public participation or approval processes, especially since administration by the rule of law was not common even a few years ago. Therefore if the government needs land to develop, it will just take the land.[82] The land issue also reveals tensions between transparency and weaknesses in China's fiscal management that have yet to be resolved. Without sufficient funding through the formal fiscal system to carry out its public service functions, cash-strapped local governments have increasingly turned to off-budget financing (through what is called extra-budgetary funds). It has been estimated that the use of such funds in the late 1990s amounted to 19–27 percent of GDP. Reforms in the early 2000s abolishing many fees and levies brought the amount of reported extra-budgetary funds down to 3.4 percent in 2003. However, without a revenue stream from these levies, governments have increasingly turned to land development for funding—and such activities do not show up in either budgetary or extra-budgetary reports.[83] These resource constraints pose a natural limit to the ability of the OGI regulations to strengthen accountability and improve governance, without reform in other parts of the system.[84]

Lack of Civil Society Autonomy

A major challenge in using transparency as a tool to improve governance is that the information disclosed is often too technical and voluminous for those whom the information affects to understand and act on. The effectiveness of the OGI regulations depends heavily on the existence of intermediary groups that can analyze and process information and push for useful information to be collected and disclosed. The challenge of interpreting and processing information is greater in developing countries where institutions are fragile and where the capacity of interpreting organizations, from think tanks to NGOs, is weaker.

Despite the constraints we described in chapter 4, China's NGOs have been playing a small but crucial role in interpreting and processing disclosed information to make it useful and relevant. In the environmental transparency arena, it is striking that much of the NGO activity has been focused on implementing the OEI measures, and highlighting areas where both local government and enterprises have fallen short of regulatory requirements. Activities of this type are attractive for NGOs to focus on, allowing them to act strictly within the scope of the law, while demonstrating their usefulness to the central government, in serving as agents to push for the implementation and enforcement of central policy initiatives.[85] Indeed, given the challenge that central agencies face in getting their policies implemented by local government, it is not unusual for central state agencies to encourage NGOs to be more confrontational with local governments. Given the central authorities' limited abilities to monitor what localities are or are not doing, and weak capacity to mete out punishments, NGOs serve as an extra set of eyes and hands. Civil society's actions in monitoring progress in state implementation and activities to promote awareness of national policies all help to increase pressure on local states in areas where central agencies have less capacity.[86]

However, there are natural limits to how much organizations such as IPE and NRDC can compensate for the weak regulatory capacity of EPBs and the MEP. Ultimately, NGOs can serve as a complement to but not a substitute for government enforcement of transparency rules. Beyond scale and capacity issues, there are also risks that enforcement capacity outside the hands of government will be inconsistent and be captured by the most organized interest groups.[87]

Weak Institutionalization: A System in Transition

One goal of the OGI regulations is also to build institutions to effectively manage state-society interactions. The process of implementation shows how difficult it is to establish and strengthen such institutions and reveals the state's own conflicted attitudes about how best to manage social grievances. On one hand the National Human Rights Action Plan in 2009–2010 announced the intent to set up a national complaints office, to reflect the government's responsiveness to the social grievances multiplying across the country.[88] Premier Wen Jiabao also officially acknowledged the need for institutions to mediate state-society issues by visiting the central complaints department and meeting personally with petitioners in January 2011.[89] On the other hand, with the petitions system being overwhelmed, petitioners are often intercepted on their journey to complaints offices and thrown into "black jails."[90]

It is also not clear if the process of institutionalizing state-society mediation efforts is working. Rising occurrences of Internet-motivated governance and "vigilante justice" suggest that citizens are exploring all available pathways to resolve social issues, some outside and some through institutionalized channels. For example, in one case in Hangzhou the son of a rich businessman ran over a citizen with his car. The citizen died, and the local transport administration authority said that the car was driving at a speed of 70 kilometers per hour. After citizens questioned the accuracy of that announcement on the Internet, the Hangzhou government stepped in and established an investigative committee, which determined that the son had been driving at a speed far greater than was first reported.[91] Although the truth came out and justice was administered in this case, the response from both government and citizens was entirely outside of institutionalized channels of complaints and redress, and reactive rather than proactive. It can be argued that these incidents have raised expectations among citizens about their right to know, but the rising number of demonstrations and Internet outcries is indicative of the current weaknesses of these nascent social mediation institutions.

Lack of Enforcement

A major challenge of scaling from local experiment to national regulation is implementation and enforcement. The fact that the OGI regulations were passed by the State Council signals the high-level importance the central government places on government transparency. However, the State Council itself has limited enforcement abilities. The Secretariat Office of the State Council has to contend with managing multiple policy objectives and has not been able to adequately enforce the implementation of the regulations across China. Instead, implementation is decentralized horizontally across individual ministries and vertically down through local governments at each level of administration. The bureaucratic fragmentation makes enforcement of these regulations highly challenging, even though the regulations were motivated in part by the desire to reduce information asymmetry in the decentralized system. Fundamental misalignments in the incentive structure stymie efforts to promote transparency. In implementing the environmental transparency measures, for example, local EPBs receive policy directives from the MEP, but their resources and promotion decisions are controlled by the local government. Local governments, in turn, tend to prioritize economic growth over the environment. Localities that do have the political will to implement the regulations make significant progress, such as the Beijing and Hunan examples described earlier. But those that do nothing face little punishment. Even in the central government, many agencies did not publish reports on their progress on OGI implementation in 2009 as required, and did so without consequence.[92] One study found that 90 percent of thirty provinces in China had, to varying extents, established specific regulations on OGI in 2009. Less than half, however, had made enough progress in actual implementation of those regulations to attain a passing score in the assessment.[93]

Legal Weaknesses

These enforcement weaknesses within the bureaucracy are exacerbated by gaps in legal clarity and a lack of judicial independence. Courts are not only not independent from the Party-state, but in each locality are subordinate to their local government. As mentioned earlier, the Archives Law and Secrecy Law supersede the OGI regulations. Within the regulation itself, there is no clear articulation of the fundamental principle of openness, and hence decisions to disclose or withhold certain information can end up being made arbitrarily.[94] Each locality is therefore left to grapple with the questions of how to define state versus commercial secrets, as well as issues of privacy, and to reconcile the OGI regulation with existing laws on secrecy and government archives.[95] As Jamie Horsley notes:

> In China . . . the Party ultimately controls the government personnel system and the courts. Although Chinese citizens can sue government agencies for abusive acts or failure to act as required under the 1989 Administrative Litigation Law, that law's coverage is narrowly drawn, and courts are frequently reluctant to accept cases that involve untested rights—since they are only supposed to apply and not interpret the law—or politically sensitive issues. Thus, Chinese citizens basically lack the means to compel government compliance with newly emerging rights of information.[96]

While an increasing number of litigation cases involve OGI issues, court decisions are rarely in favor of transparency. For example, Horsley's 2010 update on the progress of OGI implementation noted that plaintiffs in Shanghai "overwhelmingly lose their OGI cases," and that there was only one reported OGI success case out of around 400 lawsuits filed between 2004 and 2008.[97] And even though the emerging transparency in some aspects of the judiciary described earlier is encouraging, the change is marginal. In 2008, the total number of verdicts made by all the courts across China amounted to 9.84 million, while the total number of published verdicts (by April 10, 2009) was around 60,000 (less than 1 percent).[98]

Openness of Outcomes vs. Openness of Process

While progress has been made in disclosing the "outcomes" of decisionmaking processes, such as laws and regulations, open government is equally about transparency in the *process* of decisionmaking, including allowing for citizen participation. While recognition of the need for public participation mechanisms exists in formal regulations, actual practice has fallen short.[99] For example, Hunan province opened its draft OGI measures up to public comment, but found that citizens were still not accustomed to commenting and checking on draft regulations.[100] The draft measures drew more than one hundred comments, but these included comments from international experts brought in by the government; the number of comments from citizens was low. The trend in citizen awareness of the OGI regulations, however, remains positive. Beijing municipality has seen an increasing number of hits on its government websites, and by May 2009 the number of visits to the municipal OGI Center from January through April 2009 had already surpassed the total numbers for the year 2008 when the national regulations came into force.[101]

Balance between Decentralization and National Guidance

In the context of weak enforcement and widening inequality, a tricky balance has to be struck between national policy issuance and decentralized implementation. A stark trend of the OGI implementation process is how uneven the efforts have been, both vertically on different administrative levels, and horizontally in agencies at the same administrative level. The OGIWA assessment conducted by Beijing University and Yale University's law schools, for example, assessed central State Council agencies, provincial governments, and subprovincial governments in five categories: Institution Building;[102] System Building;[103] Disclosure on Own Initiative (that is, proactive disclosure); Disclosure on Request; and Supervision and Remedy). The specific indicators in each category, however, varied between central and local government assessments.[104]

One benefit of trying out reforms through small pilots is that each locality can draft trial guidelines specific to its context and development needs. In scaling up to the national level, however, policymakers need to balance between writing regulations that are not so specific as to crowd out room for area-specific needs, but not so broad as to allow for lax interpretation and weak implementation.

One government official noted that given the broad nature of the regulations, different places have different understandings of how, for example, to count requests for information.[105] Other inconsistencies lie in interpretations of what types of information the government ought to disclose.[106] These inconsistencies make it difficult to compare cases or to know how implementation is progressing overall.

A bigger problem is that leaving implementation up to individual agencies and localities means that the process tends to falter precisely where greater transparency is needed. More polluted cities (measured by the amount of sulfur dioxide emissions as a share of industrial output) tend to perform more poorly in implementing the Open Environmental Information (OEI) measures.[107] Cities with a highly concentrated industrial base (for example, those dependent on a single industrial firm) also tend to perform more poorly in OEI implementation.[108] These findings suggest that pressure to improve transparency is not having an impact on reducing pollution, either because cities whose governments know that pollution levels are high are reluctant to subject themselves to greater scrutiny or place less weight on environmental governance in the first place, or because governments whose economies are highly dependent on a single source of industry for revenue or employment are captured by industrial interests and do not have sufficient bargaining power to assert regulatory authority over polluting enterprises.

Localities that want to do more on the transparency front, however, can find themselves constrained to curtail their regulations in order to abide by national guidance. Shanghai, for example, has had to reconcile its transparency policies in ways that still allow for more openness than previous practice, but which also fall within the OGI regulatory boundaries.[109] Hunan province, in drafting its provincial level implementation regulations, had to find ways to emphasize the spirit of "disclosure as the principle, secrecy as the exception" (Article 2) without stating so explicitly, as the explicit principle would go beyond OGI regulations.[110]

This difficult balance reveals a central challenge for fostering policy innovation in China. The light touch provided by the broadness of the OGI regulations has both positive and negative effects. In terms of advantages, broad guidelines allowed committed localities to innovate and find approaches appropriate to their specific context and needs. The same space for interpretation, however, allows corrupt or less progressive local governments to do the bare minimum in terms of implementation, find ways to get around transparency requirements, or simply do nothing. The result is that the transparency regulations fail precisely where they are needed most to tackle corruption and strengthen accountability.

Conclusion

The story of these OGI regulations in China reveals both the dynamism and the difficulty of China's experimental approach to governance reform. Trial regulations in places such as Guangzhou and Shanghai provided the central government with substantive evidence of the value of transparency regulations before scaling up to the national level. While such approaches to reform have been taking place in the economic sphere for a long time, similar experiments dealing with tricky governance issues are newer. What the OGI regulations demonstrate is the active efforts by the central government to address the complex social and political issues that are arising as China continues to develop economically, and how local governments are brought into national efforts.

But the OGI experience thus far also shows the immense challenge of implementing national policy in China's decentralized administrative structure. A few show strong signs of relatively rapid and significant implementation, buoyed by a combination of strong state leadership and active engagement by citizens and civil society. But because implementation is left up to individual localities, it is precisely where the predatory elites are most deeply ensconced that we are likely to see the least progress. This challenge will apply to all efforts to scale reforms from local to national, and will have a bearing on how the innovations that were described in the preceding chapters influence the national governance architecture.

The OGI story also demonstrates how the Chinese government has moved beyond the traditional party disciplinary apparatus to adopt new regulatory tools that are based on dramatically different assumptions about how state and society relate to each other. However, as this chapter has shown, the transparency regulations here do not necessarily operate in the same frameworks as those in democratic governance systems. China's OGI regulations have a unique scope, and are implemented within a one-party system. As such, we need new mental models to understand how such regulations operate in China, and how the channels of disclosure operate to change the incentives and bargaining power within the state, as well as between state, society, and enterprises. Some welfare improvements could take place through entirely unexpected channels. In the environmental sector, for example, enterprises have had to clean up their production processes as a result of the OEI guidelines. The pressure, however, has come not from government or citizens, but through the international supply chain from client multinational corporations.

The OGI regulations therefore represent a new mode of governance that differs both from traditional CCP structures of control and from traditional democratic governance mechanisms. The potential impact of such regulations on China's future political trajectory is thus far from straightforward. Implementation is uneven across agencies at the same level and on different levels of administration; and incentives empower a wide range of actors rather than a single set of interests. If the primary effect of disclosure is to reduce corruption and promote administrative efficiency, the regulations could bolster the resilience of the one-party system, with the enhanced efficiency translating into greater legitimacy. However, as we have seen, the formal scope of the regulations is quite limited, applying only to the administrative apparatus and not to the party or the judiciary.

The party state's conflicted relationship between openness and control makes it unclear what might happen in the future. The norm of transparency could slowly spread to the party and judiciary and the entire system could move toward greater transparency, or events could lead the party to clamp down on the free flow of information, leading to normative contradictions and possibly a stalemate. At the same time, we have also seen how the OGI regulations have empowered citizens, the social elite, and civil society to advance their interests, taking advantage of the broader space provided by the disclosure regulations. As these groups continue to push for greater state accountability within the limits of the regulations, information technology and the global spread of social networking is changing the contours of citizen mobilization around the world. It is not clear whether the OGI regulations, even if comprehensively implemented, will keep up with the development of social media.

What we are left with, then, is not a single linear path forward, but several meandering and overlapping trajectories. What is clear is that the OGI regulations, in empowering multiple interest groups, are deepening the contestation between authoritarian and democratizing forces in China.

6

Where Is China Going?

To say that China is at a political crossroads is a cliché—but correct. Although the country remains far from anything that could be called a democracy in the Western sense, its increasingly complex governance is by no means straightforwardly autocratic. As the numerous detentions of 2011 reveal, China's leaders still are not constrained by rule of law or systems of accountability when they feel their grip on power may be under threat. But that same leadership also recognizes that China cannot be governed by centralized diktat. The modernizing and marketizing economy, the rapid rise of a vast middle class, and the widespread diffusion of such information technologies as cell phones and Internet access are all simultaneously requiring and enabling new approaches to running this vast country.

China's response to these pressures is to experiment, cautiously. Its experiments range from administrative improvements to loosening the reins on social organizations to freeing up the flow of information to—rarely but increasingly—holding meaningfully contested elections. Most of the experiments, often encouraged by the central authorities, aim to improve performance of the existing one-party system, not to lay the groundwork for a fundamental transformation of that system. But experiments can have unintended consequences.

This book has shown how the sweeping decentralization of economic and political authority has allowed, even required, experimentation by local officials. The resulting kaleidoscope reveals irregular patterns with enormous variation from one locality to another and from one type of experiment to another. Some experiments have met with the center's approval; others have not. In both cases the rules are fluid and ever-changing (except for the taboo against advocating the end of the party's monopoly on formal power, which remains absolute). Some innovations are welcomed or even spearheaded by the central authorities, like the government services "supermarkets" and the sweeping cuts in the suf-focating system of endless administrative approvals. But others encounter obstacles, like the objections to semi-competitive mayoral or people's congress elections. And there is little agreement up and down the vertical layers of China's party-state: some of the initiatives most warmly welcomed at the top are the ones most strenuously resisted by entrenched elites at lower levels.

This variability, fluidity, and scale of change make it extremely difficult to know whether efforts to make the party-state more effective and efficient will satisfy increasingly demanding citizens in the face of China's enormous challenges. Where some observers see the successful institutionalization of authoritarianism and others predict an inevitable democratization, we see the development of political processes that could go either way. Since 1989, the authorities have worked assiduously to ensure that dissatisfactions remain localized. But systemic shocks are likely from many directions—a slowing economy, conflicts with other countries, the accelerating pace of massive environmental degradation, or some combination that could test the resilience of the country's governing institutions. How well will China's interwoven government bodies and party structures be able to cope? Is a resilient civil society developing?

Lessons from the Experiments

This book has explored four experimental realms: administrative reforms and their implications for political change; electoral contests for both government and party posts; the growth and governance of civil society organizations; and steps toward greater transparency, particularly with the recent Open Government Information regulations. We have seen promise and repression in them all, from a party secretary defying the center's prohibition on elections to try to make a township governable, to AIDS activists called in to advise the president, to social organizations shut down arbitrarily when they infringed on official interests. Each type of reform effort deepens the competition between democratizing and authoritarian forces. Although each individual case has its own idiosyncrasies, exploring them helps to highlight which groups are empowered at the expense of which others, as well as the lines along which the competition is heating up.

The streamlining of administrative processes is clearly a priority from the center's perspective. More efficient local government that provides more services for citizens demonstrates a more effective governance capacity of the system as a whole and thus bolsters the ruling party's legitimacy. Although such reforms began as local initiatives, as subnational authorities found themselves both forced and empowered to undertake governance as the country decentralized in the 1990s, the center quickly took up the cause. Administrative reform in the form of reducing the number of items requiring administrative approval became a national campaign, catalyzed in significant part by the international negotiations over China's accession to the WTO in 2001. The growing private sector also benefits from the large reductions in the transactions costs of operating legally.

The impact on local authorities from these administrative reforms is more mixed. Local scope for arbitrary exercise of power is clearly reduced when citizens and businesses can receive licenses and services quickly and transparently. But bureaucracies have a way of springing back, as we saw in Shenzhen, where hundreds of administrative approval procedures that were eliminated in one round of reforms somehow found their way back onto the books by the beginning of the next round. Yet local officials face powerful, indeed overwhelming, pressures to keep economic growth on track. Many such officials have recognized that economic growth requires governmental administrative processes to support economic efficiency by such measures as granting licenses quickly. And such experiments as the "government supermarkets" both reflect and foster a changing mind-set on the part of government and citizens alike about the appropriate nature of the state-society relationship. This could potentially bolster a responsive and thus more legitimate but still authoritarian one-party system.

Overall, however, there is little sign that such administrative reforms in and of themselves have solved the problems of China's governance. The same years that have seen these types of reforms sweep across the country have also seen rapid escalation in the numbers of protests, demonstrations, and uprisings, with some 90,000 reported annually in recent years.

After all, good governance is not only about providing predetermined sets of services to citizens. It also must include meaningful mechanisms for holding the governors accountable to those citizens.

That issue of accountability brings us to the second category of political reforms: elections. As we have seen, "semi-competitive" elections—that is, elections that allow voters to choose between candidates, though not between organized groups—are now common at the village level, with the endorsement of the central authorities. In other words, the majority of the Chinese population now has direct, personal experience with the use of periodic elections to choose local representatives and to hold them to account through the prospect of losing office in the next election.

Within the party itself, electoral mechanisms likewise are increasingly common.[1] Such intra-party elections are significant not only because the party is the focal point of governance within China, but also because it is huge. With something on the order of 70 million members, the party is the size of a reasonably large country and includes the vast majority of the social and political elites.[2] Most strikingly, in 2007 members of the Politburo, the powerful central organ of the Central Committee of the Communist Party, were selected via a quasi-electoral process that included the equivalent of campaigning by multiple candidates for a limited number of posts. Although details on the process are not available, the very fact that a quasi-electoral mechanism was publicly known to have been used at such a rarified level indicates a degree of acceptance of the importance of elections as legitimizing mechanisms for the exercise of political authority.

At least, such is the case when the electorate consists of party members voting for party positions. Semi-competitive public elections for government positions (such as mayor or representative to a local congress) at township and higher levels have encountered a much chillier reception from the center, despite evidence of considerable public support. In small numbers, they have been cautiously tolerated. Yet here the initiative comes from the localities, not from the center. The Buyun township election that so shocked the country in the 1990s came about not as a challenge to the system, but as a desperate effort by the county party secretary to get the township's inhabitants to agree to cooperate with the township government's projects. The election of independents to county-level congresses over the opposition of the county authorities, and their subsequent activism on behalf of their constituents, has received massive publicity and widespread public support, although that support has not always kept the successful candidates in office or out of jail.

The electoral story is still in its opening chapter, and skepticism about how the storyline will develop is certainly warranted. Only something on the order of 2,000 township-level elections for government positions have occurred (out of 41,636 townships across the country), and perhaps a total of 15 at the county level (of 2,862 counties), with none at all at the larger municipal or provincial levels. A number of independent candidates do get elected, and show themselves willing to act independently. A few determined victors have opened constituent liaison offices (although the National People's Congress in 2010 banned such offices, which now must call themselves something else).[3] But this amounts to a handful of individuals in the world's most populous country, acting separately. There is still no formal capacity to organize politically around shared interests. As we and others have noted, the party plays a major role in guiding who runs for office, although some independents get through, and has generally discouraged elections for government posts beyond the village level.[4] The quasi-electoral experiments at the top level of the party could be interpreted as merely a mechanism through which factional politics play out at the highest level,[5] or as an important new approach to legitimizing political succession.[6]

To reiterate what we pointed out in chapter 3, these various interpretations are valid—but what is also true is that these experiments are making citizens and party members increasingly familiar with the ideals and mechanisms of electoral processes. The importance of these electoral experiments is not solely whether and to what extent they are changing the formal rules of governance in China today. The key questions are (1) what habits, norms, and expectations are being inculcated, and (2) whether those new norms and expectations extend not only to those at the center of power in China but also to those whose voices have not been heard before.

In the realm of civil society, we see a similarly conflicted story. The development of a larger set of civil society organizations has the potential to both strengthen and undermine authoritarianism. Social organizations provide crucial services in areas from health to education. By relieving the burden on an overtaxed state apparatus that is struggling to address the needs and wants of an enormous population enduring all the disruptions of rapid modernization, these organizations can bolster the system's legitimacy. But social organizations and networks, once created, can serve purposes beyond those approved by the authorities.

On the one hand, authorities at all levels seem to recognize the need to allow China's citizens space to develop an associational life to pursue their own interests and provide social services. Over the past three decades, China has gone from an almost complete absence of any kind of social organizing outside the party-state to perhaps millions of clubs, associations, and formally registered social organizations. In addition, the clan associations, temple associations, and other social connections of pre-revolutionary China are resurging. Without a doubt, social capital is being formed (and reconstituted) on a massive scale at an extraordinary pace.

There is, of course, a wide spectrum of types and functions of civil society organizations, from the mass organizations/GONGOs we discussed in chapters 3 and 4, to charitable service providers, clubs, and international NGOs that also operate within China. The party's effective level of control decreases along this spectrum. In terms of function, the spectrum runs from service providers, to those monitoring and helping to enforce regulations, to those participating in formulating policy, to those in advocacy roles; and the party's desired level of NGO participation in these various functions is also decreasing along this spectrum.

As long as the party is able to control the development of NGOs across type and function, it may be able to enhance its authoritarian resilience. But the party is finding it increasingly difficult to have the best of both worlds in a sustainable fashion. Within the GONGOs, critical tensions are building between the mandate to uphold official policy and the need to effectively represent the interests of members even if, as in the case of trade unions, there are conflicts between the self-interest of workers being represented by those unions and the rapid economic growth on which the system's legitimacy continues to depend. There are increasingly thick networks of communication and cooperation between GONGOs, NGOs, and INGOs, which over time can form a shared social space (and social identity) quite distinct from the space of state authority. And the authorities must also grapple with the reality that social organizations evolve over time. Today's service provider can morph into tomorrow's sharply critical advocate, as people working within nongovernmental groups come to understand the broader systemic reasons for the problems faced by their beneficiaries, or expert groups become frustrated with what they see as inadequate government responses to dealing with major policy issues such as environmental degradation. In short, tensions and contradictions abound when we consider the role of civil society organizing in determining China's political future.

Thus it is not surprising that the party-state remains extremely nervous about this whole process. It is particularly uneasy about the formal components of civil society—NGOs. The center has carefully studied both the collapse of the Soviet Union and other Warsaw Pact states and the subsequent "color revolutions" in numerous formerly Communist states, drawing lessons about the dangers to authoritarian states of permitting social organizing to get out of hand. Its capacity to constrain such social organizing is significant, although far from absolute, as its limits on foreign funding and legal registration make clear. At the same time, however, some official elements find some types of NGOs very useful: the Ministry of Environmental Protection, a relatively new and weak player on the official scene, benefits from the explosion of environmental activism in its struggles with growth-obsessed local governments and polluting businesses.

With regard to transparency, the Open Government Information regulations are a fundamental step forward in recognizing that government has an obligation to provide information to its citizens. But in comparison with some of the local experiments that came earlier, the national regulations are a substantial step backward from democratization. The single most important change is the removal of the principle of the "right to know," and its replacement with language that describes technocratic rather than rights-based rationales for the regulations. That fits with the overall story of the center driving for power-preserving technocratic reforms but attempting to limit rights-based approaches or anything that could serve as encouragement to independent political organization outside the party.

The longer-term impact of the national regulations is particularly hard to predict, given how the regulations can empower a large diversity of interest groups, and the very uneven policy implementation across the country. In terms of empowerment of different interest groups, we have seen how the regulations have been actively used by civil society groups and social elites, and how the stories have captured media attention. Pro-transparency local governments have taken the regulations seriously and undertaken significant reform to make government services and policies more transparent to citizens, as well as be more responsive to citizen requests for information. Yet the regulations appear to be failing precisely where they are needed most—that is, in localities where abuses of power are rampant. Weaknesses in rule of law and weak protection of civil liberties mean that citizens are held back from being able to fully exploit the regulations to address their social concerns.

In the context of Chinese politics, it is striking that the majority of these initiatives came from local levels, without the prior permission of the center. This is very different from political reform initiatives in the 1980s, during which local experiments were usually designed and assigned by the center. The responses from Beijing to these innovations have been highly varied. The center picked up and scaled up reforms related to administrative streamlining, with several rounds of detailed and concrete measures over the past decade. But central authorities remain deeply nervous about NGOs and broadly opposed to electoral processes outside the party itself. Local experiments in transparency regulations were encouraged by the central government, but when the time came to draw up national guidelines, authorities in Beijing significantly scaled back the scope of what had been tried out in places like Guangzhou and Shanghai.

All this points to some important lessons for both China watchers and policymakers around the world. Above all, it is key to pay attention to dynamics both at the subnational level and within the party-state system. Some of the most crucial changes occurring in China are happening not in Beijing but in tiny (by Chinese standards) townships, driven by a growing array of politically important actors that range far beyond the party. Other critical dynamics are at play within the broad party-state system. Far from being a monolithic whole, the CCP is host to an active contest of ideas about the path the country should take. These internal tensions, in turn, may create new points of access for the growing diversity of interests within the country.

These changes are not easy to understand, as they do not always fall into neat categories of democratic or authoritarian governance. Meaningful electoral contestation does sometimes happen, but it is not the clash of organized political forces familiar to the West. China is clearly becoming more pluralistic, but its civil society groups are more prone to seek ways of working with the party-state system than to directly confront it.

Signposts at the Crossroads?

As we observe China's political development in the coming years, how will we know which way the country is heading? In the Rorschach test that is modern China, virtually anything that can be said about the country is true—somewhere. It has contested elections; it has a ruthless one-party state. Citizens can successfully demand information and accountability from their government; citizens face long prison terms for making such demands. Widespread administrative reforms are making the system more efficient, effective, and accountable; corruption has skyrocketed and is reaching crippling levels.

The range of experiments described in this book could be used as evidence that China is heading in any of the four very different directions we described in chapter 1:

—Administrative reforms, limited transparency measures, and careful controls on social organizing speak to a future in which a one-party authoritarian state manages to keep the lid on a tumultuous process of modernization for decades to come—the "authoritarian resilience" scenario.

—The gradual spread of semi-competitive elections, explosive growth in civil society organizing, and widespread access to information via new social media suggest that China's road may be heading toward democracy in the Western sense of fully competitive elections and increasing freedoms—the "democracy" track.

—The limited scope and partial success of those administrative reforms and the continued repression of civil society argue for an outcome that Minxin Pei has called a "trapped transition," with corrupt local elites largely beyond the control of either the center or the people.

—And what everyone fears most, instability degenerating into chaos, is a plausible outcome of the growing combination of unaccountable government power with civil society autonomy—the failure of both authoritarianism and democratization.

In a country where everything is changing so fast, and where even "local" changes can affect tens of millions of people, all of the predictions for China's political future have a degree of plausibility. But they cannot all come true. The one certainty in China watching is that the triumph of authoritarian capitalism, the collapse of the state, stagnation in a "trapped transition," and a smooth process of democratic transition cannot ALL be the national outcomes of China's political development.

But China's politics will develop in one direction or another. How will we know what is happening? One way to get a sense of direction is to identify signposts to watch for—developments whose unfolding will indicate that the country is moving down one or another of these roads from its current crossroads. Where are the signposts that can give us such insights?

Some of the most important signals may be seen over the next several years in the ways in which the center responds to the ongoing local initiatives. As we noted in chapter 1, the center has quite deliberately decentralized authority over many things and is actively encouraging local political experimentation, up to a point, with an eye toward finding solutions that can be taken up throughout the country. Thus, what happens at the local level has clear national import. Yet it is also clear that the center has a less than perfect capacity to control these experiments and their spread, so attention must also be paid to events and reforms beyond the center's direct control.

Administration

The administrative reforms are the most important to watch with regard to the prospects for authoritarian resilience. The party-state's legitimacy is increasingly based not only on economic growth, but also on the system's capacity to redress inequality and provide services, tasks it can only carry out if it has a very high degree of administrative efficiency. China must somehow walk the tightrope, providing a highly responsive, efficient, and effective state in the absence of the feedback mechanisms that in other countries are made possible by elections and an independent civil society. The tens of thousands of public demonstrations and protests that erupt across the country every year, often violently, suggest that such a balance has not yet been achieved. Indicators of increasing authoritarian resilience would thus include a substantial ramping up of administrative streamlining across the country at all levels, with concomitant reductions in levels of corruption, and a substantial decrease in the numbers of public protests. For the authoritarian resilience prediction to hold true, these improvements would take place in the absence of broader political reform or competition.

That said, we should look deeper into what is meant by "authoritarian resilience," if the very nature of this authoritarianism is one that is experimental and continually evolving. Therefore it is also crucial to see whether and how administrative reforms affect state-society relations. There is quite a difference between administrative reforms that simply increase efficiency and enhance the government's mandate to rule and reforms that reflect the notion of the government's duty to serve. Similarly, the administrative reform process could affect the internal workings of the party, steadily raising the pressure for similar curbs on the exercise of party authority. And to the degree that administrative reforms establish feedback mechanisms that allow for public input, it will be particularly critical to watch whether these reforms create meaningful, even if controlled, space for substantive citizen participation in policy processes.

Electoral Mechanisms

In the West, a minimal definition of democracy is taken to include regular competitive elections for candidates who wish to represent constituencies in making and implementing the law of the land.[7] As we saw in the chapter on elections, electoral competition is becoming more common, at least at the village level and within the party, and with a number of experiments in semi-competitive elections for government posts. Over the next few years, we can look for several signs of whether the legitimacy and practice of competitive elections is spreading:

—Selection of Standing Committee of the Politburo: in 2012, seven of the nine members of China's most important governing institution, the Standing Committee of the Politburo of the Communist Party, are expected to retire. If their replacements are selected by a quasi-electoral process (even if the electorate is limited to a few hundred senior party officials, what China watchers refer to as the "selectorate"), this may indicate further institutionalization of the idea that political power is legitimized through electoral processes.

—Local elections: how widely will semi-competitive elections spread at the township and county levels? Or will the center crack down on all such processes?

—To date, electioneering outside the party has been "semi-competitive," meaning that non-party members are allowed to run for office and to win, but not to organize beyond their individual candidacies. A sign of radical change would be experiments with allowing any meaningful degree of political organization outside the party.

To push beyond a minimal definition of democracy, it would also be important to watch for signs of strengthening platforms for deliberation and debate. While the vote can be a powerful mechanism, it does not by itself foster stable processes of decisionmaking, equal representation of interests, or fair mediation of differences. In the Introduction, we pointed out the many ways in which citizen opinions are increasingly being voiced, across a growing range of issue areas. However, the channels of citizen and state engagement remain fragile and unstable. Oftentimes the authorities are stuck in a reactive mode, galvanized to either crack down on corruption or shut down discussion of an issue after it has erupted on social media and sparked widespread consternation. Important indicators of deepening democratic forces in China, then, would include the creation of deliberative platforms that include a diversity of interests and which enable inclusive debate on a wide range of issues. These platforms may take any shape or form, from community roundtables and town halls to their digital equivalents in the social media space. This discussion brings us naturally to the next two realms of experimentation—civil society and transparency.

Civil Society

The regulations governing registration of NGOs impose tough requirements that are clearly intended to prevent the emergence of an autonomous, independent organized civil society sector. Nonetheless, an enormous array of social organizations now exists, from formally registered membership groups or service providers to grassroots clubs and "virtual" networks that either do not fall under the registration requirements or do not bother to register. A democratizing China would likely be marked by significant changes to the registration requirements, possibly along the lines of the experiment now being conducted in Shenzhen. A resiliently authoritarian or politically trapped China would continue to impose tight controls and to integrate party structures into civil society groups in the manner of the Changzhou NGO Service Center model in Shanghai, attempting to balance the need for service provision with restrictions on political space and autonomy.

Thus, an important arena to observe will be the legal and regulatory structures for civil society organizations. Will the scrapping of the dual registration system be expanded beyond the Shenzhen experiment now under way? Will the restrictions on foreign funding be loosened, or will rules be introduced to encourage domestic philanthropy? Will the efforts of Sichuan's government-organized trade unions to foster connections with counterparts in other provinces be the first step toward broader permission for organizations to be allowed to have members in multiple regions?

It is more likely that the legal and regulatory structure will slowly catch up to more dynamic shifts on the ground. Clearer evidence about the degree to which autonomous social capital is being formed may well appear in the social response to a future natural (or man-made) disaster, as we saw in the aftermath of the Sichuan earthquake in 2008. Other indicators worth watching may include numbers of partnerships among different NGO types (for example, GONGO-INGO), and evidence of more NGOs playing more sophisticated functions, going beyond service delivery to active policy participation or advocacy. It would also be useful to pay attention to the nature of collaboration between NGOs and government departments, to observe whether modes of engagement remain informal or become thicker, more regularized, and professionalized. Finally, a real test of autonomy would be splintering interests between NGOs and government departments that used to work together.

Transparency

Despite the surprising existence of a Chinese regulatory equivalent of a freedom of information act (the Open Government Information regulations), governance in China generally remains highly opaque. The continuing information asymmetries, combined with the absence of democratic accountability mechanisms, explain why what Minxin Pei describes as the "trapped transition" has emerged: neither center nor local populace can see what corrupt local elites are doing well enough to stop them from doing it. Indeed, the OGI regulations were promulgated largely to attack exactly this problem, and so a key question for China's future will be how the OGI regulations are implemented across the country. That, in turn, will depend in part on whether national laws on secrecy and on government archives are revised to support governmental openness.

But such national laws and rules on governmental openness and secrecy are just one component of a larger set of transparency measures tied to political change. Other key indicators of whether transparency is increasing in ways that would indicate a meaningful shift in state-society relations include whether government budgets or proposed regulations or court verdicts are widely published, whether mechanisms to allow citizens to comment on government rules and proposed spending are widely established, whether efforts to constrain the circulation of news via social media and the Internet intensify or ease, and to what degree the party itself discloses information.

The direction of China's political trajectory depends on decisions made by its leaders and citizens over the next several years, and on the strength of the evolving political institutions and processes described throughout this book. Putting these pieces together, we can see several potential paths. Going down the road of long-term authoritarian resilience (continuation of the one-party system, with the party continuing to set policy and to appoint all government and SOE leaders) would require a high level of state capacity and a low capacity of non-party groups to insist on any role in allocating positions or making policy. Sustaining this over the long term would require much greater and more effective technocratic administrative reform; enhanced transparency measures leading to more efficient government and possibly somewhat lessened corruption but not transparency of the "right to know" type; elections only within the party or at the village level, with no expansion beyond the small number of semi-competitive governmental elections seen to date; and continued tight controls on social organizing. All of these developments would only be stable, however, with support from a citizenry that is in ideological agreement with the party on the values and methods of this type of governance.

At the other extreme, the road to a relatively smooth rapid transition to full democracy (incorporating multi-party contested elections, freedom of press and assembly, and political organizing of and contestation among interests) would include relatively rapid expansion of the level and scope of electoral competition, formal recognition of a citizen's right to know as the basis for government disclosure policy, and significant changes in the regulations governing civil society organizations. These formal governance regulations would be animated and fully expressed through robust participation by citizens and by political and interest groups in stable platforms for deliberation and representation, active use of disclosure laws to hold the state to account, and civil society organizations that are empowered to create and lead a widening of social initiatives.

The four reform arenas explored in this book—administrative streamlining, elections, civil society, and transparency—are clearly key areas to explore for signs of large-scale change, although certainly not the only ones. A comprehensive investigation of political reform in China would also have to examine in depth the role of the judiciary, the development of the media (including, and perhaps especially, social media), the impact of international norms on internal debates as China engages ever more intensely with the outside world, and many more topics. All of these issues are interconnected. For example, the extent to which citizens are able and motivated to use the transparency regulations to hold the state to account depends on whether their rights are protected and upheld in courts. As long as local courts continue to report to governments at their administrative level, it will be difficult for the judiciary to serve as a check on predatory local elites. The growing instances of social media catalyzing widespread outcries over stories of official abuse place even greater pressures on the government to strengthen its administrative reforms. And as China increasingly engages on global issues where transnational civil society networks are thick and active, such as in HIV/AIDS and the environment, ideas and practices on the role of NGOs in governance are steadily gaining acceptance in some domestic policy circles. This in turn leads to much greater debate and inconsistency in the government's practices in engaging with civil society.

But even without the encyclopedic treatment such a comprehensive approach would require, our four arenas provide some highly interesting explorations into China's potential political trajectories. These trajectories, in turn, could be quickly altered by various flashpoints.

Triggers and Trajectories

Whether change comes abruptly or slowly is not solely dependent on the pace of reform. Given the scale of China's internal challenges as outlined in chapter 1, there is no shortage of potential triggers of significant political upheaval.

One obvious trigger is the economy. Within China, it is widely believed that it was the economic turmoil of the 1980s, particularly inflation, that mobilized large numbers of people in the unrest that culminated in Tiananmen Square in June 1989. Thus, significant growth in inflation and/or high levels of unemployment would likely be key factors in creating the enabling conditions for political change. The leadership clearly understands this, although keeping both under control is a daunting policy challenge. The task of economic governance has become ever more complex, with multiple sources of destabilization. These include not just interdependencies resulting from global economic integration, but also the management of local government debt, the management of land and property prices, income inequality, the role of state-owned enterprises, and so on.

Environmental disasters could also provide the spark for a concerted call for change. In a country that is home to twenty of the world's thirty most polluted cities, and where nearly all rivers and lakes are badly polluted and desertification claims an area the size of New Jersey every five years, environmental degradation is a direct threat to the health and livelihoods of millions. Environmental catastrophes and mismanagement cause many of the tens of thousands of uprisings each year. Should several of these coincide, it is possible that upheaval would spread more broadly.

Corruption and mis-governance are additional issues that could trigger widespread discontent, particularly when we consider the interaction of scandals with the development of information technology and social media. The government thus far has shown itself able to respond quickly to outcries of dissatisfaction arising from regulatory weaknesses, corruption, or abuses of power. These responses have ranged from disciplinary actions (for example, sacking of incompetent officials) to stifling anti-establishment opinions (for example, censorship on the Internet). Such approaches, however, are reactive rather than proactive. The social outcry that arose after the crash of two high-speed trains in Zhejiang in July 2011 provides yet another glimpse into the depth of citizen dissatisfaction with the CCP's record of governance. The scale of public anger over the Zhejiang train crash was particularly interesting given that many of the victims of the accident were from the wealthier segments of society. Those who were affected or had close interests in the issue therefore also had a wider range of tools with which to express their discontent, including *weibo*, the Chinese micro-blogging site.[8] This incident offers a valuable glimpse into how the fragile balance of interests in China can easily be disrupted.

To its credit, the political leadership is well aware of the urgency of creating change in all of these areas. The 12th Five-Year Plan includes a wide-ranging set of priorities for reform, among which control over inflation and continued economic transformation, environmental protection, and curbing corruption were all highlighted by Premier Wen Jiabao.[9] Over the past three decades, the party-state has already fundamentally transformed China's economic structure, although that is still a work in progress. The state-society relationship has changed beyond recognition, with literally millions of civil society organizations, clan associations, social organizations, formal and informal, modern and traditional, developing myriad ways to interact with and/or avoid the authorities. The scope for political control over both society and economy has been reduced by the many measures to streamline administration and increase transparency. Even electoral mechanisms are spreading, both within and beyond the party. In short, the social and political change taking place within China is far deeper and more vast than is commonly assumed. Political liberalization is occurring in the form of streamlined administrative power and stronger transparency. We are also witnessing political pluralization in the form of a much more active and participatory civil society. Political *democratization* is developing far more slowly but is clearly not stagnant.

Putting all this together, one possible way to view China's political trajectory is as a slow-motion transformation of authoritarianism that has been under way under Communist Party management, with many ups and downs, since 1978. This Chinese-style authoritarianism is increasingly permeable and open to the spread of new ideas and institutions. The crucial question is whether China's experimental approach to reform, and the delicate balance between local initiative and central response, is sufficient to both keep up with the multiplying socioeconomic challenges and at the same time overcome entrenched interests that oppose change.

History shows numerous relevant cases of ruling authoritarian elites living on into more democratic eras, when the transition is preceded by a sufficient degree of political reform and political institutionalization. The formerly authoritarian Kuomintang actively carried out political reforms in the 1980s and 1990s in Taiwan and remains the ruling party. In Hungary, the Communist Party began to reform in 1968, and its transformation in 1989 was basically peaceful. One of the ruling parties in Hungary after 1989, the Socialist Party, was actually the reform wing of the former Communist Party, which means that a large part of the former ruling elite survived. By contrast, authoritarian elites that fail to institutionalize any reforms while still in control often have faced a more sudden, violent, and even bloody transformation, after which the former ruling elite quickly disappears from the political scene. In the 1989 wave of democratization, Romania and Yugoslavia were such cases, and Tunisia, Egypt, Libya, and Syria seem to be repeating the pattern.

If historical precedent holds, the precise timing and nature of triggers that challenge China's authoritarianism will be unpredictable. All that can be said with confidence is that such challenges will recur. The persistence of the authoritarian regime in China long after its counterparts in Central and Eastern Europe (CEE) collapsed in the late 1980s and early 1990s has led many both within and outside the country to believe that China has developed a kind of immunity to the forces that normally undermine authoritarianism. And indeed it is true that the Chinese Communist Party has to date succeeded in maintaining the appearance, and much of the reality, of a monopoly on political power. But it has done so in considerable part by reducing the scope and scale of its authority, as well as the nature of its control.

As China sits at this tantalizing crossroads, then, it can draw on its experimentalist foundations for a wide range of options for creative and new governance innovations. Making that happen will require strong and enlightened leadership. The new leadership headed by Xi Jinping and Li Keqiang that takes over in 2012 has an extraordinary opportunity to take a bolder approach to experimentation and reform in order to rise to the challenge of transforming China.

A bolder experimental strategy would comprise a few key elements. One would be to go beyond verbal endorsements and exhortations in scaling up successful innovations. This strategy so far has led reform to lag behind in precisely those localities that are the most poorly governed. New measures could be established to build in concrete incentives for both local governments *and* society to adopt new reform ideas. These incentives could range from banking credit for development projects for governments to grants to NGOs.

Another element would be providing more space for citizens and civil society to actively join in and partner with their local township, county, or provincial governments in experimentation efforts. This multi-actor approach would allow the state to tap into a wider pool of talent and ideas and dramatically strengthen problem-solving processes. The development of this more networked approach to governance in effect would lay the foundation for a more resilient set of institutions that could respond flexibly to the unpredictable challenges that arise in today's globalizing China.

Given the massive scale required for any reform effort in China, a third element would be to develop multiple platforms for cross-learning—within the government, between state and society, and globally among research institutes, civil society groups, and even transnational networks of government officials. The range of tools available to the party-state to do these things is richer and more powerful today than at any point in history. The established approach to experimentation has been to run trials in different localities and then scale up nationally. The ground is fertile for China to leapfrog from the localized approach of past decades to building networked innovation hubs for governance—clusters of collaboration across the nation where pathbreaking ideas are brainstormed, where the most interesting new trials in governance are studied and disseminated, and where hybrid partnerships can be built to tackle new and emerging problems.

Finally, the new leadership in China has to grapple with the larger question of where these experiments are headed. As China's state institutions open up to new ideas, the risk also emerges that different segments of the country may get pulled in divergent normative directions. Chinese state and society today are effectively drawing from multiple ideologies. From within the country, there are Dengist, Maoist, and Confucian traditions to draw from, and international norms are also increasingly becoming a part of daily conversation as the world and China become more tightly interlinked. This heady mix is producing multiple interpretations of what China is and what it means to be Chinese, depending on whether one is speaking to cosmopolitan urbanites, to migrant workers, to the heads of multinational corporations, to farmers, to university students and professors, or to HIV/AIDS activists, artists, or steel workers. All of these people will increasingly look to their new leaders to offer a unifying, coherent, and convincing vision of China's future that they can identify with. Thus far, the debate about which direction China should move in has been confined to the intellectual and political elite. Looking forward, however, many outside of these circles are also increasingly demanding a role in writing that future. The time is ripe for China's new generation of leaders to take the experimental approach to the next stage.

Notes

Chapter One

1. World Resources Institute and Institute of Public and Environmental Affairs, "Greening Supply Chains in China: Practical Lessons from China-Based Suppliers in Achieving Environmental Performance," 2010 (www.ipe.org.cn/Upload/Report-Green-Supply-Chain-In-China-EN.pdf).

2. "Environmental Performance Index 2010," Yale Center for Environmental Law and Policy and Columbia University Center for Earth Science Information Network, in collaboration with the World Economic Forum and Joint Research Center of the European Commission (http://epi.yale.edu/countries).

3. Kenneth Lieberthal and Michel Oksenberg, *Policy Making in China: Leaders, Structures, and Processes* (Princeton University Press, 1988).

4. David Shambaugh, *China's Communist Party: Atrophy and Adaptation* (University of California Press, 2009); Richard McGregor, *The Party: The Secret World of China's Communist Rulers* (New York: Harper Collins, 2010).

5. The phrase, widely associated with Deng Xiaoping, was said by Chen Yun at a meeting in December 1980. See *Selected Works by Chen Yun,* vol. 3 (Renmin Press, 1995), p. 279. Deng quickly agreed and said, "Yes, and we shall experiment boldly." See *Selected Works by Deng Xiaoping,* vol. 3 (Renmin Press, 1993), p. 372.

6. While the experimental approach has been used since the 1980s, its history actually stretches back to the Mao years, where the terminology of "experimental point" and spreading reforms from "point to surface" became established in the 1940s to the early 1950s. The tumultuous years of the Great Leap Forward and the Cultural Revolution in the 1950s and 1960s squeezed out most of the room for experimentation, but Deng and other leaders revived the practice in the 1980s as a useful approach to economic reform. Multiple models addressing regional differences were promoted, in a conscious departure from previous decades of

insisting on a single ideologically driven model. A more detailed account can be found in Sebastian Heilmann, "From Local Experiments to National Policy: The Origins of China's Distinctive Policy Process," *The China Journal*, no. 59 (January 2008).

7. Ibid.

8. Ibid., p. 29.

9. Elizabeth Economy, *The River Runs Black: The Environmental Challenge to China's Future* (Cornell University Press/Council on Foreign Relations, 2010); also see the numerous reports of the China Environment Forum at the Woodrow Wilson International Center for Scholars (www.wilsoncenter.org/program/china-environment-forum).

10. Nouriel Roubini, "China's Bad Growth Bet," April 14, 2011 (www.project-syndicate.org/commentary/roubini37/English), and "When Fast Growing Economies Slow Down: International Evidence and Implications for China," Working Paper 16919 (Cambridge, Mass.: National Bureau of Economic Research, March 2011).

11. Michael E. Brown, Sean M. Lynn-Jones, and Steven E. Miller, *Debating the Democratic Peace* (MIT Press, 1996).

12. Maria Csanadi, *Self-Consuming Evolution: A Model on the Structure, Self-Reproduction, Self-Destruction and Transformation of Party-State Systems Tested in Romania, Hungary and China* (Budapest: Akademia Kiado, 2006).

13. Edward Steinfeld, *Playing Our Game: Why China's Economic Rise Doesn't Threaten the West* (Oxford University Press), pp. 32–35.

14. See World Bank, Data, "China," 2011 (http://data.worldbank.org/country/china).

15. Laetitia Lipman, "Leading China's Voguish Revolution," *The Telegraph*, February 9, 2011 (http://fashion.telegraph.co.uk/news-features/TMG8311302/Leading-Chinas-voguish-revolution.html).

16. Frederik Balfour, "China's 'City Jade Men' Indulge in Mud Masks, L'Oreal Creams," Bloomberg, December 12, 2010 (www.bloomberg.com/news/2010-12-12/china-s-city-jade-men-indulge-in-mud-masks-l-oreal-creams.html).

17. Michael Wines, "Once Banned, Dogs Reflect China's Rise," *New York Times*, October 24, 2010 (www.nytimes.com/2010/10/25/world/asia/25dogs.html?_r=1&src=me).

18. Peter Ford, "How One Man in China Strengthens the Rule of Law," *Christian Science Monitor*, February 22, 2008 (www.csmonitor.com/World/Asia-South-Central/2008/0222/p01s04-wosc.html/%28page%29/2).

19. Yu Keping, "Zhongguo gongmin shehui: Gainian, fenlei yu zhidu huanjing" (Civil Society in China: Concept, Categorization, and Institutional Environment), *Zhongguo Shehui Kexue* (China Social Sciences), no. 1 (2006).

20. "Dog Rescue Sparks Pet Law Debate," April 19, 2011 (http://english.sina.com/china/p/2011/0418/369318.html?utm_source=twitterfeed&utm_medium=twitter&utm_campaign=DTN+Fashion).

21. Lai Renqiong, "Kexue de lunzheng, minzhu de juece" (Scientific Argumentation, Democratic Decisionmaking), *Renmin Ribao* (*People's Daily*), April 4, 1992.

22. Examples include four township mayoral nominees in Nanbu in the mid-1990s, the mayoral nominee for Yueyang prefecture in 2003, and the mayoral nominee for Fushun prefecture in 2002. (See http://news.sina.com.cn/c/2004-10-02/20314483782.shtml.)

23. Xie Shenghua, "An Interview with Wang Xiuhong, the Chairperson of the Court for Administrative Cases in the Supreme Court," *People's Court Daily,* April 1, 2004.

24. Yang Tao, "The Three Connotations of the Finance Ministry's Loss in a Legal Case for the First Time," *China Youth Daily,* September 2, 2006.

25. Hu Xinqiao, "A Court in Hubei Gives a Verdict on the She Xianglin Case for State Compensation," *Legal Daily,* September 1, 2005.

26. White Paper on Human Rights, Information Office of the State Council of the People's Republic of China, 1991 (http://china.org.cn/e-white/7/7-1.htm).

27. Human Rights Watch, "Promises Unfulfilled: An Assessment of China's National Human Rights Action Plan," 2011 (www.hrw.org/en/reports/2011/01/11/promises-unfulfilled).

28. On the major governmental reorganizations through 2002 and their implications, see Dali L. Yang, *Remaking the Chinese Leviathan: Market Transition and the Politics of Governance in China* (Stanford University Press, 2004).

29. Thomas Carothers, "Promoting the Rule of Law Abroad: The Problem of Knowledge," Carnegie Endowment for International Peace Working Paper 34, Rule of Law Series, Democracy and Rule of Law Project (Washington, January 2003).

30. We borrow these broad categorizations from Minxin Pei, "Is China's Transition Trapped and What Should the West Do about It?"(www.fljs.org).

31. For a detailed assessment of the development of the Chinese version of a modern regulatory state, see Dali L Yang, *Remaking the Chinese Leviathan: Market Transition and the Politics of Governance in China* (Stanford University Press, 2004).

32. Andrew Nathan, "Authoritarian Resilience," in "China's Changing of the Guard," Special Issue, *Journal of Democracy* 14, no. 1 (January 2003): 11.

33. David Shambaugh, *China's Communist Party: Atrophy and Adaptation* (Washington: Woodrow Wilson Center Press, 2009).

34. Gordon Chang, *The Coming Collapse of China* (New York: Random House, 2001).

35. Robert Wade, *Governing the Market: Economic Theory and the Role of Government in East Asian Industrialization* (Princeton University Press, 1992); Randall Peerenboom, *China Modernizes: Threat to the West or Model for the Rest?* (Oxford University Press, 2007); Suzanne Ogden, *Inklings of Democracy in China* (Harvard University Press, 2002).

36. Minxin Pei, *China's Trapped Transition: The Limits of Developmental Autocracy* (Harvard University Press 2008).

37. Andrew Mertha, "'Fragmented Authoritarianism' 2.0: Political Pluralization in the Chinese Policy Process," *The China Quarterly* 200 (2009): 995–1012.

38. Cheng Li, ed., *China's Emerging Middle Class: Beyond Economic Transformation* (Brookings Institution Press, 2010).

39. Timothy J. Kehoe and Kim Ruhl, "Why Have Economic Reforms in Mexico Not Generated Growth?" Working Paper 16580 (Cambridge, Mass.: National Bureau of Economic Research, 2010) (www.nber.org/tmp/11815-w16580.pdf).

Chapter Two

1. Jianmin Ji, "166 ge Gongzhang Wenti" (The Problem of 166 Stamps), *Qian Xian* (Front Line) 166, no. 4 (2009).

2. Andrew J. Nathan, "Authoritarian Resilience," *Journal of Democracy* 14, no. 1 (2003): 6–17.

3. He Zengke, "Corruption and Anti-Corruption in Reform China," *Communist and Post-Communist Studies* 33 (2000): 243–70.

4. Chen Zhenming, "Shenhua Xingzheng Tizhi Gaige, Jiakuai Fuwuxing Zhengfu Jianshe: Zhongguo Zhengfu Gaige he Zhili de Xin Qushi Toushi" (Deepening Administrative System Reform, Accelerating the Development of Service-Oriented Government: New Trend of Chinese Government Reform and Governance), *Fujian Xingzheng Xueyuan Xuebao* (Journal of Fujian Institute of Administration), no. 4 (2008): 7–14.

5. Wang Hongwei and Li Hong, "Woguo Xingzheng Shenpi Zhidu Gaige de Xianzhuang yu Jingyibu Shenru Fazhan Silu de Tantao" (The State of Administrative Approval Reform and the Possible Way of Deepening), *Jing Ji Shi* (China Economist), no. 1 (2004): 268–69.

6. Kenneth G. Lieberthal, "Introduction: The 'Fragmented Authoritarianism' Model and Its Limitations," in *Bureaucracy, Politics, and Decision Making in Post-Mao China*, Kenneth G. Lieberthal and David M. Lampton, eds. (University of California Press, 1992), pp. 1–30.

7. Kenneth Lieberthal and David Lampton, *Bureaucracy, Politics, and Decision-Making in Post-Mao China* (University of California Press, 1992).

8. Kenneth Lieberthal and Michel Oksenberg, *Policy Making in China* (Princeton University Press, 1990).

9. Nathan, "Authoritarian Resilience."

10. Pan Xiuzhen and Chu Tianyou, "Liyi Chongtuxing Zhidu Bianqian—Zhuanxingqi Zhongguo Xingzheng Shenpi Zhidu Gaige de Lixiang Moxing" (Interests Conflict Leading to Institutional Reform—Ideal Model of Administrative Approval Reform in the Transformation Period), *Zhongguo Xingzheng Guanli* (Chinese Public Administration), no. 5 (2010): 16–20.

11. Yifu Qin, "Lichengbei Yiyi de Gaige: Xingzheng Shenpi Zhidu Gaige de Huigu yu Zhanwang" (Milestone Reform: A Review on Reforming Administrative Approvals), *Zhongguo Jingji Zhoukan* (China Economic Weekly), no. 46 (2006): 19–22.

12. Wang Wei, "Shenru Tuijin Xingzheng Shenpi Zhidu Gaige" (Further Promoting Administrative Approval Reform), *Zhongguo Jiancha* (Supervision in China), no. 18 (2010): 8–10.

13. Yifu Qin, "Lichengbei Yiyi de Gaige."

14. Qing Hongyan, Zhu Fengjun, Yan Yan, and You Xingyu, "Shenzhen Kaiqi Xingzhen Shenpi Zhidu Gaige Xianhe" (Shenzhen Spearheaded the Reform of Administrative Approvals), *Nanfang Doushi Bao* (Southern Cosmopolitan), March 12, 2008 (http://news.sina.com.cn/c/2008-03-12/030015129989.shtml).

15. This promotion criterion is not written in any document, but is understood by all. Since 1978 the Party has repeatedly called on the whole nation and the establishment to focus on economic development. The reform and opening started in late 1978, when the third plenary session of the 11th Party Congress decided to shift the focus of the work of the Party from class struggle to economic development. It was at that point that the promotion criterion changed from ideological purity to economic performance.

16. Sun Shoushan, "Guanyu Shenhua Xingzheng Shenpi Zhidu de Jidian Sikao" (Some Thoughts on Reforming the Institution of Administrative Approval), *Guojia Xingzheng Xueyuan Xuebao* (Proceedings of the State Administrative College), no. 3 (2009): 4–7.

17. Ibid.

18. Unless otherwise noted, the following discussion of the Shenzhen reform is drawn from Yan Haibing, "Shenzhen Jianchaju Xingzheng Shenpi Dianzi Jiancha Xitong Anli Fenxi" (A Case Study of the Electronic Supervision System for Administrative Approval Procedures in Shenzhen), in *Zhongguo Difang Zhengfu Chuangxin Anli Yanjiu Baogao* (Innovations and Excellence in Chinese Local Governance: Case Study Reports 2007–2008), Yu Keping, ed. (Beijing University Press, 2009).

19. Yu Keping et al., *The Theory and Practice of Government Reform* (Zhejiang People's Publisher, 2005), pp. 197–98.

20. Mudajiang Anti-Corruption Bureau, "Guanyu Mudanjiang Xingzhen Shenpi Zhidu Gaige Gongzuo de Diaoyan Baogao" (A Study on Reforming Administrative Approval in Mudanjiang) (www.szzw.gov.cn/jlxx/gddt/201103/t20110310_1642398.htm).

21. "From the Remaining 385 Items, Another 112 Items Cropped Up," *Guangzhou Yang Chen Daily,* July 25, 2003.

22. Xing Ying, Hu Xianzhi, and Zhang Jixing, "China's WTO Entry and Government Administrative Approval System Reformation, Discussion Group Proceedings," *China Administration Control* 8 (2002): 22.

23. In our case 2, it is called Government Service Supermarket.

24. As mentioned earlier, Shenzhen prefecture established an "administrative service hall" as part of its reform process. This is a one-stop administrative service center. While in the Shenzhen case, the innovation in streamlining happened at the prefecture level, it happened at the county level in Xiaguan district. Administrative streamlining took place at all levels. We chose these two cases to highlight the pervasiveness of administrative reform across China at different levels of government and in places with very different levels of economic performance.

25. Unless otherwise noted, the following discussion of the Xiaguan reform is drawn from Wang Yongbing, "Nanjingshi Xiaguanqu 'Zhengwu Chaoshi' Diaoyan Baogao ji Fenxi" (A Case Study of the Supermarket of Governmental Affairs at Xiaguan District in Nanjing Municipality), in *Difang Zhengfu Chuangxin yu Shanzhi: Anli Yanjiu* (Case Studies of Local Governance Innovations), Yu Keping, ed. (Social Sciences Academic Press, 2003), pp. 158–86.

26. Cao Chao, "Qianxi Zhongguo Gongwuyuan Guimo Zhi Bian" (A Brief Review of the Changing Scale of Public Servants in China), *Fazhi yu Shehui* (Law and Society), no. 1 (2011). There are three definitions of "cadres": (a) staff of Party organs and state organs, the number of which is about 12 million; (b) staff of Party organs, state organs, military organs, state-owned enterprises, school teachers, and others, the number of which is around 40 million; and (c) staff of the above-mentioned organizations plus their retirees, the number of which is 60–70 million. Yang Jisheng, *Zhongguo Dangdai Shehui Jieceng Fenxi* (Analyzing Social Status in Contemporary China) (Jiangxi Gaoxiao Press, June 2011).

27. Li Yamin: "Quntixing Shijian de Goutong Jizhi Yanjiu" (A Study of Communication Mechanisms in Demonstrations), *Fazhi yu Shehui* (Law and Society), no. 16 (2010).

Chapter Three

1. Tang Jianguang, "Zhixuan Xiangzhang" (Electing the Township Mayor Directly), *Nanfang Zhoumo* (Southern Weekend), January 15, 1999, p. 2.

2. See www.uscpf.org/html/1999/April/v3-1elections.html, April 16, 2011.

3. See Lianjiang Li, "The Politics of Introducing Direct Township Elections in China," *China Quarterly*, no. 171 (Sept. 2002): 704–23.

4. Tony Saich and Xuedong Yang, "Innovation in China's Local Governance: 'Open Recommendation and Selection,'" *Pacific Affairs* 76, no. 2 (Summer 2003): 185–208.

5. Huang Weiping, "Zhongguo Minzhu Xuanju: cong Guangdu dao Shendu" (Democratic Election in China: From Width to Depth), *Makesizhuyi yu Xianshi* (Marxism and Reality), no. 5 (2001): 48–52.

6. Saich and Yang, "Innovation in China's Local Governance."

7. For details about and the implications of this kind of election, see, for example, Everett M. Jacobs, "Soviet Local Elections: What They Are and What They Are Not," *Soviet Studies* 22, no. 1 (July 1970): 61–76.

8. For example, in 1985 Hungary held its first multi-candidate elections. In 1987, the first multi-candidate local elections were permitted in the Soviet Union. However, in Hungary between 1985 and 1989 and in the Soviet Union between 1987 and 1991, the Communist Party monopolized the political process and no opposition parties were allowed.

9. This is referred to as *cha'e xuanju* (elections in which there are more candidates than available positions).

10. John L. Thornton, "Long Time Coming," *Foreign Affairs* 87, no.1 (Jan./Feb. 2008): 2–22.

11. See media report at http://news.cntv.cn/20101118/103313.

12. See media report at http://news.sohu.com/20090828/n266285079.shtml.

13. See media report at http://news.qq.com/a/20101114/000299.htm.

14. See media report at http:/qjrb.cn/2009-10/16/content_66800.htm.

15. See, for example, Amy B. Epstein, "Village Elections in China: Experimenting with Democracy," in *China's Economic Future*, U.S. Congress, Joint Economic Committee, ed. (Washington, 1996). See also Melanie Manion, "The Electoral Connection in the Chinese Countryside," *American Political Science Review* 90, no. 4 (1996): 736–48. This study evaluates the results of a survey in fifty-six villages in Anhui, Hunan, and Hebei provinces and Tianjin municipality. David Zweig, *Freeing China's Farmers: Rural Restructuring in the Reform Era* (Armonk, N.Y.: M. E. Sharpe, 1997), p. 26. Yongnian Zheng, "Zhongguo hui biande geng minzhu ma?" (Will China Be More Democratic?), in *Liang'an jiceng xuanju yu zhengzhi shehui bianqian* (Grassroots Elections and Sociopolitical Changes on the Two Sides of the Taiwan Strait), Chen Mingtong and Zheng Yongnian, eds. (Taipei: Yuedan chubanshe, 1998), pp. 437–55. Tianjian Shi, "Economic Development and Village Elections in Rural China," *Journal of Contemporary China* 8, no. 22 (1999): 425–42. Jean C. Oi and Scott Rozelle, "Elections and Power: The Locus of Decision-Making in Chinese Villages," *Journal of Contemporary China* 8, no. 22 (1999): 513–39. Kevin J. O'Brien and Lianjiang Li, "Accommodating 'Democracy' in a One-Party-State: Introducing Village Elections in China," *China Quarterly*, no. 162 (June 2000): 465–89. Robert A. Pastor and Qingshan Tan, "The Meaning of China's Village Elections," *China Quarterly*, no. 162 (June 2000): 490–512. Zhenglin Guo and Thomas P. Bernstein, "The Impact of Elections on the Village Structure of Power: The Relation between the Village Committees and the Village Party Branches," *Journal of Contemporary China* 13, no. 39 (May 2004): 257–75.

16. O'Brien and Li, "Accommodating 'Democracy.'"

17. See Article 2 of the Law of Organizing Villagers Committees, effective November 4, 1998. The text of the law is available on the National People's Congress website (www.npcnews.com.cn/gb/paper12/1/class001200006/hwz64679.htm).

18. As noted in chapter 1, within the hierarchy of the Chinese political system, there are five levels of authority: the center; 34 provinces, autonomous regions,

municipalities, and special administrative regions (including Hong Kong, Macau, and Taiwan, which are not covered by this research); 333 prefectures; 2,862 counties; and 41,636 townships. The Chinese terms for prefecture and county are confusing. *Diqu* (and *zhou* and *meng* in the ethnic minority regions) is the usual term for prefecture, and *xian* (and *qi* in the ethnic minority regions) refers to the county. Meanwhile, some *shi* are at the prefectural level while other *shi* are at the county level. Some counties are called *qu*. In this research, these administrative entities are referred to as prefectures and counties, despite the variations in Chinese. This usage corresponds with the administrative zoning practices of the Ministry of Civil Affairs. See the statistics on the website of the Ministry of Civil Affairs (http://qhs.mca.gov.cn/article/zlzx/qhtj/200711/20071100003177.shtml).

19. Li Fan, "Zhongguo Jiceng Minzhu Zhengzhi de Fazhan he Zhengzhi Gaige" (Grassroots Democracy and Political Reform in China), 2005 (www.chinaue.com/html/2005-11/2005113014134619921.htm).

20. Li Fan, "Toushi Shenzhen Renda Daibiao Xuanju de Xin Xianxiang" (Understanding the New Phenomena in the Elections for People's Congress in Shenzhen Municipality)," *Anhui Juece Zixun* (Anhui Journal of Decision-Making Consultation), no. 7 (2003): 35–37.

21. Zhao Jinliang, "Guanyu Yao Lifa Xianxiang de Jidian Sikao" (Thinking on the Case of Yao Lifa), *Renda Yanjiu* (Studying the People's Congress), no. 1 (2003): 37–38.

22. The World and China Institute, "Renda Daibiao Huanjie Xuanju Jingdian Anli Renwu 4: Zeng Jianyu" (A Representative Case and Figure in the Election for Representative to the People's Congress), 2006 (www.world-china.org/news detail.asp?newsid=1613).

23. Wang Ganlin, "Yuan Renda Daibiao Zeng Jianyu Xingman hou de Shenghuo" (The Life of the Former People's Congress Representative Zeng Jianyu after Being Released from Jail), *Shandong Renda Gongzuo* (Shandong Journal of People's Congress), no. 6 (2003): 60.

24. See the report at Wenzhou News Net (http://wznews.66wz.com/system/2007/01/17/100244289.shtml).

25. See the report at the website of Nanzhou Government in Qinghai province (www.huangnan.gov.cn/html%5C265%5C20060806091215.html).

26. See the report at the website of Liaoyang prefecture government in Liaoning province (http://liaoyang.gov.cn/listarview.asp?id=8515&flbs=61).

27. See post at the website of Kunming Prefecture People's Congress (http://renda.km.gov.cn/Html/changweihuigongbao/2008nian/di01qi08/1982289.html).

28. See the report at Public Network (www.dzwww.com/xinwen/xinwen zhuanti/07xxljrdhjxj/bd/200712/t20071210_3067240.htm).

29. Zhou Changxian, "Zizhu Canxuanren de Xingqi yu Renda Daibiao Xuanju Zhidu de Xin Zouxiang" (The Emergence of Independent Candidates and the New Direction of the Evolution of the Election System for People's Congress), *Sichuan Ligong Xuanyuan Xuebao—Shehui Kexue Ban* (Journal of

Sichuan Institute of Science and Technology—Social Sciences Edition), no. 3 (2009): 21–24.

30. "China: Vote as I Say," *The Economist,* June 18, 2011, p. 33.

31. See the report "Weile Dang he Guojia Xingwang Fada Changzhi Jiu'an—Dang de Xinyijie Zhongyang Lingdao Jigou Chansheng Jishi" (For the Prosperity and Peace of the Party and the Nation—Witnessing the Emergence of the Central Leadership of the New Party Congress), Xinhua News Net (http://news.xinhuanet.com/newscenter/2007-10/24/content_6931498.htm). October, 24, 2007.

32. "Dangzheng Lingdao Ganbu Xuanba Renyong Gongzuo Zanxing Tiaoli" (Tentative Regulation for Selecting and Appointing Party and State Cadres), Central Committee of the Communist Party, document no. 4, February 9, 1995.

33. "Dangzheng Lingdao Ganbu Xuanba Renyong Gongzuo Tiaoli" (Regulation for Selecting and Appointing Party and State Cadres), Central Committee of the Communist Party, document no. 7, July 9, 2002.

34. See, for example, Cheng Li, "From Selection to Election? Experiments in the Recruitment of Chinese Political Elites," *China Leadership Monitor,* no. 26 (2008); and Alice Miller, "The Case of Xi Jinping and the Mysterious Succession," *China Leadership Monitor,* no. 30 (2009).

35. See, for example, Joseph Fewsmith, "The 17th Party Congress: Informal Politics and Formal Institutions," *China Leadership Monitor,* no. 23 (2008).

36. Unless otherwise noted, the description of the Rushan City case is drawn from Cao Sheng, "Rushanshi Dangnei Minzhu Gaige Anli Fenxi" (A Case Study of Intra-party Democratic Reform in Rushan City), which was published in Mandarin in *Zhongguo Difang Zhengfu Chuangxin Anli Yanjiu Baogao* (Innovations and Excellence in Chinese Local Governance: Case Study Reports 2007–2008), Yu Keping, ed. (Beijing University Press, 2009). For the English translation see Sheng Cao, "The Progressing Comprehensive Promotion of Intra-Party Democracy Reform," Working Paper 025 (National University of Singapore, Lee Kuan Yew School of Public Policy, Centre on Asia and Globalisation, June 2011) (www.lkyspp.nus.edu.sg/CAG).

37. Cao Sheng, "The Progressing Comprehensive Promotion of Intra-Party Democracy Reform." Working Paper 025 (2011) (www.caglkyschool.com/pdf/working%20papers/2011/CAG_WorkingPaper_25.pdf).

38. Zhu Fangming, *Siyou Jingji zai Zhongguo* (Private Sector in China) (Beijing City Press, 1998), p. 470.

39. Chen Jianming and Qiu Haixiong, "Fubai Xina yu Minzhu—Zhongguo Zhengshang Guanxi de Zhangli" (Corruption, Absorption, and Democracy—the Tension between Politics and Business in China), in *21 Shijichu de Zhongguo* (China in the Early 21st Century), Guan Xinji and Xiong Jinming, eds. (Chinese University of Hong Kong Press, 2009).

40. Unless otherwise noted, the description of this case is drawn from Xiang Guolan, "Tuijin Dangnei Minzhu de Zhidu Chuangxin—Ya'an Dang Daibiao Dahui Changrenzhi Anli Fenxi" (A Case Study of the Regularization of the Local

Party Congress in Ya'an Prefecture—An Institutional Innovation in Promoting Intra-party Democracy), published in Mandarin in *Zhongguo Difang Zhengfu Chuangxin Anli Yanjiu Baogao* (Innovations and Excellence in Chinese Local Governance: Case Study Reports 2003-2004), Yu Keping, ed. (Beijing University Press, 2006), pp. 175–98. For the English translation see Xiang Guolan, "Institutional Innovations for the Promotion of Intra-Party Democracy," Working Paper 14 (National University of Singapore, Centre on Asia and Globalisation, Lee Kuan Yew School, June 2011) (www.lkyspp.nus.edu.sg/CAG).

41. Ya'an prefecture had 72,596 CCP members, with 293 party committees in government bodies, enterprises, and associations.

42. Unless otherwise noted, discussion of the Qianxi county case is drawn from Chen Xuelian, "Ruoshi Qunti Gonggong Canyu—Hebei Qianxi Fudaihui Zhixuan Gean Baogao" (A Case Study of Public Participation of Disadvantaged Groups in Direct Elections for the Women's Association at Qianxi County in Hebei Province), in *Difang Zhengfu Chuangxin yu Shanzhi: Anli Yanjiu* (Case Studies of Local Governance Innovations), Yu Keping, ed. (Social Sciences Academic Press, 2003), pp. 69–95.

43. Zha Qingjiu, "Minzhu Buneng Chaoyue Falv" (Democracy Must Not Surpass the Law)," *Fazhi Ribao* (Legal Daily), January 19, 1999, p. 1.

44. In semi-competitive elections for township mayor, the actors who introduce the new elections are primarily county Party secretaries. As discussed before, according to the nomenklatura in China, officials are appointed by a higher-level official. Thus a township mayor is supposed to be appointed by a county party committee (in practical terms, the county Party secretary together with two or three of his closest colleagues); a county mayor is supposed to be appointed by a prefecture party committee; a prefecture mayor is supposed to be appointed by a provincial party committee; and a provincial governor is to be appointed by the center. In other words, it is the jurisdiction of a county party committee to decide what mechanism to apply to select a township mayor, under the guidance of the general rules set by the center.

Chapter Four

1. Trudy Rubin, "NGOs a Paradox in Today's China," *Philadelphia Inquirer*, May 23, 2010 (www.internationalreportingproject.org/stories/detail/1559/).

2. The quote is from A. Seligman, *The Idea of Civil Society* (New York: Macmillan, 1982), p. 33.

3. Alexis de Tocqueville, *Democracy in America*, trans. Arthur Goldhammer (New York: Library of America, 2004).

4. Gabriel A. Almond and Sidney Verba, eds., *The Civic Culture: Political Attitudes and Democracy in Five Nations* (Newbury Park, Calif.: Sage, 1989), p. 502.

5. See, for example, Larry Diamond, "Toward Democratic Consolidation," in Larry Diamond and Jarc F. Plattner, eds., *The Global Resurgence of Democracy* (Johns Hopkins University Press, 1966).

6. Marina Ottaway and Thomas Carothers, eds., *Funding Virtue: Civil Society Aid and Democracy Promotion* (Washington: Carnegie Endowment for International Peace, 2000).

7. Robert Putnam, with Robert Leonardi and Rafaella Y. Nanetti, *Making Democracy Work: Civic Traditions in Modern Italy* (Princeton University Press, 1993), p. 3.

8. Putnam, *Making Democracy Work,* chap. 4.

9. Ibid., p. 111. In game theory terms, strong networks of associations enable participants in societies to overcome incentives to defect in noncooperative games by generating expectations of diffuse reciprocity.

10. Chan Kin-man, Qiu Haixiong, and Zhu Jiangang, "Chinese NGOs Strive to Survive," in *Social Transformations in Chinese Societies: The Official Annual of the Hong Kong Sociological Association,* Bian Yan-jie, Chan Kwok-bun, and Cheung Tak-sing, eds. (Leiden: Brill, 2005), p. 138.

11. Quisha Ma, *Non-Governmental Organizations in Contemporary China: Paving the Way to Civil Society?* (London: Routledge, 2006), p. 110.

12. Ministry of Civil Affairs website (http://files2.mca.gov.cn/cws/201101/20110130160410749.htm). Foundations are more likely to be operating foundations rather than grant-giving organizations.

13. The classic definition of corporatism comes from Philippe Schmitter's 1979 definition of a corporatist system as interests "organized into a limited number of singular, compulsory, noncompetitive, hierarchically ordered and functionally differentiated categories created or regulated by the state, which allows them to operate with constraints on the leadership and demands." Yiyi Lu, "NGOs in China: Development Dynamics and Challenges," in *China's Opening Society: The Non-State Sector and Governance,* Yongnian Zheng and Joseph Fewsmith, eds. (London: Routledge, 2008), chap. 2, p. 147, n2, quoted language from Philippe C. Schmitter and Gerhard Lehmbruch, eds., London: Sage, 1979), p. 13. For an in-depth exploration of the applications of corporatist versus civil society approaches to understanding the role of associations in China, see Jonathan Unger, ed., *Associations and the Chinese State: Contested Spaces* (Armonk, N.Y.: M. E. Sharpe, 2008).

14. Ma, *Non-Governmental Organizations in Contemporary China,* pp. 136–42.

15. For a superb analysis of the CCCP's efforts to adapt itself to the twenty-first century, see David Shambaugh, *China's Communist Party: Atrophy and Adaptation* (Woodrow Wilson Center Press and University of California Press, 2008).

16. For a discussion of China's private sector, see the special section of *The Economist,* March 11, 2011.

17. A number of Chinese scholars argue vociferously for assessing China's associational life in its own terms: "The key question here is not whether associations are autonomous from state control, but to what extent people are associated with one another in some structured forms." Shaoguang Wang and Jianyu He, "Association Revolution in China: Mapping the Landscapes," *Korea Observer* 35, no. 3 (Autumn 2004): 489. Yiyi Lu argues that the complexities of the Chinese reality call for a much deeper institutionalist analysis. The Chinese Party-state is not monolithic, but rather a rapidly changing, very complex constellation of actors that make up the party-state system. Civil society organizations span a broad spectrum, from fully state-based to fully society-based, have a wide range of specific goals, and use a variety of tools to engage that system in pursuit of those goals. Nor is it helpful to classify Chinese NGOs according to their formal degree of autonomy from the state, as such classifications usually obscure more than they illuminate about incentives and behavior. Thus, rather than focusing on organizational autonomy, a better approach to understanding the roles of civil society and the potential future political trajectory of China is to do institutional analysis that disaggregates both state and society and looks at incentives facing actors within each institution. Yiyi Lu, "NGOs in China, chap. 2.

18. Ma, *Non-Governmental Organizations in Contemporary China*, pp. 186–87.

19. Chan, Qiu, and Zhu, "Chinese NGOs Strive to Survive," in *Social Transformations in Chinese Societies*, Bian, Chan, and Cheung, eds., p. 145.

20. Wang and He, "Association Revolution in China."

21. Ma, *Non-Governmental Organizations in Contemporary China*, p. 61.

22. Wang and He, "Association Revolution in China."

23. For a good account of the role of intellectuals in the evolution of China's civil society, see Jean-Philippe Beja, "The Changing Aspects of Civil Society in China," in *China's Opening Society*, Zheng and Fewsmith, eds.

24. Ma, *Non-Governmental Organizations in Contemporary China*, p. 52.

25. Ibid., p. 87.

26. Ibid., pp. 181–82.

27. Zheng Yongnian and Joseph Fewsmith, "Introduction" in *China's Opening Society*, Zheng and Fewsmith, eds., p. 3.

28. Qi Zhi, "What a Warning Signal Given by 'Color Revolution'!" *International Strategic Studies*, no. 3 (2005), quoted in Shambaugh, *China's Communist Party*, p. 90.

29. Amy E. Gadsden, "Chinese Nongovernmental Organizations: Politics by Other Means?" (Washington: American Enterprise Institute Tocqueville on China Project, July 2010), p. 1.

30. Ng Tze-wei, "Will Stronger Social Governance Give NGOs More Leeway?" *South China Morning Post*, March 10, 2011.

31. Peh Sing Huei, "China Too Good at Quelling Protests," *Singapore Strait Times*, June 15, 2011, p. A2.

32. Willy Lam, "Beijing's Blueprint for Tackling Mass Incidents and Social Management," *China Brief*, March 25, 2011 (www.jamestown.org/programs/chinabrief/single/?tx_ttnews%5Btt_news%5D=37696&tx_ttnews%5BbackPid%5D=25&cHash=ea32c96b432552f2f027619725a91714).

33. Ng, "Will Stronger Social Governance Give NGOs More Leeway?"

34. Lily Tsai, "Solidary Groups, Informal Accountability, and Local Public Goods Provision in Rural China," *American Political Science Review* 101, no. 2 (May 2007).

35. For a discussion of social dislocations under modernization, see Karl Polanyi, *The Great Transformation: The Political and Economic Origins of Our Time* (Boston: Beacon Press), including the Foreword by Joseph E. Stiglitz.

36. Cheng Li, "Introduction: The Rise of the Middle Class in the Middle Kingdom," in *China's Emerging Middle Class: Beyond Economic Transformation*, Cheng Li, ed. (Brookings Institution Press, 2010), chap. 1.

37. Jie Chen, "Attitudes toward Democracy and the Political Behavior of China's Middle Class," in *China's Emerging Middle Class*, Li, ed. chap. 15.

38. China Internet Network Information Center, statistics as of June 2010 (www.cnnic.net.cn/en/index/).

39. Shan Philips, "Mobile Internet More Popular in China than in U.S.," Nielsen China Insights Report, August 2010 (http://cn.en.acnielsen.com/documents/NielsenChinaMobileReportInsights_FinalEN.pdf).

40. Guobin Yang, *The Power of the Internet in China: Citizen Activism Online* (Columbia University Press, 2009), pp. 31–32.

41. International Center for Not-for-Profit Law, "NGO Law Monitor—China," updated February 19, 2011 (www.icnl.org/knowledge/ngolawmonitor/china.htm).

42. Kin-Man Chan, "Commentary on Hsu: Graduated Control and NGO Responses: Civil Society as Institutional Logic," *Journal of Civil Society* 6, no. 3 (December 2010): 304.

43. A separate set of "Regulations for the Management of Foundations" took effect on June 1, 2004.

44. For private nonenterprise institutions, defined as "social organizations which are established by enterprises, institutions, associations, or other social forces as well as individual citizens using non-state assets and conduct non-profit-making social service activities," the relevant rules are the "Interim Regulations on the Registration and Administration of Private Non-Enterprise Units" issued on October 25, 1998.

45. Quasi-government public institutions are covered by the "Interim Regulations on the Registration and Administration of Public Institutions" (which took effect on June 27, 2004). These regulations define quasi-government public institutions as "social service organizations sponsored by state organs or other organizations using state-owned assets that engage in educational, science and technological, cultural, health, and other activities for the purpose of social

welfare." They are usually formed by government agencies and staffed by government employees.

46. Lu, *Non-Governmental Organisations in China,* p. 3.

47. Ministry of Civil Affairs (http://files2.mca.gov.cn/cws/201101/20110130 160410749.htm).

48. According to Article 7 of "Regulations for Registration and Management of Social Organizations" (published by the State Council at the 8th ordinary session on 25/9/98 and took effect from that date), different levels of social organizations must register with and be managed by different levels of the Civil Affairs Bureau. (Original text of Article 7: "National level social organizations must register with and be managed by State Council registration and management agencies; local social organizations must register with and be managed by the local People's Government registration and management agencies; inter-area social organizations must register with and be managed by common higher level peoples registration and management agencies.")

49. Yu Keping, "Zhong Guo Gong Min She Hui: Gai Nian, Feng Lei yu Zhi Du Huang Jin" (Civil Society in China: Concepts, Classification and Institutional Environment), *Zhongguo she hui ke xue* (China's Social Science) 1 (2006).

50. International Center for Not-for-Profit Law, "NGO Law Monitor—China."

51. Ma, *Non-Governmental Organizations in Contemporary China,* chap. 8.

52. Circular of the State Administration of Foreign Exchange on Relevant Issues Concerning the Administration of Donations in Foreign Exchange by Domestic Institutions, December 30, 2009 (http://safe.gov.cn/model_safe_en/laws_en/laws_detail_en.jsp?ID=30600000000000000,58).

53. Lei Xie, *Environmental Activism in China* (London: Routledge, 2009), pp. 33–34.

54. For an excellent assessment of the form and consequences of the obstacles to the development of social organizing in China, see Zengke He, "Institutional Barriers to the Development of Civil Society in China," in Zheng and Fewsmith, eds., *China's Opening Society,* pp. 161–73.

55. Ma, *Non-Governmental Organizations in Contemporary China,* p. 187.

56. Wang and He, "Association Revolution in China," p. 514; Chan Kin-man, Qiu Haixiong, and Zhu Jiangang, "Chinese NGOs Strive to Survive," in *Social Transformations in Chinese Societies,* Bian, Chan, and Cheung, eds., pp. 141–42.

57. Gadsden, "Chinese Nongovernmental Organizations," pp. 6–7.

58. Lu, "NGOs in China," in *China's Opening* Society, Zheng and Fewsmith, eds., pp. 89–105.

59. Ibid., p. 91.

60. Unless otherwise noted, the factual material about the Changzhou case (although not the analysis) is drawn from Zhou Hongyun, "The Partnership between Government and Civil Society: An Analysis of NGO Administrative Reforms in Putuo District, Shanghai, Using the Case Study of the 'Changzhou

Model'" (English translation), Working Paper 22, June 2011 (Centre on Asia and Globalisation, National University of Singapore).

61. Zhou, "The Partnership between Government and Civil Society."

62. International Center for Not-for-Profit Law, "NGO Law Monitor—China."

63. Ibid.

64. Act 5 of the Trade Union Law (amended) stipulates: "Trade Unions shall organize and educate employees to exercise their democratic rights pursuant to the provisions of China's Constitution and laws, to play their role as the nation's master, participate through various channels and formats in the management of national affairs, economic and cultural institutions and social matters, assist the people's governments in their work, uphold the leadership of the working classes and support the worker-peasant alliance which forms the basis of the people's democratic dictatorship of socialist state power."

65. "A Brief Introduction of the All-China Federation of Trade Unions," September 20, 2007 (http://english.acftu.org/template/10002/file.jsp?cid=63&aid=156).

66. Unless otherwise noted, the following description of the rules and practices governing China's mass trade unions is drawn from Xuedong Yang, "Path for System Formation in Resource Mobilization: A Case Study of the Rights Protection Policy in Quanzhou City's Trade Union," available in English as Working Paper 19, Centre on Asia and Globalisation, National University of Singapore, June 2011 (www.caglkyschool.com/pdf/working%20papers/2011/CAG_Working Paper_19.pdf).

67. For a useful overview of the literature on whether labor is becoming, or is likely to become, a threat to China's state authority, see Ching Kwan Lee, "Is Labor a Political Force in China?" in Elizabeth Perry and Merle Goldman, eds., *Grassroots Political Reform in Contemporary China* (Harvard University Press, 2007), pp. 228–29.

68. Ibid., p. 229.

69. The Trade Union Law has been amended twice (it was formulated in 1950, reformulated in 1992 to require trade unions "to better represent and protect the specific interests of employees while maintaining the general interest of the nation," and amended in 2001 to state that "it is the basic responsibility of the trade union to protect the legal rights and interests of the employees" (Act 6)). Similarly, the All-China Federation of Trade Unions (ACFTU) has made multiple legal and policy adjustments at its various National Congresses. In October 1983, the ACFTU's 10th National Congress stressed the role of trade unions in protecting the legal rights and interests of employees. Its next National Congress five years later redefined the union's purpose as serving "four basic functions": "safeguard specific interests of employees," "represent employees in management," "develop mass-oriented production activities," and "help raise employees' qualities," or in short, "protection, participation, development, and education." By 1998, the 13th ACFTU National Congress was according its role of protecting the

employees' political and democratic rights and fundamental economic interests a more important position. See Yang, "A Case Study of the Rights Protection Policy in Quanzhou City's Trade Union."

70. Unless otherwise noted, the discussion of the Quanzhou reforms is drawn from ibid.

71. You Jun, ed., *2005 China's Employment Report: Employment of Peasants,* chap. 3 (www.china.org.cn/10/21/2005).

72. Interview with Quanzhou Municipal Federation of Trade Unions, November 7, 2005, cited in Yang, "A Case Study." According to Yang, a survey report issued by the Business Survey Team of the Quanzhou Statistics Bureau showed that in 2001 the labor department of Quanzhou helped rural migrant workers recover some 38.95 million RMB in wage arrears. The Quanzhou Municipal Federation of Trade Unions received and handled 1,199 complaints from rural migrant workers in 2003, including complaints about salary arrears and work injuries. Among these were 637 enterprises that owed salaries totaling 2.1 million RMB. See "Labor Shortage—Caused by the Unhealthy Employment Environment of a City" (www. nanfangdaily.com.cn/south-news/tszk/nfdsb/sd/200403030060.asp).

73. Yang, "A Case Study," notes: "It is estimated that the city already has a shortage of 200,000 workers for operating flat sewing machines. The survey showed that after the Lunar Festival in 2004, industrial enterprises in Jinjiang City only operated at 80–85 percent of its normal capacity, and business enterprises [in the] ceramics industry operated at less than half of their ordinary capacity. The statistics on labor shortage in Quanzhou Economic and Technological Development Zone provided by the Quanzhou Municipal Federation of Trade Unions in March 2003, also showed that business enterprises are short of 2,330 clothing needle machine operators, 1,860 resin-coloring workers and 2,505 general shoe-making workers."

74. In Quanzhou City, one relatively famous organization is the Quanzhou branch of Fujian province Ninghua County Chamber of Commerce organized by Wu Genfa with more than 300 officially registered "members." There are also 35,000 people from Ninghua county working in Quanzhou. Mei Yongcun and Huang Hexun, "How 'Clansmen Association' becomes 'Rights-Safeguarding Committee'" (http://news.china.com/zh_cn/domestic/945/20050514/12313640. html), cited in Yang, "A Case Study,"

75. Unless otherwise noted, the discussion of the Yiwu City case is drawn from Fuguo Han, "Transformation of Labour Unions and Integration of Organisational Resources: The Development of Social Integration in the Labour Rights System of Yiwu City," Working Paper 23 (Centre on Asia and Globalisation, National University of Singapore) (www.caglkyschool.com/pdf/working%20 papers/2011/CAG_WorkingPaper_23.pdf).

76. See http://opinion.people.com.cn/GB/8213/49375/49381/3606616.html [in Chinese].

77. For a fascinating assessment of legal aid in China, see Mary E. Gallagher, "'Hope for Protection and Hopeless Choices': Labor Legal Aid in the PRC," in *Grassroots Political Reform in Contemporary China,* Perry and Goldman, eds., pp. 196–27.

78. Unless otherwise noted, discussion of the Longhua Migrant Workers' Management Association is drawn from Xijin Jia, "From Administration to Autonomy: The Innovative Model of 'Migrant Workers' Homes' in Haikou Longhua District," Working Paper 16 (Centre on Asia and Globalisation, National University of Singapore, June 2011) (www.caglkyschool.com/pdf/working%20 papers/2011/CAG_WorkingPaper_16.pdf).

79. See the description at the website of the Program of Local Governance Innovation Best Practice Awards in China (www.Chinainnovations.org/Item/26883.aspx).

80. Xie, *Environmental Activism in China,* p. 89.

81. Guobin Yang, *The Power of the Internet in China: Citizen Activism Online* (Columbia University Press, 2009), pp. 147–49.

82. Xie, *Environmental Activism in China,* p. 11.

83. Chan, Qiu, and Zhu, "Chinese NGOs Strive to Survive," in *Social Transformations in Chinese Societies,* Bian, Chan, and Cheung, eds., p. 147.

Chapter Five

1. Ariana Eunjung Cha, "In Crisis, China Vows Openness," *Washington Post,* March 5, 2009 (http://washingtonpost.com/wp-dyn/content/article/2009/03/04/AR2009030401893.html).

2. "Chinese Premier Wen chats online with Internet users" (http:/chinadaily.com.cn/china/2011-02/27/content_12084017.htm).

3. Jamie Horsley, "Toward a More Open China?" in *The Right to Know: Transparency for an Open World,* Ann Florini, ed. (Columbia University Press, 2007), pp. 60–61.

4. Ibid., pp. 61–62.

5. "CPC Pledges to Focus on Party Building for Advancement of Ruling Capacity," *People's Daily Online,* September 26, 2004 (http://english.people-daily.com.cn/200409/26/eng20040926_158383.html).

6. Jamil Anderlini, "Punished Supplicants," *Financial Times,* March 5, 2009 (http://ft.com/cms/s/0/7d13197e-09bc-11de-add8-0000779fd2ac.html#axzz1 MGWyU5IE).

7. For an overview, see Florini, ed., *The Right to Know.* For an excellent website that covers the range of national experiences and disclosure issues at intergovernmental organizations, see www.freedominfo.org.

8. In making that comparison, a very useful document is Article 19, *Global Right to Information Index* (www.article19.org/pdfs/press/rti-index.pdf).

9. Horsley, "Toward a More Open China?" in *The Right to Know*, Florini, ed.

10. Ibid., pp. 69–81.

11. Interview #7, conducted by Ann Florini and Yeling Tan, Beijing, China, May 21, 2009. Interviews cited in this chapter are identified only by number in order to preserve the anonymity of those interviewed.

12. Article 1 of the Shanghai provision states the need to "protect the right to know of citizens, legal persons, and other organizations," while Article 1 of the Guangzhou provisions states the need to "protect the right to know of individuals and organizations." Article 4 of the Guangzhou provisions further states, "Individuals and organizations are 'persons with the right of access.' They enjoy the right to obtain government information in accordance with the law." Shanghai Municipal Provisions on Open Government Information (www.law.yale.edu/documents/pdf/Shanghai_Municipal_Provisions.pdf); Decree no. 8 of the Guangzhou Municipal People's Government dated November 6, 2002, "Guangzhou Municipal Provisions on Open Government Information" (http://freedominfo.org/wp-content/uploads/documents/provisions.pdf).

13. Regulations of the People's Republic of China on Open Government Information, April 5, 2007, effective May 1, 2008 (www.law.yale.edu/documents/pdf/Intellectual_Life/CL-OGI-Regs-English.pdf).

14. Article 3 of the Shanghai Provisions states: "All government information related to economic and social management and public services should be made public or provided upon request, unless subject to one of the exemptions from making public in accordance with the law listed in Article 10 of these Provisions." Article 6 of the Guangzhou provisions states: "As a general principle, government information shall be made public, and information that is not made public shall be the exception."

15. In addition, Articles 5–7 state that information disclosed must "observe the principles of justice, fairness, and convenience to the people," be released "promptly and accurately," and cannot be released without approval if the information involved requires approval "in accordance with relevant state regulations." Article 14 notes that information is "to be disclosed in accordance with the provisions of the Law of the People's Republic of China on Safeguarding State Secrets and other laws, regulations, and relevant state provisions," and that information involving "state secrets, commercial secrets, or individual privacy" is not to be disclosed. Finally, Article 34 requires administrative agencies to establish a "secrecy examination mechanism for releasing government information," failing which the agency will suffer administrative penalties "[i]f the circumstances are serious."

16. Article 7 of Shanghai's provisions gave citizens, legal persons, and other organizations "the right, based on these Provisions, to request government agencies to provide to them relevant government information." Similarly, Article 13 of Guangzhou's provisions states that requested information should be made public, "except for information that is prohibited from being made public by law, regulation, or these Provisions."

17. Articles 3 and 4 of the OGI regulations set out bureaucratic responsibilities for implementation and call for the establishment of systems for open government. Articles 9–12 specify the types of information that governments are to disclose, which, in the Chinese context of secrecy, is useful in constraining the government's ability to withhold information. Chapter III of the regulations provides specific details on the methods and procedures of disclosure, stating for example that information is to be disclosed through gazettes, websites, newspapers, and other media, as well as the setting up of public reading places for accessing state archives. Information that is proactively disclosed is to be released within twenty business days from the formation or changing of the information, and agencies are to respond to requests for information within fifteen to thirty business days. Agencies are also to provide information on request without charge, except for cost-based fees such as postage. Chapter IV of the regulations sets forth specific safeguards and supervisory mechanisms, stating for example that all administrative agencies are to publish an annual report on OGI by March 31 of each year. Article 33 allows citizens, legal persons, or other organizations to apply for administrative reconsideration or file an administrative lawsuit if they "believe a specific administrative action of an administrative agency in its open government information work has infringed their lawful rights and interests."

18. Paul Hubbard, "China's Regulations on Open Government Information: Challenges of Nationwide Policy Implementation," *Open Government: A Journal on Freedom of Information* 4 (no. 1) (April 11, 2008).

19. Interview #9, conducted by Ann Florini and Yeling Tan, Beijing, China, May 22, 2009.

20. Jamie Horsley, "China Adopts First Nationwide Open Government Information Regulations" (http://freedominfo.org/2007/05/china-adopts-first-nationwide-open-government-information-regulations/)

21. Interview #8, conducted by Ann Florini and Yeling Tan, Beijing, China, May 22, 2009.

22. See the website of the National Security Archive at www.gwu.edu/~nsarchiv/. It describes itself as an independent nongovernmental research institute and library located at George Washington University. The archive collects and publishes declassified documents obtained through the Freedom of Information Act.

23. Interview #1, conducted by Yeling Tan, Beijing, China, July 13, 2010.

24. Jamie Horsley, "Update on China's Open Government Information Regulations: Surprising Public Demand Yielding Some Positive Results," April 23, 2010 (http://freedominfo.org/2010/04/update-on-china-open-government-information-regulations).

25. Horsley, "Toward a More Open China?" in Florini, ed., *The Right to Know*, pp. 81, 82.

26. Interview #1, conducted by Ann Florini and Yeling Tan, Changsha City, Hunan Province, China, May 18, 2009.

27. Ibid.

28. Interview #4, conducted by Ann Florini and Yeling Tan, Beijing, China, May 20, 2009.

29. Ibid.

30. Ibid.

31. Ibid.

32. Ibid.

33. Interview #1, conducted by Ann Florini and Yeling Tan, Changsha City, Hunan Province, China, May 18, 2009.

34. "Measures of Hunan Province to Implement the Regulations of the People's Republic of China on Open Government Information" (www.law.yale.edu/.../CL-OGI_Hunan_OGI_Measures_(Eng_FINAL).pdf).

35. Interview #3, conducted by Ann Florini and Yeling Tan, Yuhua District, Changsha City, Hunan Province, China, May 19, 2009.

36. Interview #1, conducted by Ann Florini and Yeling Tan, Changsha City, Hunan Province, China, May 18, 2009.

37. Laura Neuman and Richard Calland, "Making the Law Work: The Challenges of Implementation," in *The Right to Know,* Florini, ed.

38. Interview #1, conducted by Ann Florini and Yeling Tan, Changsha City, Hunan Province, China, May 18, 2009.

39. Interview #4, conducted by Ann Florini and Yeling Tan, Beijing, China, May 20, 2009.

40. Horsley, "Update on China's Open Government Information Regulations."

41. Interview #1, conducted by Yeling Tan, Beijing, China, July 13, 2010.

42. Michael Wines and Jonathan Ansfield, "Trampled in a Land Rush, Chinese Resist," *New York Times,* May 26, 2010 (https://nytimes.com/2010/05/27/world/asia/27china.html?pagewanted=1&_r=1&sq=china%20land&st=cse&scp=1).

43. Horsley, "Update on China's Open Government Information Regulations."

44. For comprehensive information about global trends, national comparisons, and other issues, see the website of the International Budget Partnership (http://internationalbudget.org/).

45. Horsley, "Update on China's Open Government Information Regulations."

46. Vivek Ramkumar and Elena Petkova, "Transparency and Environmental Governance," in *The Right to Know,* Florini, ed., pp. 279–308.

47. World Resources Institute & IPE, "Greening Supply Chains in China: Practical Lessons from China-Based Suppliers in Achieving Environmental Performance," WRI Working Paper, October 2010 (www.wri.org/publication/greening-supply-chains-in-china); Maria Shao, "Ma Jun and the IPE: Using Information to Improve China's Environment," Case SI-115 (Stanford Graduate School of Business, 2009).

48. Greenpeace, "Silent Giants," 2009 (http://greenpeace.org/raw/content/eastasia/press/reports/silent-giants-report.pdf).

49. Hua Wang and David Wheeler, "Equilibrium Pollution and Economic Development in China," *Environment and Development Economics* 8 (2003): 451–66.

50. Horsley, "Update on China's Open Government Information Regulations."

51. Ministry of Environmental Protection, "Guidelines on Cultivation and Guiding Orderly Development of Environmental Non-Government Organizations," January 10, 2011 (http://english.mep.gov.cn/News_service/news_release/201101/t20110120_200080.htm).

52. "Guanyu Renmin Fayuan Fating Zhuanyong Shebei Peizhi de Yijian" (Directive on the Equipment Required in Courts), Directive No. 21 (2002) issued by the Supreme Court of China, November 28, 2002. Full text of the directive is available at: http://law.baidu.com/pages/chinalawinfo/10/89/b793fc792a66f44f3b3c0b7e65352034_0.html. "Guanyu Tingshen Huodong Luyin Luxiang de Ruogan Guiding" (Regulations on Audio and Video Recording Debates and Judgments at Courts), Directive No. 33 (2010) issued by the Supreme Court of China, August 16, 2010. The full text of the regulation is available at: www.law-lib.com/law/law_view.asp?id=324868.

53. "Sunlight Judicature Promoted in Henan Province through Live Broadcasting Court Trials via the Internet" (http://nbcp.gov.cn/article/English/Government Transparency/201004/20100400007127.shtm).

54. "All Trials of Intermediate Courts to Be Live Broadcasted Online before the End of the Year in Liaoning Province" (http://nbcp.gov.cn/article/English/GovernmentTransparency/200911/20091100004744.shtml).

55. "Sunshine Online Grand Platform for Facilitating the People" (http://nbcp.gov.cn/article/English/GovernmentTransparency/201002/20100200005984.shtml).

56. "Various Measures Taken in Zhabei District Court of Shanghai to Make Judicial Affairs Transparent" (http://nbcp.gov.cn/article/English/Government-Transparency/200907/20090700003205.shtml).

57. Horsley, "Update on China's Open Government Information Regulations."

58. Wang Jingqiong, "Law to Promote Gov't Transparency," *China Daily,* November 3, 2009 (http://chinadaily.com.cn/bizchina/2009-11/03/content_8903259.htm).

59. "Su Xiaozhou: Panjueshu Yinyong Falu Tiaowen Jing Shi Zixuwuyou" (The Verdict Quoted a Legal Code That Doesn't Exist), *Nanguo Zaobao* (Southern Morning Post), April 2, 2010 (http://ngzb.gxnews.com.cn/html/2010-04/02/content_370610.htm).

60. Xinhua News, "Xinhua Insight: Communist Party of China Aims to Curb Corruption through Transparency Reform" (http://news.xinhuanet.com/english2010/indepth/2010-11/27/c_13624859.htm).

61. Wu Jiao, "CPC at All Levels to Have Spokesperson," *China Daily,* December 30, 2009 (http://chinadaily.com.cn/china/2009-12/30/content_9244059.htm).

62. Xin Dingding. "Central Party School Opens Doors to the Media," *China Daily,* July 1, 2010 (http://chinadaily.com.cn/china/2010-07/01/content_10042918.htm).

63. Jake Hooker, "At Shuttered Gateway to Tibet, Unrest Simmers against Chinese Rule," *New York Times,* March 26, 2008 (https://nytimes.com/2008/03/26/world/asia/26tibet.html?_r=1).

64. Interview with Jonathan Watts, conducted by Yeling Tan, Beijing, China, January 11, 2011.

65. Mark Sweney, "China Blocks Media due to Tibet Unrest," *The Guardian,* March 17, 2008 (www.guardian.co.uk/media/2008/mar/17/chinathemedia.digitalmedia).

66. BBC News, "China's Press Freedoms Extended," October 18, 2008 (http://news.bbc.co.uk/2/hi/7675306.stm).

67. *Christian Science Monitor,* July 10 2009, "Urumqi Unrest: China's Savvier Media Strategy," July 10, 2009 (www.csmonitor.com/World/Asia-Pacific/2009/0710/p06s05-woap.html).

68. Tania Branigan, "China's Jasmine Revolution: Police but No Protesters Line Streets of Beijing," *The Guardian,* February 27 2011 (http://guardian.co.uk/world/2011/feb/27/china-jasmine-revolution-beijing-police).

69. Interview #9, conducted by Ann Florini and Yeling Tan, Beijing, China, May 22, 2009.

70. Interview #1, conducted by Ann Florini and Yeling Tan, Changsha City, Hunan Province, China, May 18, 2009.

71. Ma Jun, "The Power of Public Disclosure" (www.chinadialogue.net/article/show/single/en/4001-The-power-of-public-disclosure).

72. Interview #9, conducted by Ann Florini and Yeling Tan, Beijing, China, May 22, 2009.

73. Interview #2, conducted by Ann Florini and Yeling Tan, Changsha City, Hunan Province, China, May 18, 2009. Interview #9, conducted by Ann Florini and Yeling Tan, Beijing, China, May 22, 2009.

74. Interview #3, conducted by Ann Florini and Yeling Tan, Yuhua District, Changsha City, Hunan Province, China, May 19, 2009.

75. Interview #8, conducted by Ann Florini and Yeling Tan, Beijing, China, May 22, 2009.

76. Will Clem, "Half of State Websites Miss the Mark," *South China Morning Post,* February 23, 2010.

77. *Wall Street Journal,* "Evaluating China's Drive for Budget Transparency," April 16, 2010 (http://blogs.wsj.com/chinarealtime/2010/04/16/evaluating-china%E2%80%99s-drive-for-budget-transparency/).

78. Interview #1, conducted by Ann Florini and Yeling Tan, Changsha City, Hunan Province, China, May 18, 2009. Interview #9, conducted by Ann Florini and Yeling, Tan Beijing, China, May 22, 2009.

79. Interview #1, conducted by Ann Florini and Yeling Tan, Changsha City, Hunan Province, China, May 18, 2009.

80. Interview #4, conducted by Ann Florini and Yeling Tan, Beijing, China, May 20, 2009.

81. Interview #1, conducted by Ann Florini and Yeling Tan, Changsha City, Hunan Province, China, May 18, 2009.

82. Ibid.

83. Christine Wong, "Rebuilding Government for the 21st Century: Can China Incrementally Reform the Public Sector?" BICC Working Paper Series 12 (Oxford, UK: British Inter-University China Centre, 2008).

84. Interview #9, conducted by Ann Florini and Yeling Tan, Beijing, China, May 22. 2009.

85. Interview #2, conducted by Yeling Tan, Beijing, China. January 11, 2011. Interview #4, conducted by Yeling Tan, Beijing, China, January 13, 2011.

86. Peter Ho, "Greening without Conflict? Environmentalism, NGOs and Civil Society in China," *Development and Change* 32 (2001): 893–921.

87. Susmita Dasgupta, Hua Wang, and David Wheeler, "Disclosure Strategies for Pollution Control," in *International Yearbook of Environmental and Resource Economics 2006/2007,* Tom Tietenberg and Henk Folmer, eds. (Cheltenham, UK: Edward Elgar, 2007).

88. National Human Rights Action Plan of China 2009–2010 (www.gov.cn/english/official/2009-04/13/content_1284128.htm).

89. Chris Buckley, "China's Wen Meets Petitioners in Show of Worry over Discontent," January 26, 2011 (www.reuters.com/article/2011/01/25/us-china-rights-wen-idUSTRE70O2L920110125).

90. Jamil Anderlini, "Punished Supplicants," *Financial Times,* March 5, 2009 (http:/ft.com/cms/s/0/7d13197e-09bc-11de-add8-0000779fd2ac.html#axzz1MGWyU5IE).

91. Interview #7, conducted by Ann Florini and Yeling Tan, Beijing, China, May 21, 2009.

92. Interview #8, conducted by Ann Florini and Yeling Tan, Beijing, China, May 22, 2009.

93. Center for Public Participation Studies and Support, Beijing University Law School, "Summary of the 2009 Annual Report on China's Administrative Transparency," September 2010 (translated by The China Law Center, Yale Law School).

94. Center on Asia and Globalisation, Lee Kuan Yew School of Public Policy, National University of Singapore & The Asia Foundation, International Workshop on Access to Information, March 2009. Workshop report available upon request.

95. Interview #4, conducted by Ann Florini and Yeling Tan, Beijing, China, May 20, 2009.

96. Horsley, "Toward a More Open China?" in *The Right to Know,* Florini, ed., p. 82.

97. Jamie Horsley, "Update on China's Open Government Information Regulations."

98. "Caipan Wenshu Shangwang Weihe 'Leisheng Da Yudian Xiao'" (Why Official Court Verdicts Published on the Internet Are "Loud Thunder and Small Raindrops") [meaning all bluster and little action]. See http://news.xinhuanet.com/comments/2009-04/13/content_11175545.htm [in Chinese].

99. Interview #1, conducted by Yeling Tan, Beijing, China, July 13, 2010.

100. Interview #1, conducted by Ann Florini and Yeling Tan, Changsha City, Hunan Province, China, May 18, 2009.

101. Interview #4, conducted by Ann Florini and Yeling Tan, Beijing, China, May 20, 2009.

102. Institution Building refers to whether "the level of leadership over the OGI deliberative and coordinative body was higher than that of the corresponding department in charge" (usually the General Affairs Office).

103. System Building refers to whether the OGI regulations have been reconciled with regulations on secrecy and archives management.

104. The assessment found that provinces outperformed central agencies on average. The "passing rate" on the 100-point assessment was 40 percent for provinces, and a low 4.7 percent for State Council agencies. The average score on the index for provinces was 57.4, while that for State Council agencies was more than 10 points lower, 46.1. Across the five categories of performance indicators, State Council agencies outperformed provinces in Institution Building, System Building, and Disclosure on Request, while provinces did better in the two categories that were given the heaviest weights in the assessment, Disclosure on Own Initiative and Supervision and Remedy. In addition, the assessment found that in the six pilot provinces chosen for subprovincial assessment, provincial level performance was by and large significantly better than city government performance. On average, provincial governments outperformed their city counterparts by 14.3 points. The OGIWA report assesses that this imbalance in performance reflects the concentration of resources for OGI implementation at higher levels of government. The report also makes the important point that while several of the driving motivations for open government came from concerns at the grassroots, there has not been a corresponding allocation of resources at these levels. Center for Public Participation Studies and Support, Beijing University Law School, "Summary of the 2009 Annual Report on China's Administrative Transparency," September 2010 (translated by The China Law Center, Yale Law School).

105. Interview #1, conducted by Ann Florini and Yeling Tan, Changsha City, Hunan Province, China, May 18, 2009.

106. Interview #7, conducted by Ann Florini and Yeling Tan, Beijing, China. May 21, 2009.

107. Authors' calculations.

108. Peter Lorentzen, Pierre Landry, and John Yasuda, "Transparent Authoritarianism? An Analysis of Political and Economic Barriers to Greater Governmental Transparency in China," 2010, paper presented at the APSA Annual Meeting 2010 (http://papers.ssrn.com/sol3/papers.cfm?abstract_id=1643986).

109. Interview #9, conducted by Ann Florini and Yeling Tan, Beijing, China, May 22, 2009.

110. Interview #1, conducted by Ann Florini and Yeling Tan, Changsha City, Hunan Province, China, May 18, 2009.

Chapter Six

1. As the Rushan County case shows, in some cases the two categories overlap, with villagers who are not Party members nonetheless being granted a say in the selection of the village Party secretary, but to date this occurs only at the village level.

2. Yu Keping, "Ideological Change and Incremental Democracy," in *China's Changing Political Landscape: Prospects for Democracy,* Cheng Li, ed. (Brookings Institution Press, 2008), p. 56.

3. The law that banned liaison offices is the Daibiao Fa Caoan (Draft Revision of the Representative Law), announced by the National People's Congress, August 23, 2010.

4. See, for example, Tony Saich and Xuedong Yang, "Innovation in China's Local Governance: 'Open Recommendation and Selection,'" *Pacific Affairs* 76, no. 2 (Summer 2003): 185–208.

5. See, for example, Joseph Fewsmith, "The 17th Party Congress: Informal Politics and Formal Institutions," *China Leadership Monitor* 23 (2008).

6. See, for example, Cheng Li, "From Selection to Election? Experiments in the Recruitment of Chinese Political Elites," *China Leadership Monitor* 26 (2008); and Alice Miller, "The Case of Xi Jinping and the Mysterious Succession," *China Leadership Monitor,* no. 30 (2009).

7. For a good overview of Western definitions of democracy and how they contrast with thinking and practice in China, see Cheng Li, "Introduction: Assessing China's Political Development," in *China's Changing Political Landscape: Prospects for Democracy,* Cheng Li, ed. (Brookings, 2008), pp. 1–12.

8. David Pilling, "China Crashes into a Middle Class Revolt." *Financial Times,* August 3, 2011 (www.ft.com/intl/cms/s/0/0558876e-be1b-11e0-bee9-00144feabdc0.html#axzz1XGp7vEVC).

9. Wen Jiabao, "Guanyu Zhiding Guomin Jingji he Shehui Fazhan Di Shi'er Ge Wunian Guihua Jianyi de Shuoming (Notes on Suggestions to Making the 12th 5-year Plan for National Economic and Social Development)," October 28, 2010 (http://news.xinhuanet.com/politics/2010-10/28/c_12713246.htm).

Index

Accountability: administrative reform for, 29, 41; benefits of administrative transparency, 131, 139; decentralized governance and, 124; electoral reform for, 30, 64

Administrative Approval Service Center, 51

Administrative levels of government: authority for revision of regulations, 48–49; cadre appointment system, 64–65; communication between, 124; electoral reforms, 30, 68; fragmented authoritarianism, 42–43, 55; implementation of transparency regulations, 134–35, 136–39; professionalization of staff, 25; sources of corruption in, 40–41; staffing levels, 60; structure and functions, 11, 68. *See also* Administrative reforms

Administrative Licensing and Approval Service Center, 50

Administrative Litigation Act, 18, 25, 155

Administrative reforms: to accommodate private initiatives, 44, 46; case examples, 49–58; to clarify staff responsibilities, 57; economic growth and, 162; electronic

monitoring of workplace performance, 51–56; to facilitate administrative approvals, 56–58, 59; future prospects, 169–70; to improve public understanding of regulations and processes, 57, 58, 155–56; lessons from experiences to date, 161–63; local efforts, 44–46; national efforts, 46–49; need for, 42, 44; recent experiments and outcomes, 28, 35, 43–49, 59–61; relationship to system-wide reform, 41–42, 61; to remove obstacles to economic development, 40, 44–45; scaling up, 45; transparency initiatives, 126–27, 130–31, 137. *See also* Administrative levels of government

AIDS Care China, 88–89

Aizhixing, 142

All-China Environment Federation, 120

All-China Federation of Trade Unions, 89, 108, 109, 110

All-China Women's Federation, 99

Animal welfare protection, 16

An Lidong, 16

Archives Law, 134, 154–55

Authoritarian resilience, 24–25, 43, 168, 169–70, 173

Nongovernmental organizations:
benefits of administrative transparency, 131; environmental,
118–20; example of local problem
solving, 1–3; funding, 105; government agencies cooperating with,
142–43; government classification
of, 103; government-organized, 30,
31, 73, 82–85, 108–18, 165–66;
international, 96–97, 99, 100,
104–05, 119–20; linkages among,
96–97, 106, 165, 172; local service
center for coordinating efforts of,
106–07; registration requirements,
103–04, 171, 172; sponsorship
requirements, 104, 108; trends
in formation and operations, 16,
89, 95, 101; use of transparency
laws, 140–43, 152–53. *See also*
Civil society

Oksenberg, Michel, 55
Olympic Games, Beijing, 146, 147
One Foundation, 100
Open Environmental Information,
140–41, 149, 156–57
Open Government Information regulations: access to information under,
130; conflicted relationships in
government generated by, 134, 146,
154–55, 159; coverage, 134; disclosure limits, 129–30; effects on governance, 131–34, 136–37, 158–59;
enforcement, 154; examination
of past grievances, 150–51; future
prospects, 33–34, 159, 172–73;
implementation challenges, 134–35,
137, 150–51, 154, 156–57, 158;
influence on judicial system transparency, 143–44; interaction with
other laws, 134, 145–46, 154–55;
international comparison, 130–31,
132–33; lessons for implementation
of policy reforms, 157–59; local

implementation, 33, 137–39; NGO
utilization, 140–43; objectives,
127–29, 134; origins of, 32–33,
126–27, 167; outcomes to date,
33–34, 135–43, 148, 166–67; public understanding of, 156; public
utilization, 135, 139–40, 148–49,
150, 156, 166–67; underlying principles, 33, 126, 127–30, 167; variations in government compliance
with information requests, 149–52
Open Government Information Watch
Alliance, 140
Open Government Information Watch
Audit, 156
Ownership, 13, 22

Parliamentary government in China,
11–12, 17; county congress elec-
tions, 69–73
Pei, Minxin, 26, 124, 172
People's Congress, 11
People's Political Consultative Confer-
ence, 11
Pet ownership, 15
Poland, 92
Politburo elections, 72–73, 163
Pollution Information Transparency
Index, 141
Prada, Miuccia, 15
Price regulation, 13
Private sector: benefits of administra-
tive reforms, 162; government
encouragement of, 44, 46, 47; out-
comes of government transparency
regulations, 131; ownership struc-
ture of Chinese economy, 13; rela-
tionships with foreign counterparts,
47–48; representation in local party
committees, 78–79; Socialism with
Chinese Characteristics, 22
Privatization: local experimentation in
China, 5; trends, 13
Putnam, Robert, 93, 94